Carleton Olegario Máximo (Ed.)

HTC 7 Surround

Carleton Olegario Máximo (Ed.)

HTC 7 Surround

Windows Phone 7, AT&T Mobility, HTC Corporation

Ject Press

Imprint

All parts of this book are extracted from Wikipedia, the free encyclopedia (www.wikipedia.org).

You can get detailed informations about the authors of this collection of articles at the end of this book. The editors (Ed.) of this book are no authors. They have not modified or extended the original texts.

Pictures published in this book can be under different licences than the GNU Free Documentation License. You can get detailed informations about the authors and licences of pictures at the end of this book.

The content of this book was generated collaboratively by volunteers. Please be advised that nothing found here has necessarily been reviewed by people with the expertise required to provide you with complete, accurate or reliable information. Some information in this book maybe misleading or wrong. The Publisher does not guarantee the validity of the information found here. If you need specific advice (f.e. in fields of medical, legal, financial, or risk management questions) please contact a professional who is licensed or knowledgeable in that area.

Cover image: www.ingimage.com
Concerning the licence of the cover image please contact ingimage.

Publisher:
Ject Press is a trademark of
International Book Market Service Ltd., 17 Rue Meldrum, Beau Bassin, 1713-01 Mauritius
Email: info@bookmarketservice.com
Website: www.bookmarketservice.com

Published in 2011

Printed in: U.S.A., U.K., Germany. This book was not produced in Mauritius.

ISBN: 978-613-6-55531-7

Contents

References

Article Licenses

HTC 7 Surround

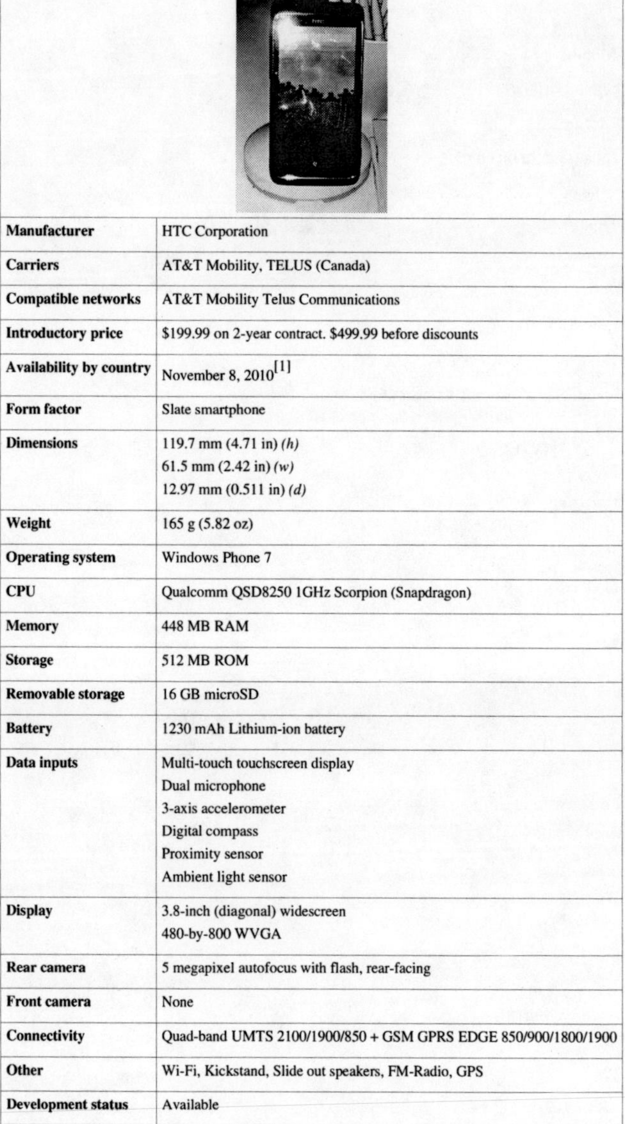

Manufacturer	HTC Corporation
Carriers	AT&T Mobility, TELUS (Canada)
Compatible networks	AT&T Mobility Telus Communications
Introductory price	$199.99 on 2-year contract. $499.99 before discounts
Availability by country	November 8, 2010[1]
Form factor	Slate smartphone
Dimensions	119.7 mm (4.71 in) *(h)* 61.5 mm (2.42 in) *(w)* 12.97 mm (0.511 in) *(d)*
Weight	165 g (5.82 oz)
Operating system	Windows Phone 7
CPU	Qualcomm QSD8250 1GHz Scorpion (Snapdragon)
Memory	448 MB RAM
Storage	512 MB ROM
Removable storage	16 GB microSD
Battery	1230 mAh Lithium-ion battery
Data inputs	Multi-touch touchscreen display Dual microphone 3-axis accelerometer Digital compass Proximity sensor Ambient light sensor
Display	3.8-inch (diagonal) widescreen 480-by-800 WVGA
Rear camera	5 megapixel autofocus with flash, rear-facing
Front camera	None
Connectivity	Quad-band UMTS 2100/1900/850 + GSM GPRS EDGE 850/900/1800/1900
Other	Wi-Fi, Kickstand, Slide out speakers, FM-Radio, GPS
Development status	Available

The **HTC 7 Surround** (also known as the **HTC Surround**) is a smartphone created by HTC running on the Windows Phone 7 operating system. The HTC Surround launched on November 8, 2010 on AT&T.

History

Release

The Surround was released on November 8, 2010. Initial sales data has not been reported yet.

Features

The HTC Surround, like its European cousin, the HTC Mozart, was one of the first phones to use the Windows Phone 7 OS. Its main feature is its slide-out speaker, which also reveals a kick stand.

Screen and input

The HTC Surround uses a modest 3.8 inch WVGA LCD touchscreen with a resolution of 480 x 800 pixels. It can produce up to 16 million colors.[2] The display is designed to be used with a bare finger or multiple fingers at one time for multi-touch sensing.

The Surround has 6 hardware buttons: 3 physical and 3 touch. It has a dedicated power button, camera button, and a volume rocker. The device also has a back button, a home button and a search button. The back button takes the user back to the previous application or screen. The home button brings the user to the home screen. The search button opens up a Bing search screen.[3]

The device contains a GPS chip to show the location of the phone, a Proximity sensor to turn the screen off during phone calls so that the face doesn't accidentally click the screen, a G-sensor, an Ambient light sensor to dim the light in dark rooms and increase the brightness in direct sunlight, and a Digital Compass.[4]

Processor and memory

The Surround uses a 1 GHz Qualcomm QSD8250 Snapdragon Chipset.[5] It features 512MB of ROM and 448MB of RAM.[4]

Cameras

The surround comes with a 5 megapixel Camera with built in Auto Focus and Flash located on the rear of the phone. The camera can also shoot in 720p HD at 24-frames per second.[4]

Storage

As is with most other Windows Phone 7 phones, the HTC Surround doesn't support external memory. The phone comes with 16GB of memory: in the form of a 16GB internal MicroSD card.

Audio and output

Audio is undoubtedly the most distinguishing aspect of the HTC Surround. When the phone is slid open, the Dolby powered speakers are shown. Most people have been underwhelmed with the speakers stating that "The overall volume of the speakers was enough to fill a small room, but not 'take the party to another level,' as HTC claims on its website."[6] Engadget writes that "there's a lot of promise here, but unless the phone delivers the extra size and weight simply won't be worth it. Unfortunately, we're here to report... that they're simply not worth it."[7]

Smartphone connectivity

The device runs on AT&T's 3G network. It also offers WiFi as another means on connection to the internet. The phone comes with built-in Bluetooth 2.1 and a MicroUSB slot to plug in a MicroUSB to USB wire which can be used to connect the device to the computer or to the wall charger.

Battery and power

The Surround comes with a 1230mAh battery is user-replaceable by removing the back cover. The average talk and standby time are 4.16 and 255 hours respectively.[1]

Software

The device runs Windows Phone 7 as its operating system. It has a number of HTC exclusive apps available.

Entering Field Test Mode

At the phone dialer, dial **##3282#** then press the "Call" button

See also

- Windows Phone 7

References

[1] HTC Surround specs - Phone Arena (http://www.phonearena.com/phones/HTC-Surround_id4916)

[2] HTC Surround price and specifications, HTC surround Windows phone review, photos, launch date and cost in India (http://www.mobiclue.com/htc-surround-price-and-specifications.html)

[3] HTC Surround Review (http://www.ubergizmo.com/15/archives/2010/10/htc-surround-review.html)

[4] HTC - Products - HTC 7 Surround - Specification (http://www.htc.com/www/product/7surround/specification.html)

[5] HTC 7 Trophy,Mozart,Surround,Pro,HD7 Features &Availability of Windows Phone 7 (http://geniusgeeks.com/2010/10/htc-released-five-windows-phone-7/)

[6] HTC Surround (AT&T) Review - A Review of the HTC Surround (AT&T) (http://www.laptopmag.com/review/cellphones/htc-surround.aspx?page=1#axzz15kNQr5Go)

[7] HTC Surround review - Engadget (http://www.engadget.com/2010/10/20/htc-surround-review/)

External links

- Official HTC 7 Surround homepage (http://www.htc.com/www/product/7surround/overview.html)

Windows Phone

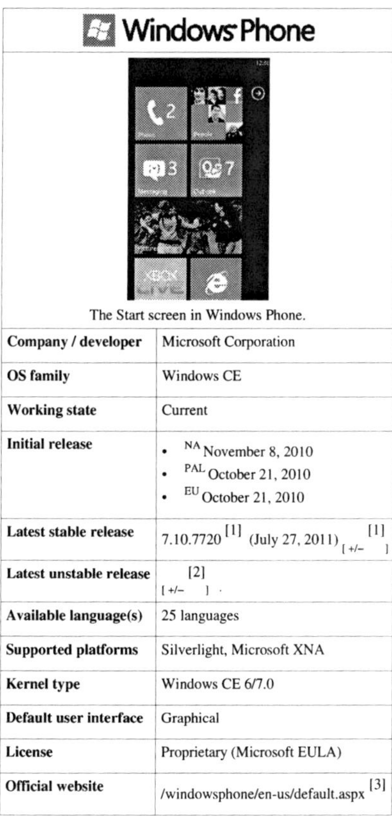

The Start screen in Windows Phone.

Company / developer	Microsoft Corporation
OS family	Windows CE
Working state	Current
Initial release	• NA November 8, 2010 • PAL October 21, 2010 • EU October 21, 2010
Latest stable release	7.10.7720 [1] (July 27, 2011) [1] [+/-]
Latest unstable release	[2] [+/-]
Available language(s)	25 languages
Supported platforms	Silverlight, Microsoft XNA
Kernel type	Windows CE 6/7.0
Default user interface	Graphical
License	Proprietary (Microsoft EULA)
Official website	/windowsphone/en-us/default.aspx [3]

Windows Phone (previously **Windows Phone 7 Series**) is a mobile operating system developed by Microsoft, and is the successor to its Windows Mobile platform.[1] Unlike its predecessor, it is primarily aimed at the consumer market rather than the enterprise market.[2] It was launched in Europe, Singapore, Australia, and New Zealand on October 21, 2010, and in the US and Canada on November 8, 2010, Mexico on November 24, 2010, the PAL region on December 3, 2010, and Asia in early 2011.[3] With Windows Phone, Microsoft offers a new user interface with its design language named Metro, integrates the operating system with third party and other Microsoft services, and controls the hardware it runs on.[4]

History

Development

Work on a major Windows Mobile update may have begun as early as 2004 under the codename "Photon", but work moved slowly and the project was ultimately cancelled.[5] In 2008, Microsoft reorganized the Windows Mobile group and started work on a new mobile operating system.[6] The product was to be released in 2009 as Windows Phone, but several delays prompted Microsoft to develop Windows Mobile 6.5 as an interim release.[7]

Timeline of Windows Phone related events

Windows Phone was developed quickly. One result was that Windows Mobile applications do not run on it. Larry Lieberman, senior product manager for Microsoft's Mobile Developer Experience, told eWeek: "If we'd had more time and resources, we may have been able to do something in terms of backward compatibility."[8] Lieberman said that Microsoft was attempting to look at the mobile phone market in a new way, with the end user in mind as well as the enterprise network.[8] Terry Myerson, corporate VP of Windows Phone engineering, said, "With the move to capacitive touch screens, away from the stylus, and the moves to some of the hardware choices we made for the Windows Phone 7 experience, we had to break application compatibility with Windows Mobile 6.5."[9]

Naming

The name Windows Phone 7 is a rebranding of Microsoft's old mobile OS called Windows Mobile. Before the official announcement of Windows Phone 7, Microsoft began to refer to devices running Windows Mobile as "Windows Phones". Microsoft at first announced its new platform as "Windows Phone 7 Series" which initially came under criticism as being too wordy and difficult to say casually. Responding to this, on April 2, 2010 Microsoft announced that the "Series" would be dropped from the name, leaving the platform named Windows Phone 7.[10] The official statement on the matter was:

> "Customers want a simpler way to say and use the name consistently. The important thing is keeping the focus on the Windows Phone brand, which we introduced in October and will continue investing in through Windows Phone 7 and beyond."

Launch

In February 2010, a Microsoft press release listed the companies that would help make and operate Windows Phone. Many hardware makers were listed in the release.

Microsoft unveiled Windows Phone on February 15, 2010, at Mobile World Congress 2010 in Barcelona[11] and revealed additional details at MIX 2010 on March 15, 2010. The final SDK was made available on September 16, 2010.[12]

HP later decided not to build devices for Windows Phone, citing that it wanted to focus on devices for its newly purchased webOS.[13]

Windows Phone supports twenty-five languages and Windows Phone Marketplace allows buying and selling applications in 35 countries and regions.[14]

Partnership

Launch partners

On October 11, 2010, Microsoft's CEO Steve Ballmer announced 10 devices operating Windows Phone, made by HTC, Dell, Samsung, and LG, with sales beginning on October 21, 2010 in Europe and Australia and November 8, 2010 in the United States. The devices were available on 60 carriers in 30 countries, with additional devices to be launched in 2011.[15]

Partnership with Nokia

On 11 February 2011, at a press event in London, Microsoft CEO Steve Ballmer and Nokia CEO Stephen Elop announced a partnership between their companies in which Windows Phone would become the primary smartphone operating system for Nokia.[16] The event was largely focused on creating "a new global mobile ecosystem", suggesting competition with Android and iOS by saying "It is now a three horse race". Integration of Microsoft services with Nokia's own services were announced; specifically that Bing would power search across Nokia devices, and an integration of Nokia Maps with Bing Maps, as well as Nokia's application store being integrated with the Windows Phone Marketplace.[16] The partnership involves "funds changing hands for royalties, marketing and ad-revenue sharing", which Microsoft later announced was, "measured in billions of dollars."[17]

Concept render of a Nokia smartphone running Windows Phone

Other OEM partners

Microsoft, on May 25, 2011, has announced expansion of partners who plan to release Windows Phone. Acer, Fujitsu, and ZTE, in addition to Nokia, plan to release their first Windows Phones based on the first major upgrade to Windows Phone platform.[18]

Features

User interface

Windows Phone features a new user interface, based upon Microsoft's Windows Phone design system, codenamed Metro.[19] The home screen, called the "Start screen", is made up of "Live Tiles". Tiles are links to applications, features, functions and individual items (such as contacts, web pages, applications or media items). Users can add, rearrange, or remove Tiles.[20] Tiles are dynamic and update in real time - for example, the tile for an email account would display the number of unread messages or a Tile could display a live update of the weather.[21]

Several features of Windows Phone are organized into "**hubs**", which combine local and online content via Windows Phone's integration with popular social networks such as Facebook, Windows Live, and Twitter.[21] For example, the Pictures hub shows photos captured with the device's camera and the user's Facebook photo albums, and the People hub shows contacts aggregated from multiple sources including Windows Live, Facebook, and Gmail. From the Hub, users can directly comment and 'like' on social network updates. The other built-in hubs are Music and Video (which integrates with Zune), Games (which integrates with Xbox Live), Windows Phone Marketplace, and Microsoft Office.[21]

Windows Phone uses multi-touch technology.[21] The default Windows Phone user interface has a dark theme that prolongs battery life on OLED screens as fully black pixels don't emit light.[22] The user may choose a light theme instead, and can also choose from several accent colors.[23] User interface elements such as tiles are shown in the user's chosen accent color. Third-party applications can be automatically themed with these colors.[24] [25]

Text input

Users input text by using an on-screen virtual keyboard, which has a dedicated key for inserting emoticons,[26] and features spell checking[26] and word prediction.[27] Users may change a word after it has been typed by tapping the word,[28] which will invoke a list of similar words. Pressing and holding certain keys will reveal similar characters. The keys are somewhat larger and spaced farther apart when in landscape mode. Phones may also be made with a hardware keyboard for text input.[29]

Messaging

Windows Phone combined messaging through "threads". Threads allow the Windows Phone user to engage with his contacts through Windows Live Messenger and Facebook Chat as well as traditional text messages. Text message can also be composed through voice recognition. Voice recognition allows speech to be convert to text message and also allows text message to be converted to speech which can be read aloud.

Web browser

Windows Phone features a version of Internet Explorer Mobile with a rendering engine that is based on Internet Explorer 9.[30]

Internet Explorer on Windows Phone allows the user to maintain a list of favorite web pages and tiles linking to web pages on the Start screen. The browser supports up to 6 tabs, which can all load in parallel.[31] Other features include multi-touch gestures, a streamlined UI, smooth zoom in/out animations, the ability to save pictures that are on web pages, share web pages via email, and support for inline search which allows the user to search for a word or phrase in a web page by typing it.[32] Microsoft has announced plans to regularly update the Windows Phone web browser and its layout engine independently from the Windows Phone Update system.[33]

In a demo, Microsoft said that users will be able to stream YouTube videos from the browser. Clicking on a video from the mobile YouTube website will launch the video in a standalone app and will also add the YouTube video to the Music + Video Hub.[34]

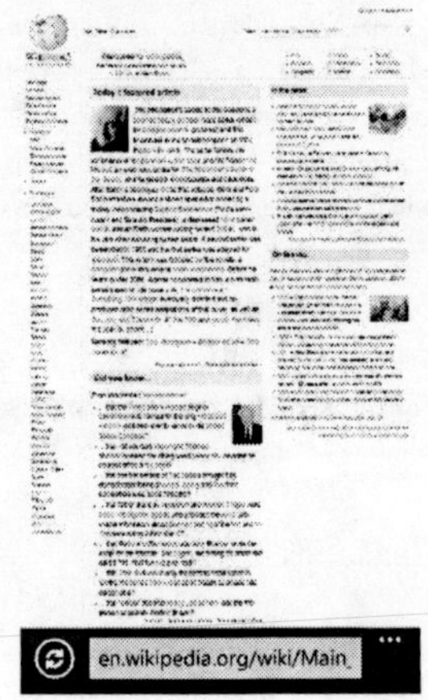

Internet Explorer Mobile on Windows Phone.

Contacts

Contacts are organized via the "**People hub**". Contacts can be manually entered into contacts or imported from Facebook, Windows Live Contacts, Twitter, and LinkedIn. A "What's New" section show news feed and a "Pictures" section show pictures from those social networks made by the contacts. A "Me" section show the phone user's own social networks status and wall, allow the user to update his status, and check-in to Bing and Facebook Places. Contacts can be added to the home screen by pinning them to the start. The contact's "**Live Tile**" displays his social network status and profile picture on the homescreen and the contact's hub displays his Facebook wall as well as all of the rest of his contact information and information from his other social networks.

Contacts can also be be sorted into "Groups". Feed and pictures from social networks made by each of the contacts are combined.

E-mail

Windows Phone supports Hotmail, Outlook, Yahoo! Mail, Gmail natively and supports many other services via the POP and IMAP protocols. For the native account types, contacts and calendars may be synced as well. Users can also search through their e-mail by searching in the subject, body, senders, and receivers. Emails are shown in threading view and multiple e-mail inboxes can be combined or kept separate.

Multimedia

The Music + Video Hub on Windows Phone.

Zune for Windows Phone is an application providing entertainment and synchronization capabilities between PC and Phone.[35] Windows Phone multimedia experience is divided in to two distinct hubs, Music + Videos hub and Pictures hub, both of which are similar in appearance and functionality to that of the Zune HD.

The "**Music + Videos hub**" plays music, videos, and podcasts, and allows users to access the Zune Marketplace to buy music or rent it with the Zune Pass subscription service, and view artist biographies and photos.[26] This hub also includes Smart DJ which can suggest songs similar to those locally stored on the phone.

The "**Pictures hub**" displays the user's Facebook and Windows Live photo albums alongside photos taken with the phone's camera. Users can also tag and upload photos to social networks and comment on online photos directly from the Pictures hub.[26] Multi-touch gestures permit zooming in and out of photos.

Media support

According to Brandon Miniman's test review for pocketnow.com, he stated "*if Zune can play it, your Windows Phone 7 device can play it*" - this refers to the supported playback of files.[36] The audio file formats, supported, include WAV, MP3, WMA, AMR, AAC/MP4/M4A/M4B and 3GP/3G2 as standards. The video file formats, supported, include WMV, AVI, MP4/M4V, 3GP/3G2 and MOV (QuickTime) standards. These supported audio and video formats would be dependent on the codecs contained inside them. It has also been previously reported that the DivX and Xvid codecs within AVI are also playable on the system.[37] [38] Unlike the previous Windows Mobile operating system, there are currently no third-party applications for handling other video formats. The image file formats that are supported include JPG/JPEG, PNG, GIF, TIF and Bitmap (BMP).[39] [40]

Games

Xbox Live on Windows Phone brings Console-like gaming experience to phones by displaying the user's avatar in a 3D fashion. Via "**Games hub**", the users are able to interact with the avatar, view gamerscore and leaderboards, message Xbox Live friends, and Spotlight.[41] Multiplayer (turn-based) gaming with live multiplayer are also released.[42] Microsoft has unveiled more than 50 premium Windows Phone Games titles at Gamescom that makes use of Xbox Live on mobile.[43] Xbox Live on Windows Phone currently doesn't offer real-time multiplayer games, but will be added in the future.[44] Some key features of Xbox Live on Windows Phone include ability to be signed in simultaneously on the console and phone, send and receive messages between Console and Phone, unlock unique gamer points only available by purchasing the gaming title on the phone, etc.

Search

Microsoft's hardware requirements stipulate that every Windows Phone must have a dedicated Search button on the front of the device that performs different actions.[21] Pressing the search button while an application is open will allow users to search within applications that take advantage of this feature; for example, pressing Search in the People hub will let the users search their contact list for specific people.[45]

The Bing application on Windows Phone.

In other cases, pressing the Search button will allow the user to perform a search of web sites, news, and map locations using the Bing application.[46]

Windows Phone also has a voice recognition function, powered by TellMe, which allows the user to perform a Bing search, call contacts or launch applications by speaking. This can be activated by pressing and holding the phone's Start button.

Bing is the default search engine on Windows Phone handsets due to its deep integration of functions into the OS (which also include the utilization of its map service for location-based searches and queries). However, Microsoft has stated that other search engine applications can be used.[46] [47] [47]

Aside from location-based searches, Bing Maps also provide turn-by-turn navigation service to Windows Phone user and Local Scout shows interest points such as attractions and restaurants in the nearby area.

Bing Audio allows the user to match a song with its name and Bing Vision allows the user to match barcodes and tags with the product online.

Office suite

Microsoft Office Mobile on Windows Phone

The "**Office hub**" organizes all Microsoft Office apps and documents. Microsoft Office Mobile provides interoperability between Windows Phone and the desktop version of Microsoft Office. Word Mobile, Excel Mobile, PowerPoint Mobile, OneNote Mobile, and SharePoint Workspace Mobile allow most Microsoft Office file formats to be viewed and edited directly on a Windows Phone device.

Microsoft Office files from SkyDrive and Office 365, as well as files stored locally on the phone, can be accessed through the Office Hub. Office files are sorted by tiles: Word documents (blue tile), Excel spreadsheets (green tile), PowerPoint presentations (red tile), and OneNote documents (purple tile).

Multitasking

In Windows Phone 7, multitasking is limited to bundled apps. Starting with Windows Phone 7.5, a card-based task switcher can be accessed by pressing and holding the back button. The screenshot of last five open app are shown as cards. Apps can be kept running even when out of view through "Live Agents".[48] In other cases, apps are suspended and can be quickly resumed.

Sync

Zune Software manages the contents on Windows Phone devices and Windows Phone can wirelessly sync with Zune Software. In addition to accessing on the Windows Phone devices, Zune software can also access the Zune Marketplace to purchase music, videos, and all apps for Windows Phone. While music and videos are both stored locally on the PC and on the phone, apps are only stored on the phone even if purchased from the Zune Software. Zune Software can also be use to update all Windows Phone devices. Although Zune Software is unavailable on Mac OS X operating system, Microsoft has released Windows Phone Connector which allow Windows Phone devices to sync with iTunes for Mac and iPhoto.[49] [50] [51]

Updates

According to Microsoft documentation, software updates will be delivered to Windows Phone users via Microsoft Update, as is the case with other Windows operating systems.[52] Microsoft has the intention to directly update any phone running Windows Phone instead of relying on OEMs or wireless carriers.[53] The software component, called Windows Phone Update, exists both on the phone (for smaller updates, over-the-air) and in the Zune Software for Windows PCs (for larger updates, via USB connection). Users will be notified to attach their phones to a PC if such an update is required.[54] Microsoft has said that in the future, all updates, both large and small will eventually support over-the-air downloads.[55] Charlie Kindel, Program Manager for the developer experience of Windows Phone, confirmed that the update infrastructure system for Windows Phone was available and that Microsoft is "in a position where we have the systems in place to effectively and reliably deliver updates to (Windows Phone) users".[56]

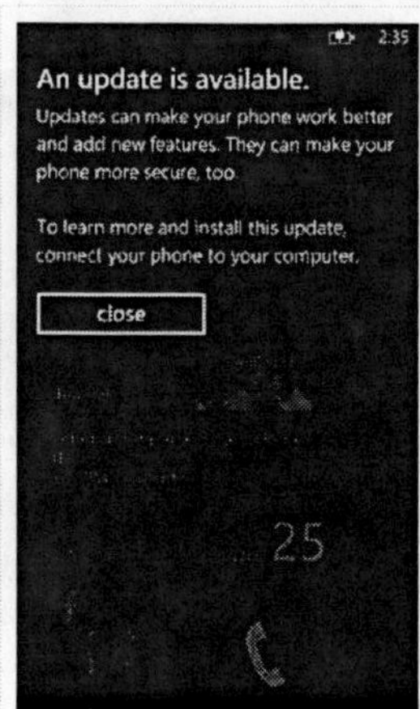

A test notification of an "update available" pop-up in the Windows Phone emulator.

Microsoft plans to regularly ship minor updates that add features throughout the year, and major updates once a year.[57]

All third-party applications can be updated automatically from the Windows Phone Marketplace.[58]

Advertising platform

Microsoft has also launched an advertising platform for the Windows Phone platform. Microsoft's General Manager for Strategy and Business Development, Kostas Mallios, said that Windows Phone will be an "ad-serving machine", pushing advertising and brand-related content to the user. The platform will feature advertising tiles near applications and toast notifications, which will bring updating advertising notifications. Mallios said that Windows Phone will be able to "preserve the brand experience by going directly from the web site right to the application", and that Windows Phone "enables advertisers to connect with consumers over time".[59] Mallios continued: "you're now able to push information as an advertiser, and stay in touch with your customer. It's a dynamic relationship that is created and provides for an ongoing dialog with the consumer."[60]

Marketplace

Windows Phone Marketplace on Samsung Focus

The Windows Phone Marketplace is used to digitally distribute music, video content, podcasts, and third party applications to Windows Phone handsets. The marketplace is accessible using the Zune Software client or the marketplace hub on devices (though videos and podcasts are not downloadable through the marketplace hub and must be downloaded and synced through the Zune software).[61] The marketplace is managed by Microsoft, which includes an approval process.

Music and videos

Zune Marketplace offers 10 million songs up to 320 kbit/s in DRM-free MP3 format from the big four music groups (EMI, Warner Music Group, Sony BMG and Universal Music Group), as well as smaller music labels. It offer movies from Paramount, Universal, Warner Brothers, and other studios and also offer television shows from popular television networks.

Microsoft also offer Zune Pass music subscription service which allows subscribers to download an unlimited number of songs for as long as their subscription is active.

Applications and games

Development

Third party applications and games for Windows Phone must be based on XNA or a WP7 specific version of Silverlight[62] only.[63] For Windows Phone apps to be designed and tested within Visual Studio 2010 or Visual Studio 2010 Express editions, Microsoft offers Windows Phone Developer Tools as an extension. Windows Phone Developer Tools run only on Windows Vista SP2 and later. [64] Windows XP and Windows Server 2003 are not supported. Microsoft also offers Expression Blend for Windows Phone for free.[65] On November 29, 2009, Microsoft announced the Release to web (RTW) version of its Visual Basic .NET Developer Tool, to allow development in Visual Basic.[65]

Submission

Registered Windows Phone and Xbox Live developers can submit and manage their third party applications for the platforms though the App Hub web applications.[66] The App Hub provides development tools and support for third-party application developers. The submitted applications undergo an approval process for verifications and validations to check if they qualify the applications standardization criteria set by Microsoft.[67] The cost of the applications that are approved is up to the developer, but Microsoft will take 30% of the revenue (the other 70% goes to the developer).[68] Microsoft will only pay developers once they reach a set sales figure, and will withhold 30% tax from non-US developers, unless they first register with the United States Government's Internal Revenue Service. Microsoft only pays developers from a list of thirty countries.[69] A yearly fee is also payable for developers wishing to submit apps.[70]

In order to get an application to appear in the Windows Phone Marketplace, the application must be submitted to Microsoft for approval.[69] Microsoft has outlined the content that it will not allow in the applications, which includes content it deem "sexually suggestive". This includes content depicting nudity (nipples, genitals, buttocks, pubic hair), prostitution, and sexual fetishes.[71]

Hardware

System requirements

Microsoft has said that it is issuing "tough, but fair" hardware requirements to manufacturers.[72] All Windows Phone devices, at minimum, must include the following:[73] [74]

Samsung Omnia 7, on the 3 Austria network, running Windows Phone

Minimum Windows Phone device requirements
Capacitive, 4-point multi-touch screen with WVGA (480x800) resolution
ARM v7 "Cortex/Scorpion" – Snapdragon QSD8X50, MSM7X30, and MSM8X55
DirectX9 rendering-capable GPU
256 MB of RAM with at least 8 GB of Flash memory
Accelerometer with compass, ambient light sensor, proximity sensor, Assisted GPS, and Gyroscope
5-megapixel camera with an LED flash
FM radio tuner
Six (6) dedicated hardware buttons – back, Start, search, 2-stage camera, power/sleep and Volume Up and Down.[75]

Reception

Reviews

Reception to Windows Phone has been generally positive, with special note to certain shortcomings, which Engadget and Gizmodo felt were notable omissions in a modern smartphone OS. ZDNet praised the OS's virtual keyboard and noted the excellent touch precision as well as powerful auto-correct and revision software.[26] [76] The touch responsiveness of the OS has also been universally praised by all three sites with reviewers noting the smoothness of scrolling and gestures like pinch to zoom in web browsing.[77]

The reception to the "Metro" UI and overall interface of the OS has also been highly praised for its style, with ZDNet noting its originality and fresh clean look.[78] Engadget and ZDNet applauded the integration of Facebook into the People Hub as well as other built in capabilities, such as Windows Live, etc.

Engadget found the OS's greatest shortcomings to be a lack of some features found in other smartphone operating systems, the most notable being lack of multitasking, a universal search, and unified email inbox. Generally all three sites found the core experience of Windows Phone to be a positive one, but few pointed to these omissions as potential deal-breakers for some consumers.[79] [80] However, Microsoft plans to address many of these shortcomings in an update codenamed Mango, which will be released in fall 2011 and will be provided to all existing Windows Phone users free of charge. Microsoft has announced many of the features which will be included in Mango, such as third-party multitasking, conversation view for email, improved Office apps, a full HTML5 web browser, custom ringtones, integrated instant messaging via Facebook and Windows Live Messenger, new Bing search features, and more.[81] [82]

Market share

According to Gartner, 3.6 million smartphones using a Microsoft mobile OS were sold world wide in the first quarter of 2011, for a 3.6% market share. Specifically, Windows Phone sold 1.6 million units, hence achieving a 1.6% market share. [83] A study carried out by Nielsen Company indicated that in the US, WP7 achieved a smart phone market share of 1% in the period Mar to May 2011.[84]

Awards

Windows Phone was presented with a total of three awards at the 2011 International Design Excellence Awards; Gold in Interactive Product Experience, Silver in Research and Bronze in the Design Strategy.

"The Windows Phone 7 was built around the idea that the end user is king. The design team began by defining and understanding the people who would use this phone. It was convinced that there could be a better user experience for a phone, one that revolves more around who the users are rather than what they do. The Windows Phone 7 lets users quickly get in, get out and back to their lives.""Windows Phone Wins Three IDEA Awards" [88].

See also

- List of Windows Phone devices
- Microsoft Silverlight
- Microsoft XNA
- Mobile operating system
- Zune HD
- Windows Mobile
- Xbox Live
- Windows 8

References

[1] Damian Koh (2010-02-18). "Q&A: Microsoft on Windows Phone 7" (http://asia.cnet.com/reviews/mobilephones/0,39050603,62061278,00.htm). CNET Asia. . Retrieved 2010-06-03.

[2] Peter Bright (2010-03-16). "Windows Phone 7 Series in the Enterprise: not all good news" (http://arstechnica.com/microsoft/news/2010/03/windows-phone-7-series-in-the-enterprise-not-all-good-news.ars). . Retrieved 2010-11-20.

[3] Sean Hollister (2010-09-26). "Microsoft prepping Windows Phone 7 for an October 21st launch? (update: US on Nov. 8?)" (http://www.engadget.com/2010/09/26/microsoft-prepping-windows-phone-7-for-an-october-21st-launch/). . Retrieved 2010-09-29.

[4] "Everything Is Different Now" (http://gizmodo.com/5471805/windows-phone-7-series-everything-is-different-now). .

[5] "What Windows Phone 7 Could Have Been" (http://gizmodo.com/5480387/what-windows-phone-7-could-have-been). 2010-02-25. . Retrieved 2010-06-05.

[6] "Thoughts on Windows Phone 7 Series (BTW: Photon is Dead)" (http://pocketnow.com/thought/thoughts-on-windows-phone-7-series-btw-photon-is-dead). 2010-02-17. . Retrieved 2010-06-05.

[7] "Steve Ballmer wishes Windows Mobile 7 had already launched, but they screwed up" (http://www.mobiletechworld.com/2009/09/24/steve-ballmer-wishes-windows-mobile-7-had-already-launched-but-they-screwed-up/). MobileTechWorld. 2009-09-24. .

[8] Nicholas Kolakowski (15 March 2010). "Microsoft Explains Windows Phone 7 Lack of Compatibility" (http://www.eweek.com/c/a/Mobile-and-Wireless/Microsoft-Explains-Windows-Phone-7-Lack-of-Compatibility-588900/). *eWeek*. .

[9] "Windows Phone 7: A New Kind of Phone (36:47 min. in)" (http://www.msteched.com/2010/NorthAmerica/WPH201). Microsoft. 2010-06-13. . Retrieved 2010-09-09.

[10] Bonnie Cha. "Microsoft drops 'Series' from Windows Phone 7" (http://www.cnet.com/8301-17918_1-20001674-85.html?tag=mncol). cnet. .

[11] "Mobile World Congress 2010 – day one overview" (http://www.techcentral.co.za/mobile-world-congress-2010-day-one-overview/12826/). 2010-02-15. . Retrieved 2010-06-03.

[12] Vlad Savov (2010-09-16). "Microsoft demoes Twitter and Netflix apps for Windows Phone 7, releases final dev tools" (http://www.engadget.com/2010/09/16/microsoft-demoes-twitter-and-netflix-apps-for-windows-phone-7-r/). Engadget. . Retrieved 2010-09-29.

[13] "HP: No More Windows Phone 7 Smartphones" (http://www.pcmag.com/article2/0,2817,2366954,00.asp). PCMAG.com. 25 July 2010. . Retrieved 13 December 2010.

[14] http://windowsteamblog.com/windows_phone/b/windowsphone/archive/2011/07/06/windows-phone-around-the-world-language-support-in-mango.aspx

[15] "Microsoft announces ten Windows Phone 7 handsets for 30 countries: October 21 in Europe and Asia, 8 November in US (Update: Video!)" (http://www.engadget.com/2010/10/11/microsoft-announces-ten-windows-phone-7-handsets-for-30-countrie/). Engadget. 11 October 2010. . Retrieved 12 October 2010.

[16] http://www.microsoft.com/presspass/press/2011/feb11/02-11partnership.mspx

[17] http://www.microsoft.com/presspass/press/2011/apr11/04-21msftnokia.mspx

[18] http://www.slashgear.com/windows-phone-mango-official-acer-fujitsu-and-zte-onboard-24153926/

[19] http://download.microsoft.com/download/F/F/C/FFCF79B1-C2EB-42C2-8E2D-665705380DA0/Windows%20Phone%20Design%20System%20-%20Codename%20Metro.PDF

[20] "Windows Phone 7 is official, and Microsoft is playing to win" (http://www.engadget.com/2010/02/15/windows-phone-7-is-official-and-microsoft-is-playing-to/). 2010-02-15. . Retrieved 2010-2-15-10.

[21] "Windows Phone 7: the complete guide" (http://www.engadget.com/2010/03/18/windows-phone-7-series-the-complete-guide/). March 18, 2010. . Retrieved September 19, 2010.

[22] Rubenstein, Benjamin (2010-03-17). "Interview: Windows Phone 7 battery life, copy/paste, multitasking, and more" (http://www.neowin.net/news/interview-windows-phone-7-battery-life-copypaste-multitasking-and-more). *Neowin.net*. . Retrieved 2010-08-21.

[23] "The Most Comprehensive Windows Phone 7 Demo to Date" (http://pocketnow.com/windows-phone/comprehensive-windows-phone-7-demo). July 27, 2010. . Retrieved September 19, 2010.

[24] "Channel 9 Demos Some Windows Phone 7 Apps" (http://pocketnow.com/windows-phone/channel-9-demos-some-windows-phone-7-apps). August 10, 2010. . Retrieved September 19, 2010.

[25] "HTC HD7: Hello, All 4.3-Inches of Windows Phone 7" (http://www.wp7forum.com/htc-hd7/htc-hd7-hello-all-4-3-inches-of-windows-phone-7). October 10, 2010. .

[26] Topolsky, Joshua (2010-07-19). "Windows Phone 7 in-depth preview" (http://www.engadget.com/2010/07/19/windows-phone-7-in-depth-preview/). . Retrieved 2010-09-04.

[27] "AutoCompleteBox in Windows Phone 7" (http://rgullhaug.wordpress.com/2010/09/08/autocompletebox-in-wp7). September 8, 2010. . Retrieved September 21, 2010.

[28] "Windows Phone 7 Keyboard Demoed, Deemed Fast, Responsive, Accurate" (http://pocketnow.com/windows-phone/windows-phone-7-keyboard-demoed-deemed-fast-responsive-accurate). August 10, 2010. . Retrieved September 19, 2010.

[29] "Windows Phone 7 Series Text Entry: Strict Hardware Requirements" (http://pocketnow.com/deals/windows-phone-7-series-text-entry-strict-hardware-requirements). August 17, 2010. . Retrieved September 19, 2010.

[30] "Windows Phone 7.5 Mango in-depth preview" (http://www.engadget.com/2011/06/27/windows-phone-7-5-mango-in-depth-preview-video/). Engadget. 2010-02-15. . Retrieved 2010-02-19.

[31] Exclusive: Windows Phone 7 Web Browser Comparison (Video) (http://pocketnow.com/windows-phone/exclusive-windows-phone-7-web-browser-comparison)
[32] "First Look: Internet Explorer on Windows Phone 7 Series" (http://pocketnow.com/software-1/first-look-internet-explorer-on-windows-phone-7-series). March 15, 2010. . Retrieved September 19, 2010.
[33] "IE Mobile Updates, Program Manager for IE Mobile team comments on update system for the browser" (http://www.mobiletechworld.com/2010/05/20/the-windows-phone-7-ie-mobile-browser-upgradable-without-a-firmware-update/). 2010-05-20. .
[34] Official YouTube support for Windows Phone 7 revealed | WMExperts (http://www.wmexperts.com/official-youtube-support-windows-phone-7-revealed)
[35] "Zune for Windows Phone 7" (http://www.zune.net/en-US/products/windowsphone7/default.htm). Microsoft. . Retrieved 16 December 2010.
[36] Miniman, Brandon (21 September 2010). "Windows Phone 7: Which Video and Audio File Formats are Supported?" (http://pocketnow.com/windows-phone/windows-phone-7-which-video-and-audio-file-formats-are-supported). *Pocketnow Win Phone 7*. pocketnow.com. . Retrieved 06 August 2011.
[37] "Updates codec support list for Windows Phone 7 released, XVID and DIVX supported" (http://wmpoweruser.com/updates-codec-support-list-for-windows-phone-7-released-xvid-and-divx-supported/). wmpoweruser.com. 18 September 2010. . Retrieved 06 August 2011.
[38] "AVI/DivX support - Microsoft Answers" (http://answers.microsoft.com/en-us/winphone/forum/wp7-wpdevices/avidivx-support/4966f233-bf3a-4495-87f4-ad130e6539ea). *Microsoft Answers*. answers.microsoft.com. 21 October 2010. . Retrieved 06 August 2011.
[39] "Supported Media Codecs for Windows Phone" (http://msdn.microsoft.com/en-us/library/ff462087(v=vs.92).aspx). *Microsoft Developer Network (MSDN)*. . Retrieved 06 August 2011.
[40] "Audio file formats supported by the Zune software" (http://support.microsoft.com/kb/928191). *MS zune file-formats*. Microsoft support.microsoft.com. 12 October 2010. . Retrieved 06 August 2011.
[41] "Games Hub for Windows Phone 7" (http://www.microsoft.com/windowsphone/en-us/howto/wp7/apps/games-hub.aspx). *Microsoft*. .
[42] "Alphajax is turn-based game" (http://social.answers.microsoft.com/Forums/en-US/windowsphone7/thread/8ec431b8-2d95-4177-8a28-4c6dd731ee87). .
[43] "Xbox Live games for Windows Phone 7 from Gamescom 2010" (http://www.bestwp7games.com/xbox-live-games-for-windows-phone-7-from-gamescom-2010.html). *BestWP7Games*. 18 August 2010. .
[44] "Windows Phone 7 Online Multiplayer Games" (http://electronictheatre.co.uk/index.php/mobile/mobile-phone-game-news/6791-windows-phone-7-online-multiplayer-now-available). Kev J.. . Retrieved 23 December 2010.
[45] "Windows Phone 7 Series hands-on" (http://www.slashgear.com/windows-phone-7-series-hands-on-1573973/). *SlashGear*. 15 February 2010. .
[46] Mary Jo Foley (15 February 2010). "Will all Xbox games work on Windows Phone 7 devices?" (http://www.zdnet.com/blog/microsoft/will-all-xbox-games-work-on-windows-phone-7-devices/5272). ZDNet. .
[47] "Windows Phone 7: Bing only default search option" (http://www.pocket-lint.com/news/34446/bing-only-default-search-option). Pocket-lint. 21 July 2010. .
[48] http://arstechnica.com/microsoft/news/2011/04/windows-phone-7-mango-one-heck-of-an-upgrade.ars
[49] Mary Branscombe. "Hands on: Windows Phone 7 Connector for Mac review" (http://www.techradar.com/news/phone-and-communications/mobile-phones/hands-on-windows-phone-7-connector-for-mac-review-902191). TechRadar. .
[50] Matthew Miller. "Windows Phone 7 Connector syncs your Mac with your WP7 smartphone" (http://www.zdnet.com/blog/cell-phones/windows-phone-7-connector-syncs-your-mac-with-your-wp7-smartphone/4878). ZDNet. .
[51] Chris Davies. "Windows Phone 7 Connector for Mac demo" (http://www.slashgear.com/windows-phone-7-connector-for-mac-demo-21109410). SlashGear. .
[52] Paul Thurrott (April 19, 2010). "Windows Phone OS 7.0 Architecture Guide" (http://windowsphonesecrets.com/2010/04/19/windows-phone-os-7-0-architecture-guide/). . Retrieved 2010-09-09.
[53] "Microsoft talks Windows Phone 7 features, native code, multi-tasking and update process" (http://www.mobiletechworld.com/2010/04/11/microsoft-talks-windows-phone-7-features-native-code-multi-tasking-and-update-process). MobileTechWorld. .
[54] M. Daou (2010-05-16). "Confidential Windows Phone 7 Development Guides leaked" (http://www.mobiletechworld.com/2010/05/16/confidential-windows-phone-7-development-guides-leaked/). . Retrieved 2010-06-03.
[55] "Windows Update for Windows Phone: This is What You've Been Waiting For" (http://www.windowsphonethoughts.com/news/show/100826/windows-update-for-windows-phone-this-is-what-you-ve-been-waiting-for.html). .
[56] Paul Thurrott (2010-05-19). "Windows Phone Update: May 2010" (http://www.winsupersite.com/mobile/wp7_update.asp). . Retrieved 2010-06-03.
[57] Ina Fried. "Ballmer talks Windows Phone 7 with CNET (Q&A)" (http://news.cnet.com/8301-13860_3-20019259-56.html?tag=cnetRiver). .
[58] Chris Ziegler (2010-03-15). "Windows Phone Marketplace for Windows Phone 7 Series unveiled" (http://www.engadget.com/2010/03/15/windows-phone-marketplace-for-windows-phone-7-series-unveiled/). Engadget. . Retrieved 2010-06-03.
[59] "MS Sees Windows Phone 7 as an 'Ad-Serving Machine'" (http://www.newsfactor.com/news/Phone-7-Seen-as--Ad-Serving-Machine-/story.xhtml?story_id=12100BWDYBSP&full_skip=1). NewsFactor Network. 25 June 2010. .

[60] "Microsoft's Ad-Serving Machine" (http://www.informationweek.com/blog/main/archives/2010/06/microsofts_adse.html). *InformationWeek*. 25 June 2010. .
[61] http://www.microsoft.com/windowsphone/en-us/howto/wp7/music/get-music-videos-and-podcasts-from-marketplace.aspx
[62] http://msdn.microsoft.com/en-us/library/ff426931(v=VS.95).aspx
[63] http://create.msdn.com/en-US/home/about/how_it_works_create
[64] Installing Windows Phone Developer Tools (http://msdn.microsoft.com/en-us/library/ff402530(v=vs.92).aspx#BKMK_SysReqs)
[65] http://create.msdn.com/en-us/home/getting_started
[66] http://create.msdn.com/en-gb/App Hub
[67] "Introducing App Hub for Windows Phone & Indie Game Developers" (http://windowsteamblog.com/windows_phone/b/wpdev/archive/2010/10/11/introducing-app-hub-for-windows-phone-7-amp-indie-game-developers.aspx). Microsoft. . Retrieved 16 December 2010.
[68] http://windowsteamblog.com/windows_phone/b/wpdev/archive/2010/03/15/the-right-mix.aspx
[69] http://create.msdn.com/en-us/home/faq
[70] http://create.msdn.com/en-US/home/about/how_it_works
[71] http://go.microsoft.com/fwlink/?LinkID=183220
[72] "Live from Microsoft's Windows Phone press event at MWC 2010" (http://www.engadget.com/2010/02/15/live-from-microsofts-windows-phone-7-series-windows-mobile-press-event-at-mwc-2010/). engadget.com. 2010-02-15. . Retrieved 2010-03-21.
[73] "What Is Windows Phone 7?" (http://recombu.com/news/what-is-windows-phone-7_M12576.html). .
[74] Standardized Hardware Foundation (http://y.msmobiles.com/microsoft/wp7s/requirements.jpg)
[75] Anton D. Nagy. "Windows Phone 7 Actually Requires Six Hardware Buttons" (http://pocketnow.com/tech-news/windows-phone-7-actually-requires-six-hardware-buttons). pocketnow. .
[76] "Windows Phone 7 In Depth: A Fresh Start" (http://gizmodo.com/5590327/windows-phone-7-in-depth-a-fresh-start). .
[77] Matthew Miller (2010-07-18). "Microsoft Windows Phone 7 technical preview: A definitive guide" (http://www.zdnet.com/blog/cell-phones/microsoft-windows-phone-7-technical-preview-a-definitive-guide/4286). ZDNet. . Retrieved 2010-10-23.
[78] http://www.zdnet.com/blog/cell-phones/microsoft-windows-phone-7-technical-preview-a-definitive-guide/4286
[79] http://www.engadget.com/2010/10/20/windows-phone-7-review/
[80] http://gizmodo.com/5668738/windows-phone-7-review
[81] http://windowsteamblog.com/windows_phone/b/windowsphone/archive/2011/05/24/microsoft-officially-unveils-mango-hundreds-of-improvements-on-the-way.aspx
[82] http://www.engadget.com/2011/06/27/windows-phone-7-5-mango-in-depth-preview-video/
[83] Reisinger, Don (2011-05-19). "Gartner: Android leads, Windows Phone lags in Q1" (http://news.cnet.com/8301-13506_3-20064223-17.html#ixzz1POqi39Fa). CNET. .
[84] "In US, Smartphones Now Majority of New Cellphone Purchases: Apple iOS up, Android flat, RIM down among recent acquirers" (http://blog.nielsen.com/nielsenwire/?p=28237). Nielsen Wire. 2011-06-30. .

External links

- Official website (http://http://www.microsoft.com/windowsphone/en-us/default.aspx)
- Windows Phone 7 developer resources (http://msdn.microsoft.com/en-au/windowsmobile/default.aspx?WT.mc_id=soc-c-au-loc--2010oct)
- Windows Phone 7 on Microsoft Wave (http://www.microsoft.com/uk/wave/hardware-windowsphone7.aspx)
- Windows Phone 7 for government (http://www.microsoft.com/industry/government/products/WindowsPhone7.aspx)

AT&T Mobility

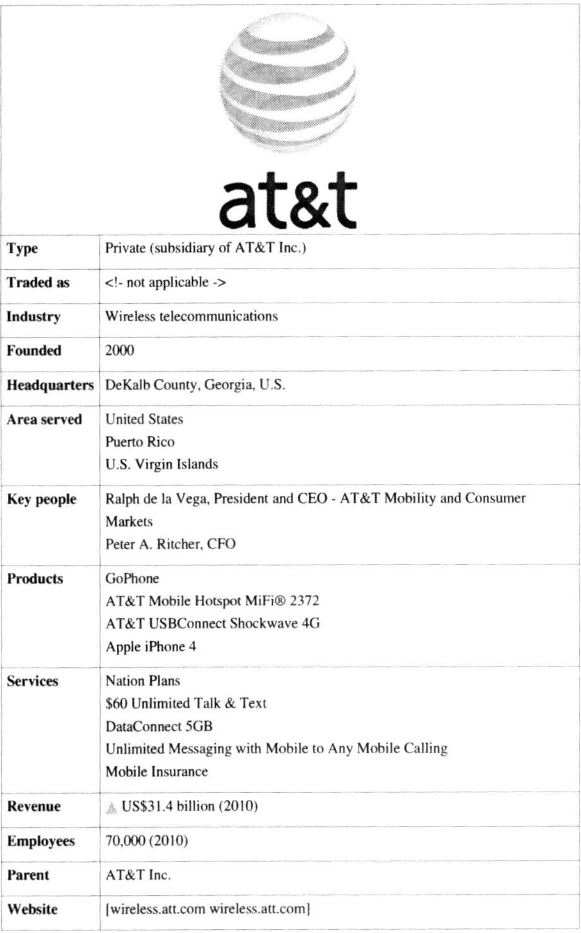

Type	Private (subsidiary of AT&T Inc.)
Traded as	<!- not applicable ->
Industry	Wireless telecommunications
Founded	2000
Headquarters	DeKalb County, Georgia, U.S.
Area served	United States Puerto Rico U.S. Virgin Islands
Key people	Ralph de la Vega, President and CEO - AT&T Mobility and Consumer Markets Peter A. Ritcher, CFO
Products	GoPhone AT&T Mobile Hotspot MiFi® 2372 AT&T USBConnect Shockwave 4G Apple iPhone 4
Services	Nation Plans $60 Unlimited Talk & Text DataConnect 5GB Unlimited Messaging with Mobile to Any Mobile Calling Mobile Insurance
Revenue	▲ US$31.4 billion (2010)
Employees	70,000 (2010)
Parent	AT&T Inc.
Website	[wireless.att.com wireless.att.com]

AT&T Mobility LLC is a wholly owned subsidiary of AT&T Inc. that provides wireless services to 98.6 million subscribers in the United States, Puerto Rico and the U.S. Virgin Islands. AT&T Mobility is the second largest wireless telecommunications provider in the United States behind Verizon Wireless, which has 106.3 million customers as of the second quarter of 2011.[1] AT&T Mobility is headquartered in the Lenox Park area of DeKalb Co. Georgia, just outside Atlanta.[2]

Originally **Cingular Wireless LLC**, a joint venture between SBC Communications and BellSouth, the company acquired the old AT&T Wireless in 2004; SBC later acquired the original AT&T and re-branded as "The New AT&T". Cingular became wholly owned by AT&T in December 2006 as a result of AT&T's acquisition of BellSouth.

In January 2007, Cingular confirmed it would re-brand itself under the AT&T name. Although the legal corporate name change occurred immediately, for both regulatory and brand-awareness reasons both brands were used in the company's signage and advertising during a transition period.[3] The transition concluded in late June, just prior to the rollout of the Apple iPhone.

On March 20, 2011, AT&T Mobility announced its intention to acquire T-Mobile USA from Deutsche Telekom for $39 billion. If AT&T receives government and regulatory approval, AT&T will be the largest wireless network in the United States, with more than 130 million subscribers. [4]

Services

Among the services that AT&T aggressively promotes is its Rollover Minutes service which allows customers to keep unused minutes from month to month on a twelve-month rolling cycle on its popular nationwide plans. Beginning in July 2007, AT&T allows its AT&T Unity plan users to have Rollover, a service which was exclusive to the Nation plans. AT&T also launched video share in 2007, in which a mobile caller can stream live video from one phone to another over the 3G network with video share capable phones. This allows one mobile phone user to view video from another user's camera through the mobile phone in real time. At&T also has A-list. The former competitor Alltel, who is now part of Verizon Wireless, had a program called "My Circle". This allowed for free calls to popular numbers, regardless of the carrier. This program was adopted company wide in February 2009 by Verizon Wireless,[5] and was renamed Friends & Family. AT&T rolled out their version of the program on September 20, 2009. Customers with individual Nation plans of $59.99 or higher can use A-List with Rollover to select up to five domestic phone numbers to call anytime—including landlines and wireless numbers on any network—without using any of the minutes in their plan. FamilyTalk customers with plans of $89.99 or more can select up to ten numbers which any person in the FamilyTalk plan can call as much as they want.[6]

Employees

A large number of AT&T Mobility employees are unionized, belonging to the Communications Workers of America. The CWA represented roughly 15,000 of the previous 20,000 formerly AT&T Wireless employees as of early 2006.[7] As of the end of 2009, the CWA website claims roughly 40,000 workers of AT&T Mobility are represented by the union.[8]

AT&T Mobility Headquarters in DeKalb County (near Atlanta), Georgia

History

Cingular Wireless LLC was founded in 2000 as a joint venture of SBC Communications and BellSouth. The joint venture created the nation's second-largest carrier. Cingular grew out of a conglomeration of more than 100 companies,[9] with 12 well-known regional companies with Bell roots. The 12 companies included:

Cingular Wireless logo, 2000–2004

- Three companies spun off from Advanced Mobile Phone Service, Inc.
  - Ameritech Mobile Communications, LLt
  - BellSouth Mobility, LLC

- Southwestern Bell Mobile Systems, Inc.
- BellSouth Mobility DCS, Inc.
- BellSouth Wireless Data, LLC
- CCPR Services Inc. d/b/a Cellular One of Puerto Rico and US Virgin Islands
- Pacific Bell Wireless, LLC
- Pacific Bell Wireless Northwest, LLC
- SBC Wireless, LLC
- SNET Mobility, LLC
- Southwestern Bell Wireless, Inc.

SBC Wireless had previously operated in several northeast markets under the "Cellular One" brand, while BellSouth's wireless operations incorporated the former Houston Cellular.

Cingular's lineage can be traced back to Advanced Mobile Phone Service, which was a subsidiary of AT&T created in 1978 to provide cellular service nationwide. AMPS, Inc. was divided among the Regional Bell Operating Companies as part of the Bell System divestiture.

With the exception of Pacific Bell and BellSouth Mobility DCS, the digital network consisted of D-AMPS technology. The Pacific Bell and BellSouth Mobility DCS networks used GSM technology on the PCS frequency band (1900 MHz).

In October 2007, AT&T's president and chief executive officer Stan Sigman announced his retirement. Ralph de la Vega, group president-Regional Telecom & Entertainment, was named as president and CEO, AT&T Mobility.[10]

AT&T Wireless merger

In February 2004, after a bidding war with Britain's Vodafone Plc (45% owners of Verizon Wireless) Cingular announced that it would purchase its struggling competitor, AT&T Wireless Services, Inc., for $41 billion. This was more than twice the company's trading value.

The merger was completed on October 26, 2004. The combined company had a customer base of 46 million people at the time, making Cingular the largest wireless provider in the United States. AT&T Wireless was then legally renamed **New Cingular Wireless Services, Inc.** [11] Shortly after, new commercials were shown with the "AT&T" transforming into the Cingular logo, and with the Cingular logo's text turned blue to acknowledge the change. First announced on June 22, 2005, Cingular Wireless announced the intention to divest its Caribbean and Bermuda operations and licenses which it acquired from the acquisition of AT&T Wireless, to Irish-owned and Jamaica-based Digicel Group under undisclosed financial terms.[12] [13] [14] [15]

AT&T Wireless logo

Cingular Wireless logo, 2004–2006

In 2006, one year following the deal, a high ranking source allegedly close to the sale pointed the Barbados Daily Nation Newspaper towards some SEC filings made by Cingular which were said to establish an idea of the approximate sale price of the deal. According to the SEC filings Cingular was paid around US$122 million, with much of that $122m cost to Digicel going towards the purchasing of the former AT&T Wireless assets in Barbados.

At the time of the merger, there were two networks: the historic AT&T *Blue* Network and the Cingular *Orange* Network. Both networks contained a mix of both TDMA and GSM facilities. Approximately 50,000 cell sites had to be melded together. From a technical standpoint, the "blue" and "orange" networks were considered different networks until integration was completed in 2005.[16] Enhanced Network Selection (ENS) was used to home cellular devices on either the "blue" or "orange" network during this process.

GSM facilities

In California, Nevada, Northern New Jersey and New York City, Cingular and T-Mobile USA maintained and shared a GSM-1900 network prior to the acquisition of AT&T Wireless, through a joint venture known as *GSM Facilities*. The network sharing agreement allowed Cingular to offer local service in northern New Jersey and New York City and T-Mobile USA to offer service in California and Nevada. On May 25, 2004, Cingular and T-Mobile USA announced their intention to dissolve the agreement contingent on Cingular's successful acquisition of AT&T Wireless, the Cingular network was transferred to T-Mobile USA, with Cingular continuing work on the GSM facilities at AT&T Wireless sites.[17]

Radio Frequency Summary

The following is a list of known frequencies which AT&T employs in the United States:

Frequencies used on the AT&T Network

Frequency	Protocol	Class
850 MHz	GSM/GPRS/EDGE	2G
1900 MHz	GSM/GPRS/EDGE	2G
850 MHz	UMTS/HSPA	3G
1900 MHz	UMTS/HSPA	3G

Network coverage

As a result of its formation through mergers and acquisitions, as well as the rapid technological change in the wireless industry, AT&T Mobility operates the largest digital voice and data network within its United States footprint reaching over 300 million people or 97% established coverage using different wireless communication standards. The core technology standard for the AT&T Mobility wireless network is called Global System for Mobile Communications, or GSM. Much of the AT&T Mobility network footprint now uses GSM-standard 3G wireless technologies (UMTS/HSPA) for simultaneous circuit switched voice and packet switched data communications. AT&T Mobility also offers Push To Talk (PTT) service using network technology from Kodiak Networks.

An AT&T Mobility Device Support Center in Las Vegas, Nevada

Cingular, the predecessor to AT&T Mobility, supported legacy D-AMPS/TDMA and analog wireless networks. In March 2006, Cingular announced that these networks would be shut down by February 2008. As of March 31, 2007 Cingular ended TDMA supported for GoPhone (pre-paid) customers. On February 18, 2008, AT&T Mobility officially ended service on their AMPS and TDMA network, except for in areas previously operated by Dobson Communications; the Dobson AMPS and TDMA network was shut down March 1, 2008.

Networks formerly operated by AT&T Mobility predecessors including Cingular also include various paging services and the Cingular Interactive division, which became Velocita Wireless. Velocita was later purchased by Sprint Nextel.[18]

The AT&T Mobility wireless data network began in 2002 as a Cingular initiative called "Project Genesis" that involved a GPRS (General Packet Radio Service) overlay of the entire wireless network. Project Genesis was completed by the end of 2004. Later, this network was upgraded to EDGE (Enhanced Data rates for GSM Evolution) across the GSM footprint.

In 2005, AT&T Mobility launched a broadband network known as "BroadbandConnect," based on UMTS and High-Speed Downlink Packet Access (HSDPA), to counter Verizon Wireless and Sprint's EV-DO networks. UMTS service was launched on December 6, 2005 in Seattle, Portland, San Francisco, Salt Lake City, San Jose, San Diego, Las Vegas, Phoenix, Puerto Rico, Austin, Houston, Dallas, Detroit, Chicago, Boston, Baltimore and Washington D.C. and expanded to all major metropolitan markets by the end of 2006. As of early 2009, AT&T Mobility has completed its upgrade of the 3G network to HSUPA,[19] and will begin a new round of upgrades to the HSPA+ standard.[20]

Future networks

AT&T Mobility, Verizon Wireless, and most other mobile phone companies (Sprint being the sole US network to be migrating to the competing WiMAX standard) have chosen to build their new "4G" networks, with "Long Term Evolution" or LTE technology. Long Term Evolution LTE is the next step from 3G/WCDMA & HSPA for many already on the GSM technology curve, including AT&T. This new radio access technology will be optimized to deliver very fast data rates of up to 100 Mbit/s downlink and 50 Mbit/s uplink (peak rates). AT&T Networks will be throttling down the speeds to ensure all customers will be able to use LTE efficiently. Speeds are expected to be actually 6 Mbit/s to 8 Mbit/s with the exception of around 20 Mbit/s (Peak Rate), however this will change in time.

Designed to be backwards-compatible with GSM and HSPA, LTE incorporates Multiple In Multiple Out (MIMO) in combination with Orthogonal Frequency Division Multiple Access (OFDMA) in the downlink and Single Carrier FDMA in the uplink to provide high levels of spectral efficiency and end user data rates exceeding 100 Mbit/s, coupled with major improvements in capacity and reductions in latency. LTE will support channel bandwidths from 1.25 MHz to 20 MHz and both FDD and TDD operation. MetroPCS has activated the first LTE network, which is fully operational. AT&T Mobility has not set an official date to begin building their LTE network. Depending on the amount of spectrum the carrier deploys it is expected AT&T will deploy 10 MHz = 70 Mbit/s.

AT&T has noted that they will begin their upgrade to HSPA 14.4 as a part of their effort to enhance their 3G wireless network as well as the transition to LTE. AT&T has stated that their upgrades will be complete at the end of 2010 after backhaul connections leading from cell sites to AT&T switching facilities .[21] In addition, AT&T has stated that their LTE network will be completed by year end 2013.

"Cingular is now The New AT&T"

On November 20, 2005, Ed Whitacre, then CEO of the newly merged SBC/AT&T, announced plans to market Cingular's service under the *AT&T* brand. BellSouth spokesman Jeff Battcher countered that the terms of the joint venture allow either party to sell the service under another name, and that he believes they will be using the brand to market to business customers.[22] Cingular president Stan Sigman concurred with BellSouth's position, indicating that the Cingular brand would continue but be sold under the AT&T brand where offered in packages with other AT&T services, such as data and wireline telephony.

However, AT&T, Inc. announced on March 5, 2006[23] that it would acquire BellSouth. The acquisition was finalized on December 29, 2006 when the FCC gave its final approval. According to AT&T, the company began the rebranding of Cingular Wireless to "AT&T".[24]

On January 12, 2007 AT&T announced[25] a major rebranding transition campaign to transition Cingular to *the new AT&T* ("in February 2009 "new" was removed). The former Cingular stores, after being rebranded to AT&T, sold all AT&T products and services: wireless, landline, Internet, U-Verse, and more.

Cingular to AT&T Rebranding Transition:

- On January 14, 2007, AT&T launched the transition of the Cingular brand to AT&T in television advertising and customer communications, by creating the "Cingular is now The New AT&T" logo.
- On April 15, 2007, AT&T Mobility began to introduce new AT&T branded mobile phones and devices. The alpha tag (portion of phone's screen which displays the name of the network on which the phone is connected) on new phone activations also started reading "AT&T".
- Around May 11, 2007, Cingular's name was replaced with "AT&T" in most advertisements.
- On May 19, 2007, the AT&T logo replaced the Cingular logo on the NASCAR NEXTEL Cup Series car it sponsors, owned by Richard Childress Racing and driven by Jeff Burton. (But it was soon removed; see below for details.)
- On May 24, 2007, Palm, Inc. issued an update for Cingular-branded Treo 680 smartphones that, among other things, updated the phone's branding (startup and shutdown screens, wallpaper backgrounds) from Cingular to AT&T.[26]
- As of May 31, 2007, the former cingular.com [27] website redirects to wireless.att.com [28] and no longer features any Cingular logos whatsoever.
- In June 2007, customer service phone lines started being answered "Thank you for calling The New AT&T, about your wireless service." Additionally, all new SIM cards are branded with the AT&T logo.
- By June 16, 2007, most of the phones on the company's network displayed AT&T as the carrier instead of Cingular.
- By early 2009, AT&T had dropped "The New" part of its brand from all advertising and communications. Customer service phone lines are answered "Thank you for calling AT&T."
- As of August 2011, www.cingular.com [27] can still be used to access AT&T's website.

Acquisition of Dobson Communications

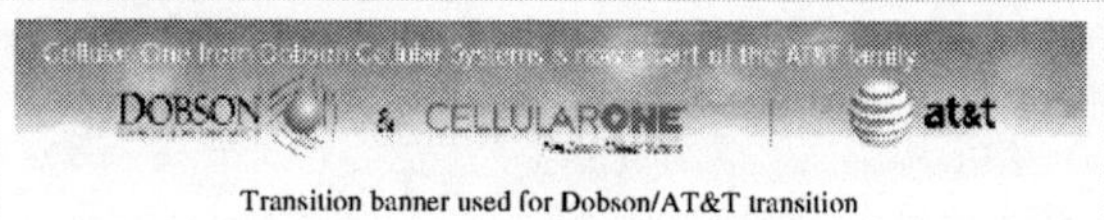

Transition banner used for Dobson/AT&T transition

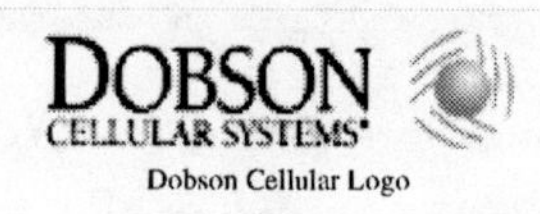

Dobson Cellular Logo

Cellular One logo used by Dobson until acquisition by AT&T in November 2007

On November 15, 2007, AT&T completed its acquisition of Dobson Communications. Dobson marketed the Cellular One brand in rural and suburban locations in various areas of the United States, including Alaska. AT&T bought Dobson for $13 per share, as well as assuming the regional carrier's debt, which cost the nation's largest carrier about $5.1 billion total. The U.S. Justice Department had ordered AT&T Inc. to sell assets in five U.S. states to complete its $2.8 billion Dobson Communications Corp. takeover. The department ordered AT&T to divest certain cell-phone assets in Kentucky, Oklahoma, Missouri, Pennsylvania and Texas where AT&T and Dobson are most competitive. At the time, AT&T was the largest U.S. cell-phone provider, with more than 81 million subscribers in 50 states. Dobson's Cellular One was the ninth largest, with 1.7 million subscribers in 17 states. Dobson had been an AT&T roaming partner since 1990, and the acquisition is expected to bring growth to Dobson's current markets. The purchase allowed AT&T to operate in the more rural areas of the United States including Alaska & West Virginia.[27]

Acquisition of Centennial Communications

On November 7, 2008, AT&T announced its plans to acquire Centennial Wireless for $944 million. AT&T said that the acquisition would provide customers with better coverage in the Southeast, Midwest, Puerto Rico, and the US Virgin Islands. The deal will also give AT&T more highly-coveted 850 MHz spectrum in the current Centennial Wireless coverage area. In addition, Centennial also provides switched voice and high-capacity data and Internet Protocol solutions for business customers in Puerto Rico. The transaction will give AT&T a wired network presence in Puerto Rico and will allow the company to better serve its multinational business customers with a presence in this U.S. territory. AT&T will gain Centennial's 893,000 subscribers after divestiture requirements. The deal was finalized on November 6, 2009.[28]

Acquisition of T-Mobile USA

On March 20, 2011, AT&T and Deutsche Telekom announced that AT&T had agreed to acquire T-Mobile USA from Deutsche Telekom in a deal estimated to be worth $39 billion in cash and stock. AT&T said the deal is expected to close in 12 months and is subject to regulatory approval. As of June 2011, it is being examined by the FCC. [29]

Marketing

"Fewest dropped calls"

During the first quarter of 2006, Telephia reported that during an extensive nationwide test of major wireless carriers in 350 metropolitan markets around the country, Cingular dropped the fewest number of calls across the country. Cingular in turn began aggressively advertising the "Allover Network", citing Telephia as "the leading independent research company." Telephia's report was in stark contrast to the Consumers Union publication, Consumer Reports, based on a survey of 50,000 of its members in 18 cities, which criticized Cingular for static and dropped calls.[30] Furthermore, J.D. Power and Associates consistently ranked Cingular at or near the bottom of every geographical region in its 2006 Wireless Call Quality Study, which is based on a smaller survey of 23,000 wireless users. This campaign had to come to an abrupt end.

Telephia, which tests wireless networks by making over 6 million calls per year in what it claims is the world's largest wireless network test program, initially refused to provide details on its study, and a spokesman for the company has said, according to the *Boston Globe*, that "Cingular shouldn't have even mentioned the company's name to a reporter."[31] The research company later stated that Cingular did indeed have a "statistically-significant lower dropped-call rate than the competition across some market/time period groupings", but that Telephia had "no knowledge of the specific methodology (markets, time periods or statistical thresholds) that Cingular used for its 'lowest dropped call' claim."[32] While AT&T has abandoned its verbal claim of "The Fewest Dropped Calls" in its commercials, it continues to show situations where two persons are speaking with each other on their phones, and one of the users' call drops. AT&T now states "We are still continuing to run ads that emphasize the importance of not dropping calls. That campaign is continuing.[33]

iPhone

On June 29, 2007 the Apple iPhone was introduced to the U.S. market, which made AT&T the exclusive carrier for the device within the United States until February 10, 2011, when the iPhone 4 was launched on the Verizon network.

Teething problems with AT&T's billing process emerged soon after the iPhone's release, as early adopters started receiving exceptionally detailed monthly telephone bills[34] [35] with one of the most notable being the 300-page iPhone bill that was featured in an online video by blogger Justine Ezarik.[36] [37]

Apple launched the iPhone 3G with AT&T on July 11, 2008. Although specific AT&T sales numbers are unavailable, Apple announced that over 1 million iPhone 3G devices were sold during the first three days – in contrast, according to Steve Jobs, Apple's CEO, "It took 74 days to sell the first one million original iPhones." [38] In August 2008, Best Buy announced that it would begin selling the iPhone 3G for use on the AT&T network.[39] In September 2008, AT&T announced that it would also sell the iPhone 3G in Puerto Rico and the US Virgin Islands.[40]

In the United States, the iPhone 3G is available for purchase with or without an AT&T contract, as most big box retailers, like Best Buy, will gladly sell it sans contract. AT&T is rumored to have heavily subsidized the iPhone's price to reach a broader spectrum of consumers.

On December 27, 2009 reports began to surface that AT&T had suspended online sales of the iPhone.[41] Spokesman Fletcher Cook said that the phone company periodically "modifies" its distribution channels, but had no further comment on the suspension of sales in the New York City area.[42] One AT&T employee incorrectly stated that, "New York wasn't ready for the iPhone," and that it lacked a sufficient number of cell towers to meet the heavy data demands imposed upon the network by iPhone users.[43] Sales of the popular iPhone resumed December 30, 2009.[44] This incident has revived speculation that AT&T's wireless network is not up to the demands of the current generation of 3G smartphones.[41] [45] The official AT&T statement is that a large amount of fraudulent activity caused the withdrawal of sales in the area.

The latest version of the iPhone is called the iPhone 4. It was released June 24, 2010. It brought a number of new features like an upgraded camera, flash, a new exterior design, upgraded screen, and the new version of Apple's software. According to Apple, over 1.7 million iPhone 4s were sold in the first few days, which is the most out of any phone ever sold. These sales propelled AT&T to strong Q2 results.

Android-based smart phones

On February 18, 2010, AT&T announced that on March 7, 2010 it would introduce its first smart phone based on Google's Android operating system,[46] the Motorola Backflip.[47] [48] On March 22, 2010, AT&T announced that its second Android handset would be the Dell Aero, a revised version of the Dell Mini 3.[46] However, the second Android phone AT&T released was the HTC Aria [49] [50] [51] which was announced on June 14, 2010 and released on June 20, 2010. The Samsung Captivate, which is part of the Galaxy S family, was released on AT&T's network on July 18, 2010. In addition to devices released on AT&T were a line of handsets manufactured by Motorola. The Motorola Flipout, followed by the Motorola Flipside and the Motorola Bravo all run Android 2.1 and were all released Q4 2010. Three new 4G Android devices were announced for release within the first and second quarter of the fiscal year 2011 including the Motorola Atrix 4G, the HTC Inspire 4G, and the Samsung Infuse 4G. HTC Inspire 4G being the first, proceeded by the Motorola Atrix 4G are currently available through AT&T's 4G network. [52] These three devices are all running Android 2.2 (froyo) and are expected to be upgraded to Android 2.3 gingerbread later in the year along with an update to 'enable' 4G uploads. Unlike other US networks with Android-based phones, AT&T did not allow non-Market Apps to be installed. However on May 16th, 2011 AT&T announced that some current and future Android devices will come with an option to allow the installation of unofficial applications. [53]

webOS-based smart phones

On January 6, 2010, Ralph de la Vega, CEO of AT&T Mobility announced during the AT&T Developer summit @ CES 2010 that AT&T will have 2 webOS devices in the first half of 2010. Silence by both Palm & AT&T after the event put this announcement in a limbo, although Palm later cleared the air by issuing a press release on March 22 that AT&T will showcase the Pre Plus and Pixi Plus, updated versions of the Palm Pre & Pixi with better memory and updated hardware at CTIA Wireless. The announced pricing for these devices is $149.99 and $49.99, respectively, with a two-year service agreement and after a $100 mail-in rebate. They were released on May 16, 2010. These will be the first webOS devices on AT&T and thereby bring Palm's webOS devices to Sprint, Verizon, and AT&T.

Microsoft Windows Phone 7

On November 8, 2010, AT&T and Microsoft released three Windows Phone 7s. One is made by HTC known as the HTC Surround. It is known for having a slide out Dolby-Surround sound speaker. One is made by Samsung known as the Focus. The Focus includes a 4-inch (100 mm) Super-amoled screen and is very similar to the Galaxy S line also made by Samsung. And the last is the LG Quantum which is known for having a slide-out QWERTY keyboard. All phones include a 5-mp camera with flash, a display with WVGA (800x480) resolution, and a 1 GHz Snapdragon processor. In 2011, HTC released its latest phone called the HTC HD7S. It has an 8 megapixel camera with dual flash, a 4.3 screen, and runs HTC Sense. It also has a stand which is he metal piece surrounding the camera, making it one of possibly 4 of the HTC line-up, the others being the HTC EVO, the Surround, and the HD7.

Phones offered

- Apple iPhone 3GS
- Apple iPhone 4
- AT&T F160
- Blackberry Bold 9700
- Blackberry Curve 8520
- Blackberry Curve 8900
- Blackberry Curve 9300
- Blackberry Pearl 9100
- BlackBerry Torch 9800
- HP iPAQ Glisten
- HTC Aria
- HTC HD7S
- HTC Inspire 4G
- HTC Surround
- HTC Tilt2
- LG Encore
- LG GU295
- LG Neon II
- LG Phoenix
- LG Quantum
- LG Vu Plus
- Motorola Atrix 4G
- Motorola Backflip
- Motorola Bravo
- Motorola Flipout

- Motorola Flipside
- Motorola Tundra
- Nokia 2330
- Nokia 6350
- Palm Pixi Plus
- Palm Pre Plus
- Pantech Breeze II
- Pantech Ease
- Pantech Impact
- Pantech Laser
- Pantech Link
- Pantech Pursuit
- Pantech Reveal
- Samsung A777
- Samsung Captivate
- Samsung Eternity II
- Samsung Evergreen
- Samsung Flight
- Samsung Flight II
- Samsung Focus
- Samsung Impression
- Samsung Infuse
- Samsung Jack
- Samsung Mythic
- Samsung Rugby II
- Samsung Solstice II
- Samsung Strive
- Samsung Sunburst
- Sharp FX
- Sony Ericsson w518a
- Sony Ericsson Vivaz
- Sony Ericsson Xperia X10

Calling plans and features

AT&T Mobility sells a variety of wireless services, including individual plans, family plans, and GoPhone (prepaid) plans.

Mobile to Mobile

All postpaid monthly rate plans (and most prepaid plans) include unlimited minutes for calls to or from any of AT&T's wireless subscribers. Night & weekend minutes were deducted before unlimited M2M minutes until March 2010, in which AT&T stated on wireless bills that M2M minutes would no longer deplete N/W minutes on plans without unlimited N/W minutes. As of November 2009, all postpaid voice plans (except for the "Nation 450") include unlimited night & weekend usage. If all N&W voice minutes are used, calls placed to non-AT&T wireless customers are deducted from the monthly package of anytime minutes . Any unused "anytime" minutes rollover to the next month, and expire after 12 months if not used.

AT&T Unity

AT&T Unity is a service offered for users of landline and wireless AT&T service. It provides free unlimited calling to users of AT&T landline and wireless services. AT&T Unity customers also receive "Rollover" minutes and night and unlimited weekend minutes. (As of early 2010 "AT&T Unity" is no longer offered, although it is still supported for existing customers who have it.)

Mobile phone insurance

AT&T Mobility allows its customers to have mobile phone insurance in case of loss or accidental damage. Asurion is the administrator of the insurance program from AT&T. All phones are covered under the mobile phone insurance plan except AT&T GoPhones.[54] Customers are required to pay a deductible for each time they make an insurance claim, and are only allowed two claims per 12-month period.

As of July 17, 2011 AT&T and Asurion announced that the Apple iPhone will be insurable with their Mobile Protection Pack service.

Slogans

- "Your world. Delivered" (2006-1st quarter of 2010)
- "Rethink possible" (2010–present.)

Controversies

Cingular/AT&T NASCAR sponsorship controversy

Cingular Wireless began its sponsorship of the #31 Chevrolet, owned by Richard Childress Racing, in the NASCAR Winston Cup Series in 2002. Two years later, when Nextel Communications (now Sprint Nextel) purchased the naming rights to NASCAR's top division (rebranding the division as the Nextel Cup, and later the Sprint Cup), Cingular and Alltel, sponsor of the #12 Dodge (owned by Penske Racing and driven by Ryan Newman), were allowed to stay as sponsors under a grandfather clause. In early 2007, following its purchase by AT&T, Cingular began a re-branding effort to the AT&T Mobility brand. NASCAR quickly claimed that a clause in their contract with Sprint Nextel would not allow Cingular to change either the name or brand advertised on the #31 car.

After trying and failing to persuade NASCAR to approve the addition of the AT&T globe logo to the rear of the car, AT&T filed a lawsuit against NASCAR on March 16, 2007. On May 18, AT&T won a preliminary injunction in the United States District Court for the Northern District of Georgia in Atlanta and, following a failed emergency motion for a stay by NASCAR on May 19, re-branded the #31 car, now driven by Jeff Burton, in time for the Nextel All-Star Challenge that evening.[55] [56] NASCAR was later granted an appeal to be heard on August 2.

On June 17, NASCAR announced it had filed a US$100 million dollar lawsuit against AT&T and would like AT&T and all other telecommunications companies out of the sport in 2008.[57]

On August 13, a ruling by the United States Court of Appeals for the Eleventh Circuit cleared the way for NASCAR to prevent AT&T Inc. from featuring its logo on the car. The 11th Circuit threw out a lower court's ruling that prevented NASCAR from stopping AT&T's plans. The appeals court remanded the case to the district court.[58]

At first practice for the Sharpie 500 at Bristol Motor Speedway on August 24, the #31 car was colored orange and black, but was bare; that is, no primary sponsor (but associate sponsors appeared) were on the car, similar to Formula One cars run in races where tobacco advertising was prohibited. The pit crew wore grey Richard Childress Racing shirts and Burton had a plain orange fire suit with associate sponsors. The car which carried a "subliminal advertising" scheme arrived in a black hauler with only the number 31 on the side. NASCAR officials said the car would not have made it through inspection with the AT&T logos.[59] During that weekend, AT&T claimed that two alternate paint schemes proposed by AT&T—one advertising its "go phone" and another with the old Cingular slogan "more bars in more places" that AT&T recently brought back—were rejected by NASCAR. The Go Phone scheme had been used in the past.[60] NASCAR later denied these claims.[61]

The car remained bare on race night on August 25, although ESPN aired the AT&T logo during shots from its in-car camera. Fox Sports had done so earlier in the dispute, with the words "Cingular is the new AT&T" on-screen during these shots.

On September 7, 2007, a settlement was reached where AT&T Mobility could remain on the #31 car until the end of 2008, but the associate sponsorship of the #29 Nationwide Series Holiday Inn Chevrolets not affected because they are in lower series. [62]

Richard Childress Racing announced the AT&T Mobility sponsorship will move to Grand American Road Racing Association sportscar racing in 2009 with the sponsorship of the Childress-Howard Motorsports #4 AT&T Pontiac Daytona Prototype sportscar. Childress is a part-owner of this team.

Competitors

AT&T is the second largest mobile carrier in the United States, based on customer totals. AT&T's competitors are (from largest to smallest):

- Verizon
- Sprint
- T-Mobile USA
- TracFone Wireless
- MetroPCS
- U.S. Cellular
- Cricket
- Claro in Puerto Rico

If the planned acquisition of T-Mobile USA is completed, AT&T will be the largest network provider in the U.S., with 129.2 million subscribers, overtaking Verizon Wireless with 101.1 million subscribers.[29]

References

[1] http://newscenter.verizon.com/press-releases/verizon/2011/verizon-reports-accelerated.html

[2] "10.2 Percent Wireless Revenue Growth, Record Net Adds and Smartphone Sales Highlight AT&T's First-Quarter Results" (http://www.att.com/gen/press-room?pid=19727&cdvn=news&newsarticleid=31831&mapcode=financial). www.att.com. . Retrieved 2011-04-21.

[3] " Cingular is now the new AT&T (http://www.att.com/gen/press-room?pid=4800&cdvn=news&newsarticleid=23308)." AT&T press release. January 12, 2007.

[4] Raice, Shayndi (March 21, 2011). "AT&T to Buy Rival in $39 Billion Deal" (http://online.wsj.com/article/SB10001424052748704433904576212810008230654.html?mod=e2tw). *The Wall Street Journal*. .

[5] http://www.phonescoop.com/news/item.php?n=3949

[6] AT&T Customers Enjoy Unlimited Calling to Their A-List (http://www.att.com/gen/press-room?pid=4800&cdvn=news&newsarticleid=27093), ATT.com, September 9, 2009

[7] DeKok, David (2006-01-11). "Employees at Cingular join union, get contract." (http://www.accessmylibrary.com/coms2/summary_0286-12292441_ITM). *The Patriot-News* (Harrisburg, Pennsylvania: Knight-Ridder/Tribune Business News).

[8] Communication Workers of America, AT&T Mobility/Cingular section (http://cwa-union.org/cingular/).

[9] CINGULAR WIRELESS LLC Annual Report 10-K, 2004 (http://sec.edgar-online.com/2004/02/24/0000950144-04-001647/Section50.asp)

[10] AT&T's Sigman to Retire; de la Vega to Lead Wireless Unit; Stankey to Lead Telecom Operations : CEOWORLD.BIZ (http://www.ceoworld.biz/?p=68)

[11] Pennsylvania Bulletin Doc. No. 06-1740 (http://www.pabulletin.com/secure/data/vol36/36-35/1740.html)

[12] Caribbean Net News "Digicel to acquire Cingular's Caribbean wireless operations", June 23, 2005 (http://www.caribbeannetnews.com/2005/06/23/acquire.shtml)

[13] Caribbean Net News "Cingular denies leaving Caribbean because of losses or poor performance", June 23, 2005 (http://www.caribbeannetnews.com/2005/06/24/denies.shtml)

[14] Caribbean Net News "Digicel awaits regulatory approval from Caribbean territories", June (http://www.caribbeannetnews.com/2005/06/24/awaits.shtml)

[15] Caribbean Net News "Digicel officially takes over Cingular in Barbados", December 21, 2005 (http://www.caribbeannetnews.com/2005/12/21/over.shtml)

[16] http://www.seattlepi.com/business/204374_cingularqa20.htm

[17] Wallack, Todd (November 1, 2004). "Cingular services up in air / Customers await effects of merger with AT&T Wireless" (http://www.sfgate.com/cgi-bin/article.cgi?f=/c/a/2004/11/01/BUGTK9HFFK1.DTL). *The San Francisco Chronicle*. .

[18] Sprint press release (http://www2.sprint.com/mr/news_dtl.do?id=10500)

[19] (http://www.engadgetmobile.com/2008/05/22/atandt-closing-in-on-completion-of-hsupa-upgrade/)

[20] (http://www.macblogz.com/2009/02/02/att-set-to-deploy-14-mbps-hspa-speeds-in-3rd-quarter-of-2009/)

[21] http://www.att.com/gen/press-room?pid=14153

[22] Redherring.com (http://www.redherring.com/Article.aspx?a=14568&hed=Cingular+to+Become+AT&T)

[23] AT&T Press Release (http://att.sbc.com/gen/press-room?pid=4800&cdvn=news&newsarticleid=22140)

[24] New York Times Article on Approved BellSouth merger (http://www.nytimes.com/2006/12/30/business/30tele.html)

[25] AT&T Prepares to 'De-Brand' the Cingular Wireless Name (http://www.nytimes.com/2007/01/12/technology/12phone.html?_r=1&ref=business&oref=slogin)

[26] Palm - Support - Product Update 2.11 for Palm Treo 680 smartphone for AT&T (http://www.palm.com/us/support/downloads/treo680update/att.html)

[27] AT&T Completes Acquisition of Dobson Communications to Enhance Wireless Coverage (http://www.att.com/gen/press-room?pid=4800&cdvn=news&newsarticleid=24739) Company press release, retrieved November 16, 2007

[28] AT&T's purchase of Centennial gets final approval from FCC (http://www.telegeography.com/cu/article.php?article_id=30858&email=html)

[29] Duryee, Tricia (2011-03-20). "AT&T Agrees to Acquire T-Mobile USA for $39 Billion" (http://emoney.allthingsd.com/20110320/att-agrees-to-acquire-t-mobile-usa-for-39-million/). *All Things Digital*. Dow Jones & Company Inc. . Retrieved 2011-03-20.

[30] "Best cell service" (http://www.consumerreports.org/cro/electronics-computers/cell-phones-service/cell-phone-service-1-07/overview/0107_serve_ov_1.htm). *Consumer Reports* (Consumers Union of U.S.). January 2007. . Retrieved 2007-03-13.

[31] Mohl, Bruce (2006-04-23). "The fewest dropped calls" (http://www.boston.com/business/articles/2006/04/23/the_fewest_dropped_calls/?page=1). *Boston Globe* (The New York Times Company). . Retrieved 2006-04-27.

[32] Belson, Ken (2006-05-03). "Best Cellphone Company? All of Them, to Hear Them Say It" (http://www.nytimes.com/2006/05/03/business/media/03adco.html?ex=&en=b376483a9562df2b&ei=5088&partner=rssnyt&emc=rss). *The New York Times* (The New York Times Company). .

[33] AT&T: 'More Bars in More Places' is the New 'Fewest Dropped Calls' | Epicenter from Wired.com (http://blog.wired.com/business/2007/08/att-more-bars-i.html)

[34] Ho, David (2007-08-25). "A 300-page iPhone bill? Too much information, users say" (http://web.archive.org/web/20070930041407/http://www.ajc.com/news/content/business/stories/2007/08/15/ibill_0815.html?imw=Y). *Atlanta Journal-Constitution*. Cox Newspapers. Archived from the original (http://www.ajc.com/news/content/business/stories/2007/08/15/ibill_0815.html?imw=Y) on 2007-09-30. . Retrieved 2007-08-19. "Internet message boards and blogs are buzzing with talk of paper iPhone bills dozens and even hundreds of pages long."

[35] http://money.aol.com/news/articles/_a/iphone-frenzy-not-an-option-for-some/n20070629193909990004

[36] Keizer, Gregg (2007-08-16). "A 300-page iPhone Bill? : iPhone owners rail at AT&T for paper waste with overly detailed bills." (http://www.pcworld.com/article/id,136068/article.html). *Computerworld*. PC World Communications. . Retrieved 2007-08-19. "One blogger, in fact, is in the middle of her 15 minutes of fame after posting a video that shows her unwrapping a 300-page AT&T bill."

[37] Graham, Jefferson (2007-08-25). "How many trees did your iPhone bill kill?" (http://www.usatoday.com/tech/wireless/phones/2007-08-14-iphone-bill_N.htm?imw=Y). *USA Today* (Gannett). . Retrieved 2007-08-19. "Justine Ezarik, a Pittsburgh graphic designer and active Internet blogger, got her first bill on Saturday. She says it was so huge — 300 pages — it was delivered in a box."

[38] "Apple Sells One Million iPhone 3Gs in First Weekend" (http://www.apple.com/pr/library/2008/07/14iphone.html). *apple.com*. Apple Inc.. 2008-07-14. . Retrieved 2010-03-06.

[39] Quinn, Michelle; Semuels, Alana (2008-08-14). "Apple looks to Best Buy to boost iPhone's reach" (http://articles.latimes.com/2008/aug/14/business/fi-iphone14). *Los Angeles Times*. . Retrieved 2010-03-06.

[40] "AT&T to Sell iPhone 3G in Puerto Rico and U.S. Virgin Islands On Oct. 17" (http://www.att.com/gen/press-room?pid=4800&cdvn=news&newsarticleid=26136). *www.att.com*. AT&T Inc.. 2008-09-30. . Retrieved 2010-03-06.

[41] http://www.businessweek.com/technology/content/dec2009/tc20091228_366556.htm

[42] http://consumerist.com/2009/12/att-customer-service-new-york-city-is-not-ready-for-the-iphone.html

[43] http://www.geek.com/articles/mobile/nyc-ready-for-the-iphone-did-att-halt-online-sales-due-to-unlockers-20091229/

[44] Sales of the popular iPhone resumed December 30, 2009

[45] http://news.cnet.com/wireless/?keyword=AT%26T

[46] "AT&T Announces Availability of First Device on Android Platform with Motorola" (http://www.att.com/gen/press-room?pid=4800&cdvn=news&newsarticleid=30522). *www.att.com*. AT&T Inc.. 2010-02-18. . Retrieved 2010-03-06.

[47] "Motorola BACKFLIP with MOTOBLUR" (http://www.motorola.com/Consumers/US-EN/Consumer-Product-and-Services/Mobile-Phones/Motorola-BACKFLIP-with-MOTOBLUR-US-EN?localeId=33). *www.motorola.com*. Motorola Inc.. . Retrieved 2010-03-06.

[48] "MOTOROLA BACKFLIP with MOTOBLUR and Android" (http://www.wireless.att.com/cell-phone-service/cell-phone-sales/promotion/motobackflip.jsp). *wireless.att.com*. AT&T Inc.. . Retrieved 2010-03-06.

[49] "Pocket-Sized HTC Aria to Premiere on Nation's Fastest 3G Network" (http://www.htc.com/us/press/pocket-sized-htc-aria-to-premiere-on-nations-fastest-3g-network/17). *www.htc.com*. HTC Inc.. . Retrieved 2010-07-14.

[50] "HTC Aria Android" (http://www.att.com/shop/wireless/devices/aria.jsp). *www.wireless.att.com*. AT&T Inc.. . Retrieved 2010-06-14.

[51] "HTC Mobile Phones - Aria AT&T - Overview" (http://www.htc.com/us/products/aria-att). *www.htc.com*. HTC Inc.. . Retrieved 2010-07-14.

[52] "AT&T releases new 4G Android Smartphones in 2011" (http://www.atrix4gsmartphone.com/att-android-phones/att-android-smartphones-motorola-htc-samsung/). *www.atrix4gsmartphone.com*. Motorola Atrix 4G. . Retrieved 2011-02-15.

[53] http://www.androidcentral.com/att-joins-sideloading-party-fashionably-late-still-attending?utm_source=feedburner&utm_medium=feed&utm_campaign=Feed%3A+androidcentral+%28Android+Central%29

[54] http://www.wireless.att.com/cell-phone-service/cell-phone-plan-details/?q_sku=sku3830293&q_planCategory=cat1370011

[55] http://www.nascar.com/2007/news/headlines/cup/05/18/att.wins.lawsuit.ap/index.html

[56] http://www.nascar.com/2007/news/headlines/cup/05/19/nascar.loses.stay.att.ap/index.html

[57] http://www.nascar.com/2007/news/headlines/cup/06/17/nascar.sues.att.ap/index.html

[58] Appeals court sides with NASCAR in AT&T dispute (http://www.nascar.com/2007/news/headlines/cup/08/13/jburton.nascar.lawsuit/index.html) NASCAR - August 13, 2007.

[59] As the logo turns: Burton's car missing AT&T again (http://sports.espn.go.com/rpm/news/story?seriesId=2&id=2989526) ESPN.

[60] NASCAR rejects proposed paint schemes for No. 31 (http://www.scenedaily.com/stories/2007/08/20/scene_daily452.html)

[61] NASCAR losing patience with AT&T court battle (http://sports.espn.go.com/rpm/news/story?seriesId=2&id=2990201) ESPN.

[62] http://hosted.ap.org/dynamic/stories/C/CAR_NASCAR_ATT?SITE=GENERIC&SECTION=HOME&TEMPLATE=DEFAULT&CTIME=2007-09-07-14-41-18

External links

- AT&T Mobility (http://www.wireless.att.com/)
- AT&T Mobility LLC (http://finance.google.com/finance?cid=850108) at Google Finance
- AT&T Mobility LLC (http://www.hoovers.com/at&t-mobility/--ID__102492--/free-co-factsheet.xhtml?cm_ven=Biz_Dev&cm_cat=Wikipedia&cm_pla=Free&cm_ite=Factsheet) at Hoover's
- AT&T Mobility LLC (http://biz.yahoo.com/ic/102/102492.html) at Yahoo! Finance

HTC Corporation

htc quietly brilliant

Type	Public
Traded as	TWSE: 2498 [1]
Industry	Telecommunications
Founded	1997
Headquarters	Taoyuan, Taoyuan County, Taiwan, ROC
Area served	Worldwide
Key people	Cher Wang, Chairwoman Peter Chou, CEO and President Fred Liu, COO
Products	Smartphones, Tablets
Revenue	$9.57 billion USD (2010)[1]
Operating income	$1.544 billion USD (2010)
Net income	$1.357 billion USD (2010)
Total assets	$6.535 billion USD (2010)
Total equity	$2.565 billion USD (2010)
Employees	5,569
Website	[3]

HTC Corporation (traditional Chinese: ; pinyin: *Hóngdá Guójì Diànzǐ Gǔfèn Yǒuxiàn Gōngsī*) (TWSE: 2498 [1]), formerly **High Tech Computer Corporation**,[2] is a Taiwanese manufacturer of smartphones. The company initially made smartphones based mostly on Microsoft's Windows Mobile operating system (OS) software, but in 2009 it began to shift its core focus away from Windows Mobile devices to devices based on Android OS, and in 2010 to Windows Phone OS as well.

HTC is also a member of the Open Handset Alliance, a group of handset manufacturers and mobile network operators dedicated to the advancement of the Android mobile device platform.[3] The HTC Dream, marketed by T-Mobile in many countries as the T-Mobile G1, was the first phone on the market to use the Android mobile device platform.[4]

History

HTC was founded in 1997 by Cher Wang, HT Cho, and Peter Chou.[5] Initially a manufacturer of notebook computers, HTC began designing some of the world's first touch and wireless hand-held devices in 1998.[6] The company has a rich heritage of many "firsts", including creating the first Microsoft-powered smartphone (2002) and the first Microsoft 3G phone (2005).[5] Their first major product was made in 2000 and was one of the world's first touch screen smartphones. The Palm Treo 650 and the iPAQ were created by HTC.[7] They started producing 3G-capable phones in early 2005 and made the world's first Android phone in 2008, the HTC Dream (also marketed as the T-Mobile G1). It was first released in the United States for pre-order through T-Mobile USA on September 23, 2008, and became available in U.S. T-Mobile stores on October 22, 2008.[8] The G1 was available in the UK several days after its USA launch, and has since been introduced in many countries including Australia and Singapore. In 2009, the company launched the HTC Sense interface for the platform with the HTC Hero.[9]

In March 2010, Apple Inc. filed a complaint with the US International Trade Commission claiming infringement of 20 of its patents covering aspects of the iPhone user interface and hardware.[10] HTC disagreed with Apple's actions and reiterated its commitment to creating innovative smartphones.[11] HTC also filed a complaint against Apple for infringing on 5 of its patents and sought to ban Apple products imported into the US from manufacturing facilities in Asia.[12] [13] Apple expanded its original complaint by adding two more patents.[14]

In June 2010, the company launched the HTC Evo 4G, the first 4G-capable phone in the United States.[15] In July 2010, HTC announced it would begin selling smartphones in China under its own brand name in a partnership with China Mobile.[16] In 2010, HTC sold over 24.6 million handsets, up 111% over 2009.[17]

HTC was named the "Device Manufacturer of the Year" for 2011 by the GSMA at the Mobile World Congress on 16 February 2011.[18] In April 2011, the company's market value surpassed that of Nokia to become the third largest smartphone maker in the world, only behind Apple and Samsung.[19]

On July 6, 2011 it was announced that HTC would buy VIA Technologies stake in S3 Graphics thus becoming the majority owner of S3.[20] [21] On August 6 2011, HTC acquired Dashwire for $18.5M

Corporate information

HTC's chairwoman is Cher Wang who is the daughter of the late Wang Yung-ching, Taiwan's petrochemical industrial giant and one of Taiwan's wealthiest men.[6] Peter Chou serves as President and CEO,[22] and HT Cho as Director of the Board and Chairman of HTC Foundation.[23] HTC's CFO is Hui-Ming Cheng.[24] In addition to being chair of HTC, Cher Wang is also acting chair of VIA Technologies.[6] HTC's main divisions, including the IA (Information Appliance) engineering division and the WM (Wireless Mobile) engineering division, are ISO 9001/ISO 14001-qualified facilities.[25]

The company's growth has accelerated dramatically since being chosen by Microsoft as a hardware platform development partner for the Windows Mobile operating system (based on Windows CE). HTC is also currently working with Google to build mobile phones running Google's Android mobile OS. HTC's sales revenue totalled $2.2 billion for 2005, a 102% increase from the prior year. It was listed as the fastest-growing tech company in *BusinessWeek*'s Info Tech 100.[26]

HTC has invested strongly in research and development, which accounts for a quarter of its employees.[5] HTC runs a software design office in Seattle (near its North American headquarters) where it designs its own interface for its phones.[27] In 2011, HTC will also open a research and development office in Durham, North Carolina, a location the company chose over Seattle and Atlanta,[28] to focus on multiple areas of wireless technology.[29]

HTC's North American headquarters are located in Bellevue, Washington.[30]

Product range

When HTC was founded it was strictly an original design manufacturer,[24] selling devices such as the HTC Wizard as the T-Mobile MDA and the Cingular 8125. The company focused on telecom operators who were willing to pay a contract manufacturer for customized products.[31] Today, many HTC devices (e.g., Incredible, Evo 4G) are marketed and sold under the HTC brand, though its main focus still remains with smartphones.[22] [31]

Innovations

On February 17, 2010, *Fast Company* ranked HTC as the 31st most innovative company in the world.[32] Bloomberg reports that HTC is assessing creating its own mobile operating system to compete with Apple's iOS, Google's Android, and Microsoft's Windows Phone 7.[33] On May 27th 2011 In response to customer feedback HTC decided that they will no longer lock bootloaders on their phones.[34]

Sports Sponsorship

HTC sponsored the HTC-Highroad cycling team, currently the most successful team in professional cycling from 2009 to 2011. The Team will disband in 2012 due to lack of sponsorship and investment.

See also

- List of HTC phones
- TouchFLO
- TouchFLO 3D
- HTC Sense

References

[1] "HTC Corporation 4Q10 Business Review" (http://www.corpasia.net/taiwan/2498/financial/40/EN/4Q10 Investor Conference(English)_GbmLFMHggKfN.pdf). . Retrieved 2011-01-24.
[2] "HTC Corporation: Snapshot" (http://investing.businessweek.com/research/stocks/snapshot/snapshot.asp?ticker=2498:TT). Bloomberg Business Week. . Retrieved 2011-01-06.
[3] "Google unveils cell phone software and alliance" (http://news.cnet.com/8301-17939_109-9810937-2.html). CNET News. 2007-11-05. . Retrieved 2010-07-08.
[4] "T-Mobile G1, aka First 'Googlephone,' Carries High Expectations" (http://www.wired.com/gadgetlab/2008/09/since-apple-lau/). Wired. 2008-09-22. . Retrieved 2010-07-08.
[5] "About HTC: HTC History" (http://www.htc.com/us/about). HTC Corporation. . Retrieved 2010-07-07.
[6] Laura Holson (2008-10-26). "With Smartphones, Cher Wang Made Her Own Fortune" (http://www.nytimes.com/2008/10/27/technology/companies/27wang.html?_r=1). The New York Times. . Retrieved 2010-07-08.
[7] "HTC History" (http://www.htc.com/history/). HTC. .
[8] HTC names Google phone, 'Dream' (http://wireless.itworld.com/4267/htc-google-phone-080320/page_1.html)
[9] "TELUS brings the HTC Hero(TM) to Canada" (http://www.bloomberg.com/apps/news?pid=21072065&tkr=2498:TT&sid=aFufuZp2mhfc). Bloomberg. 2009-11-05. . Retrieved 2010-07-08.
[10] Andrew Vanacore (2010-03-02). "Apple suing phone maker HTC over iPhone patents" (http://www.businessweek.com/ap/financialnews/D9E6LEN01.htm). Bloomberg Businessweek. . Retrieved 2010-07-07.
[11] "HTC Disagrees with Apple's Actions" (http://www.htc.com/us/press/htc-disagrees-with-apples-actions/10). HTC Corporation. 2010-03-17. . Retrieved 2010-07-08.
[12] "HTC Sues Apple for Patent Infringement" (http://www.htc.com/us/press/htc-sues-apple-for-patent-infringement/15). HTC Corporation. 2010-05-12. . Retrieved 2010-07-08.
[13] "US trade body to look into HTC complaint against Apple" (http://www.google.com/hostednews/afp/article/ALeqM5j6FKAUf2-59RZdpkQdEcPL3MHyfw). AFP. 2010-06-11. . Retrieved 2010-07-07.
[14] "Apple expands patent infringement suit against HTC" (http://news.cnet.com/8301-31021_3-20008584-260.html). CNET News. 2010-06-23. . Retrieved 2010=07-07.
[15] "The Wait is Over - America's First 3G/4G Phone, HTC EVO(TM) 4G, Available Nationwide Today,..." (http://www.forbes.com/feeds/businesswire/2010/06/04/businesswire140622846.html). Forbes. 2010-06-04. . Retrieved 2010-07-08.

[16] Chao, Loretta (2010-07-27). "HTC to Sell Branded Smartphones in Mainland Push" (http://online.wsj.com/article/SB10001424052748703700904575392313710556170.html?mod=googlenews_wsj). The Wall Street Journal. . Retrieved 2010-07-27.

[17] "HTC mobile phone shipments and revenues skyrocket in 2010" (http://www.intomobile.com/2011/01/21/htc-mobile-phone-shipments-and-revenues-skyrocket-in-2010/). IntoMobile. 2011-01-21. . Retrieved 2011-01-22.

[18] HTC Wins Device Manufacturer of the Year at Annual Global Mobile Awards (http://phandroid.com/2011/02/16/htc-wins-device-manufacturer-of-the-year-at-annual-global-mobile-awards/)

[19] "Smartphone Upstart HTC Triples Earnings As Sales Double" (http://www.forbes.com/2011/04/08/htc-earnings-triple-sales-double-in-q1-marketnewsvideo.html). Forbes. 2011-04-08. . Retrieved 2011-04-08.

[20] http://www.dailytech.com/VIA+WTI+Sell+Stakes+in+S3+Graphics+to+HTC/article22078.htm

[21] http://www.htc.com/europe/press.aspx?id=172438&lang=1033

[22] Elizabeth Woyke (2009-10-28). "HTC CEO on Android, Verizon, Microsoft" (http://www.forbes.com/2009/10/28/google-verizon-android-technology-wireless-htc.html). Forbes. . Retrieved 2010-07-08.

[23] "HTC June 2009 Sales Report" (http://www.redorbit.com/news/technology/1730652/htc_june_2009_sales_report/). redOrbit. 2009-08-03. . Retrieved 2010-07-08.

[24] "Update 1: Taiwan's HTC sees 2008 sales at high end of target" (http://uk.reuters.com/article/idUKTP35359820080912). Reuters UK. 2008-09-12. . Retrieved 2010-07-08.

[25] "HTC company profile" (http://www.phonedog.com/cell-phone-research/companies/htc.aspx). PhoneDog. . Retrieved 2010-07-08.

[26] The IT 100 Companies: The Leading Tech Companies of 2005 (http://www.businessweek.com/magazine/toc/06_27/B399106it100.htm)

[27] "HTC Launches Multi-Million Dollar Ad Campaign About 'You' To Become Household Name" (http://moconews.net/article/419-htc-launches-multi-million-dollar-ad-campaign-about-you-to-become-house/). *mocoNews*. 26 October 2009. .

[28] Bracken, David (2010-12-22). "HTC will come to Triangle" (http://www.newsobserver.com/2010/12/22/875610/htc-will-come-to-triangle.html). *News & Observer*. . Retrieved 2010-12-22.

[29] Lance Whitney (2010-12-21). "HTC opening R&D office to focus on wireless tech" (http://news.cnet.com/8301-1023_3-20026287-93.html). CNET News. . Retrieved 2010-12-22.

[30] "About HTC - Contact Us" (http://www.htc.com/us/about/contact-us/). . Retrieved 6 August 2010.

[31] Russell Flannery (2006-01-09). "Cher Dividend" (http://www.forbes.com/global/2006/0109/045A.html). Forbes. . Retrieved 2010-07-08.

[32] Macsai, Dan (2010-02-17). "Most Innovative Companies - 2010: HTC" (http://www.fastcompany.com/mic/2010/profile/htc). Fast Company. . Retrieved 2010-07-08.

[33] Nosowitz, Dan (April 14, 2010), "HTC "Continues to Assess" Making Their Own Smartphone OS--or Buying One from Palm" (http://www.fastcompany.com/1615647/htc-continues-to-assess-making-their-own-smartphone-os-or-buying-one-from-palm), *Fast Company*,

[34] Hildenbrand, Jerry (May 27, 2011), *HTC: No more locked bootloaders* (http://www.androidcentral.com/htc-announced-new-bootloader-policy),

External links

- Official website (http://http://www.htc.com)

HTC 7 Mozart

Manufacturer	HTC Corporation
Carriers	Orange (France, United Kingdom), Deutsche Telekom AG (Germany), Telstra (Australia)[1]
Compatible networks	GSM, HSDPA, Wi-Fi
Availability by country	October 2010 (Europe/Asia Pacific)
Related	HTC 7 Surround, HTC HD7
Dimensions	119 x 60.2 x 11.9 mm
Weight	130 g (4.59 oz)
Operating system	Windows Phone 7
CPU	Qualcomm QSD8250 1 GHz Scorpion (Snapdragon)
Memory	8 GB internal flash / 16 GB with T-Mobile Germany branding 512 MB ROM 576 MB RAM
Battery	Rechargeable 1300mAh Li-ion battery (Extended Battery Available)
Data inputs	Multi-touch capacitive touchscreen, proximity sensor, ambient light sensor, 3-axis accelerometer, digital compass
Display	3.7 in. LCD capacitive touchscreen 480x800 px 16m-color WVGA, backlit TFT LCD
Rear camera	8 Megapixel autofocus CMOS sensor with Xenon flash, video up to 720p resolution
Connectivity	Bluetooth 2.1, 802.11b/g/n, G-Sensor, Digital Compass, A-GPS, micro-USB, 3.5mm audio jack
Other	Dolby Mobile Sound
Development status	Released
Test mode	##3282#

The **HTC 7 Mozart** (also known as the **HTC Mozart**), is a mobile smartphone running the Windows Phone 7 operating system. The phone was designed and manufactured by HTC.

The HTC 7 Mozart is one of three Windows Phone 7 handsets available from HTC in the UK at launch, and has a focus on high-fidelity audio with Dolby Mobile and SRS surround sound built in.

Available exclusively on Orange from 21 October, the HTC 7 Mozart is very similar in size and styling to many other HTC handsets, save that it boasts the three standard buttons below the screen specified by Microsoft across all Windows Phone 7 devices.

Specifications: Windows Phone 7 OS, 1 GHz Snapdragon QSD8250 processor, 512MB ROM, 576MB RAM, 8GB internal storage, 3.7in touch screen with 480 x 800 pixels, HSPA up to 7.2Mbit/s, quad-band GSM, 802.11 b/g/n Wi-Fi, Bluetooth, GPS, 8-megapixel camera with xenon flash (supports 720p video capture).

Announcement

Announced at the Windows Phone 7 event in New York City on October 11.

See also

- Windows Phone 7

References

[1] Thomas Ricker, Engadget http://www.engadget.com/2010/10/11/htc-7-mozart-and-7-trophy-set-out-to-conquer-the-wp7-world-7-pr/

External links

- Official HTC 7 Mozart homepage (http://www.htc.com/www/product/7mozart/overview.html)
- V3.co.uk Review HTC 7 Mozart (http://www.v3.co.uk/v3/hardware/2271885/htc-mozart-review)
- (http://www.gsmarena.com/htc_7_mozart-3530.php)

Snapdragon (system on chip)

WARNING: Article could not be rendered - ouputting plain text.

Potential causes of the problem are: (a) a bug in the pdf-writer software (b) problematic Mediawiki markup (c) table is too wide

Qualcomm Snapdragon LogoSnapdragon is a family of mobile system on chips by Qualcomm. Qualcomm considers Snapdragon a "platform" for use in smartphones, tablets, and smartbook devices.The Snapdragon application processor core, dubbed Scorpion, is Qualcomm's own design. It has many features similar to those of the ARM architectureARM ARM Cortex-A8Cortex-A8 core and it is based on the ARM architectureARM v7 instruction set, but theoretically has much higher performance for multimedia-related SIMD operations.http://www.dspdesignline.com/showArticle.jhtml?articleID=204700527All Snapdragon processors contain the circuitry to decode high-definition video (HD) resolution at 720p or 1080p depending on the Snapdragon chipset. "Snapdragon - Technical Features". Qualcomm. . Retrieved 29 December 2009. Adreno, the company's proprietary GPU technology, integrated into Snapdragon chipsets (and certain other Qualcomm chipsets) is Qualcomm's own design, using assets the company acquired from AMD. "Qualcomm Acquires Handheld Graphics and Multimedia Assets from AMD". Qualcomm. 20 January 2009. . Retrieved 14 September 2010.The first chipsets in the Snapdragon family were the QSD8650 and the QSD8250 (System-on-a-Chip), available since the fourth quarter of 2008, both integrating a 1 HertzGHz applications processor, a Wireless modemcellular modem and Global Positioning SystemGPS. In 2010, the Snapdragon family was expanded to include MSM (Mobile Station Modem) and APQ (Accelerated processing unitApplication Processor) series. HistoryQ4 2008 The first chipsets in the Snapdragon family, the QSD8650 and the QSD8250, were made available. June 2009 Qualcomm presented an ASUS Eee PC using the Snapdragon SoC and running Google's Android (operating system)Android operating system. Qualcomm shows Eee PC running Android OS At the same event, ASUS also showed a Snapdragon-based device, then withdrew it abruptly.Steven J. Vaughan-Nichols (2009-06-02). "Microsoft strikes back at Linux netbook push". . Retrieved 2009-06-20.Charlie Demerjian (2009-06-12). "MS steps on a Snapdragon". . Retrieved 2009-06-20.December 7, 2009 The LG eXpo was the first US phone to utilize the Snapdragon SoC. "AT&T and LG

Mobile Phones Announce the First 1Ghz Smartphone in the United States, the LG Expo". ATT.com. .January 5, 2010 The Google Nexus One was released, manufactured by HTC, and featured Android OS 2.1 powered by a Snapdragon running at 1 GHz (Qualcomm QSD8250). Nexus One Phone, Google.comApril 29, 2010 The HTC Droid Incredible was released, using the Snapdragon QSD8650 1 GHz SoC, and was the first Snapdragon device available on the Verizon Wireless network. June 1, 2010 Qualcomm announced sampling of the MSM8x60 series of Snapdragon SoC's. "Qualcomm Ships First Dual-CPU Snapdragon Chipset". Qualcomm. 1 June 2010. .June 4, 2010 The HTC EVO 4G was released, using the Snapdragon QSD8650 1 GHz SoC, and was available on the Sprint NextelSprint network. The HTC EVO 4G was the United States' first WiMAX phone. "HTC EVO 4G is Sprint's Android-powered knight in superphone armor, we go hands-on". Engadget. 23 March 2010. . "The Dirty Secret of Today's 4G: It's not 4G". Gizmodo. 5 November 2010. .October 22, 2010 The HTC Desire HD is released, featuring the MSM8255 SoC. November 17, 2010 Qualcomm announces the roadmap for Next-Gen Snapdragon SoC development, including the MSM8960, citing future improvements in CPU and GPU performance and lower power consumption "Qualcomm Reveals Next-Gen Snapdragon MSM8960: 28nm, dual-core, 5x Performance Improvement". Anandtech. 17 November 2010. .January 5, 2011 A version of Microsoft Windows compiled for ARM is shown running on the Snapdragon SoC at CES 2011. "BBC News - Windows runs on Arm's mobile phone chips". BBC. 6 January 2011. .February 13, 2011 The HTC Inspire 4G is released, featuring the MSM8255 SoC. "HTC Inspire 4G". HTC. .March 21, 2011 The HTC EVO 3D features the MSM8660 Dual-Core SoC with Adreno 220 GPU. The HTC Thunderbolt features the MSM8655 SoC with Adreno 205 GPU. August 3, 2011 Qualcomm announces plan to use simple names (S1, S2, S3 and S4) for Snapdragon processors so that the public can better understand the products. The bigger the number is, the more advanced functions that the processor has, which means S4 can perform better than S3. Anand Lal Shimpi, AnandTech. " Qualcomm's Updated Brand: Introducing Snapdragon S1, S2, S3 & S4 Processors." Jul 18, 2011. Retrieved Jul 18, 2011. Current & Future Specifications "Snapdragon Chipset Product Page". Qualcomm. . "Qualcomm Ships First Dual-CPU Snapdragon Chipset". Qualcomm. 1 June 2010. . "The World's Largest PDA Database". PDAdb. .http://www.anandtech.com/show/4024/qualcomm-reveals-nextgen-snapdragon-msm8960-28nm-dualcore-5x-performance-improver http://www.mobiletechworld.com/2011/07/05/new-qualcomm-2011-2012-roadmap-and-soc-specifications/ Family name / generation Model Number Semiconductor Technology CPU Instruction Set CPU CPU Cache GPU Memory Technology Wireless Radio Technologies Sampling Availability Utilizing Devices Snapdragon S1 QSD8250 65 nm ARMv7 1 GHz Scorpion Adreno 200 GSM (GPRS, EDGE), UMTS/WCDMA (HSDPA, HSUPA), Multimedia Broadcast Multicast ServiceMBMS Q4 2008 Acer Liquid A1Acer Stream/Liquid, Acer neoTouch S200, Dell Venue Pro (Lightning), Dell Streak, Fujitsu Toshiba Mobile REGZA Phone T-01C, HP Compaq AirLife 100, HTC Desire, HTC HD2, HTC 7 Mozart, HTC 7 Surround, HTC 7 Trophy, HTC HD7, HTC 7 Pro, Google Nexus One, Huawei SmaKit S7, Lenovo LePhone, LG eXpo, LG Optimus Q, LG Optimus Z, LG Quantum, LG Panther, Pantech IM-A600S, Pantech IM-A650S, Sharp LYNX SH-10B, Sharp LYNX 3D SH-03C, Samsung Focus, Samsung Omnia 7, Sony Ericsson Xperia X10, Toshiba dynapocket T-01B/KG01, Toshiba TG01/TG02/TG03. QSD8650 65 nm ARMv7 1 GHz Scorpion Adreno 200 GSM (GPRS, EDGE), W-CDMA/UMTS (HSDPA, HSUPA), MBMS, CDMA2000 (1xRTT, 1xEvolution-Data OptimizedEV-DO Rel.0/Rev.A/Rev.B, 1xEV-DO MC Rev.A) Q4 2008 Fujitsu Toshiba Mobile REGZA Phone IS04(TSI04), Fujitsu Toshiba Mobile T006(TS006)/iida X-RAY(TSX06), HTC Arrive, HTC Droid Incredible, HTC Evo 4GHTC Supersonic/EVO 4G, LG Apollo GW990, LG Fathom VS750, LG GW820 eXpo, LG GW825 IQ, LG Optimus 7, Sharp IS01(SHI01)/IS03(SHI03)/, Sony Ericsson S004(SO004)/S005(SO005)/S006(SO006)/iida G11(SOX02), Toshiba dynapocket IS02(TSI01)/K01, Toshiba T004(TS004), Pantech SIRIUS α IS06(PTI06), Kyocera Echo, 4Geek Horus Snapdragon S2 QSD8250A 45 nm ARMv7 1.3 GHz Scorpion Adreno 205 GSM (GPRS, EDGE), W-CDMA/UMTS (HSDPA, HSUPA), MBMS Q4 2009 QSD8650A 45 nm ARMv7 1.3 GHz Scorpion Adreno 205 GSM (GPRS, EDGE), W-CDMA/UMTS (HSDPA, HSUPA), MBMS, CDMA2000 (1xRTT, 1xEV-DO Rel.0/Rev.A/Rev.B, 1xEV-DO MC Rev.A) Q4 2009 Lenovo LePad MSM7230 45 nm ARMv7 800 MHz Scorpion Adreno 205 GSM (GPRS, EDGE), W-CDMA/UMTS (HSDPA, HSUPA, HSPA+), MBMS Q2 2010 HTC Desire Z/T-Mobile G2,

Acer_Liquid_A1#Acer_Liquid_MTAcer Liquid Metal, HP Veer, Huawei U8800, HTC Ignite, HTC Prime, NEC Casio MEDIAS N-04C MSM7630 45 nm ARMv7 800 MHz Scorpion Adreno 205 GSM (GPRS, EDGE), W-CDMA/UMTS (HSDPA, HSUPA, HSPA+), MBMS, CDMA2000 (1xRTT, 1xEV-DO Rel.0/Rev.A/Rev.B, 1xEV-DO MC Rev.A, SV-DO) Q2 2010 HTC Evo Shift 4G, Casio G'zOne Commando MSM8255 45 nm ARMv7 1 GHz Scorpion Adreno 205 Dual-channel 333 MHz LPDDR2 GSM (GPRS, EDGE), W-CDMA/UMTS (HSDPA, HSUPA, HSPA+), MBMS Q2 2010 Acer Iconia Smart, HTC Desire HD, HTC Desire S, HTC Incredible S, HTC Inspire 4G, Huawei Vision, Sony Ericsson Xperia Arc, Sony Ericsson Xperia Neo, Sony Ericsson Xperia Play, Sony Ericsson Xperia Pro, Sony Ericsson Xperia Mini/Mini Pro, Sony Ericsson Xperia ray, Sony Ericsson Xperia active, T-Mobile myTouch 4G, Sharp GALAPAGOS 003SH/005SH, Sharp DM009SH, Blackberry Bold 9900/9930, Blackberry Torch 9810, Blackberry Torch 9860, CSL Mi410, Huawei U9000 IDEOS X6 MSM8655 45 nm ARMv7 1 GHz Scorpion Adreno 205 Dual-channel 333 MHz LPDDR2 GSM (GPRS, EDGE), W-CDMA/UMTS (HSDPA, HSUPA, HSPA+), MBMS, CDMA2000 (1xRTT, 1xEV-DO Rel.0/Rev.A/Rev.B) Q2 2010 HTC Thunderbolt, HTC Droid Incredible 2 , LG Revolution, Sharp IS05(SHI05), Motorola Triumph, Samsung Conquer 4G "Samsung Conquer™ 4G fact sheet". . MSM8255T 45 nm ARMv7 1.4 GHz Scorpion Adreno 205 Dual-channel 333 MHz LPDDR2 GSM (GPRS, EDGE), W-CDMA/UMTS (HSDPA, HSUPA, HSPA+), MBMS 2011 Samsung Galaxy S Plus , Samsung Galaxy S II Mini Sharp Aquos SH-12C , HTC Flyer MSM8655T 45 nm ARMv7 1.4 GHz Scorpion Adreno 205 Dual-channel 333 MHz LPDDR2 GSM (GPRS, EDGE), W-CDMA/UMTS (HSDPA, HSUPA, HSPA+), MBMS, CDMA2000 (1xRTT, 1xEV-DO Rel.0/Rev.A/Rev.B) 2011 HP Pre 3 Snapdragon S3 APQ8060 45 nm ARMv7 1.2 GHz Dual-core Scorpion Adreno 220 Single-channel 333 MHz ISM/266 MHz LPDDR2 Connectivity features not included 2011 HP TouchPad MSM8260 45 nm ARMv7 1.2-1.5 GHz Dual-core Scorpion Adreno 220 Single-channel 333 MHz ISM/266 MHz LPDDR2 GSM (GPRS, EDGE), W-CDMA/UMTS (HSDPA, HSUPA, HSPA+), MBMS Q3 2010 ASUS Eee Pad MeMO, HTC Sensation, HTC myTouch 4G Slide MSM8660 45 nm ARMv7 1.2-1.5 GHz Dual-core Scorpion Adreno 220 Single-channel 333 MHz ISM/266 MHz LPDDR2 GSM (GPRS, EDGE), W-CDMA/UMTS (HSDPA, HSUPA, HSPA+), MBMS, CDMA2000 (1xRTT, 1xEV-DO Rel.0/Rev.A/Rev.B, 1xEV-DO MC Rev.A) Q3 2010 Pantech Vega Racer, HTC EVO 3D, HTC "Puccini" tablet QSD8672 45 nm ARMv7 1.5 GHz Dual-core Scorpion Adreno 220 GSM (GPRS, EDGE), W-CDMA/UMTS (HSDPA, HSUPA, HSPA+), MBMS, CDMA2000 (1xRTT, 1xEV-DO Rel.0/Rev.A/Rev.B, 1xEV-DO MC Rev.A) originally Q1 2010; cancelled Snapdragon S4 MSM8960 28 nm ARMv7 1.5-1.7 GHz Dual-core Krait L2: 1 MB Adreno 225 Dual-channel 500 MHz LPDDR2 GSM (GPRS, EDGE), W-CDMA/UMTS (HSDPA, HSUPA, HSPA+, DC-HSPA+ High-Speed Downlink Packet Access#User Equipment (UE) categoriescat.29), MBMS, 3GPP Long Term EvolutionLTE E-UTRA#User Equipment (UE) categoriescat.3, CDMA2000 (1xRTT, 1xEV-DO Rel.0/Rev.A/Rev.B, 1xEV-DO MC Rev.A), TD-SCDMA Q4 2011 MSM8270 28 nm ARMv7 1.5-1.7 GHz Dual-core Krait L2: 1 MB Adreno 225 Dual-channel 500 MHz LPDDR2 GSM (GPRS, EDGE), W-CDMA/UMTS (HSDPA, HSUPA, DC-HSPA High-Speed Downlink Packet Access#User Equipment (UE) categoriescat.21), MBMS Q4 2011 MSM8260A 28 nm ARMv7 1.5-1.7 GHz Dual-core Krait L2: 1 MB Adreno 225 Dual-channel 500 MHz LPDDR2 GSM (GPRS, EDGE), W-CDMA/UMTS (HSDPA, HSUPA, HSPA+ High-Speed Downlink Packet Access#User Equipment (UE) categoriescat.14), MBMS, CDMA2000 (1xRTT, 1xEV-DO Rel.0/Rev.A/Rev.B, 1xEV-DO MC Rev.A), TD-SCDMA Q4 2011 MSM8230 28 nm ARMv7 1.0-1.2 GHz Dual-core Krait L2: 1 MB Adreno 305 Single-channel 533 MHz LPDDR2 GSM (GPRS, EDGE), W-CDMA/UMTS (HSDPA, HSUPA, HSPA+ High-Speed Downlink Packet Access#User Equipment (UE) categoriescat.14), MBMS Q3 2012 MSM8930 28 nm ARMv7 1.0-1.2 GHz Dual-core Krait L2: 1 MB Adreno 305 Single-channel 533 MHz LPDDR2 GSM (GPRS, EDGE), W-CDMA/UMTS (HSDPA, HSUPA, HSPA+, DC-HSPA+ High-Speed Downlink Packet Access#User Equipment (UE) categoriescat.29), MBMS, 3GPP Long Term EvolutionLTE E-UTRA#User Equipment (UE) categoriescat.2, CDMA2000 (1xRTT, 1xEV-DO Rel.0/Rev.A/Rev.B, 1xEV-DO MC Rev.A), TD-SCDMA Q3 2012 APQ8064 28 nm ARMv7 2.5 GHz Quad-core Krait Adreno 320 Connectivity features not included 2012 MSM8974 28 nm ARMv7 2.0-2.5 GHz Quad-core Krait L2: 2 MB Adreno 320 Dual-channel 667/800 MHz LPDDR3 GSM (GPRS, EDGE), W-CDMA/UMTS (HSDPA, HSUPA, HSPA+, DC-HSPA+

High-Speed Downlink Packet Access#User Equipment (UE) categoriescat.29), MBMS, LTE E-UTRA#User Equipment (UE) categoriescat.4, CDMA2000 (1xRTT, 1xEV-DO Rel.0/Rev.A/Rev.B, 1xEV-DO MC Rev.A, 1xAdv Rev.A/Rev.B), TD-SCDMA Q1 2013 Some Snapdragon designs like QSD8672 were announced but have never made it into production and were superseded by a newer generation of chips. Similar platformsTexas Instruments OMAPOMAP by Texas InstrumentsNvidia TegraTegra by NvidiaSamsung (System on Chip)Apple Ax (System on Chip)XScale#PXAPXA by Marvell Technology GroupMarvelli.MX by Freescale SemiconductorFreescaleSuperHSH-Mobile by Renesas TechnologyRenesasNomadik (discontinued) by ST-EricssonNovaThor by ST-Ericsson "ST-Ericsson NovaThor platform". .ZiiLabs ZMS series See alsoMSM7000Qualcomm MSM7000Smartbook, a new netbook-like class of devices, first models of which are powered by Snapdragon NotesReferenceshttp://www.anandtech.com/show/4024/qualcomm-reveals-nextgen-snapdragon-msm8960-28nm-dualcore-5x-perfor links Snapdragon Chipset Product Page

Accelerometer

An **accelerometer** is a device that measures proper acceleration. This is *not necessarily* the same as the coordinate acceleration (change of velocity of the device in space), but is rather the type of acceleration associated with the phenomenon of weight experienced by a test mass that resides in the frame of reference of the accelerometer device. For an example of where these types of acceleration differ, an accelerometer will measure a value when sitting on the ground, because masses there have weights, even though they do not change velocity. However, an accelerometer in gravitational free fall toward the center of the Earth will measure a value of zero because, even though its speed is increasing, it is in an inertial frame of reference, in which it is weightless.

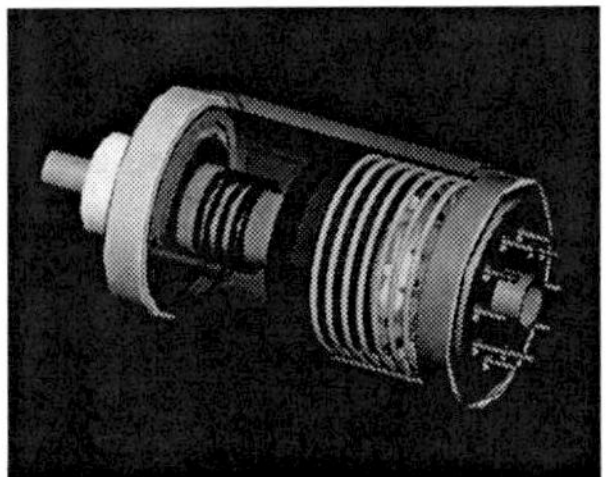

A depiction of an accelerometer designed at Sandia National Laboratories.

An accelerometer thus measures **weight per unit of (test) mass**, a quantity also known as specific force, or g-force. Another way of stating this is that by measuring weight, an accelerometer measures the acceleration of the free-fall reference frame (inertial reference frame) relative to itself.

Most accelerometers do not display the value they measure, but supply it to other devices. Real accelerometers also have practical limitations in how quickly they respond to changes in acceleration, and cannot respond to changes above a certain frequency of change.

Single- and multi-axis models of accelerometer are available to detect magnitude and direction of the proper acceleration (or g-force), as a vector quantity, and can be used to sense orientation (because direction of weight changes), coordinate acceleration (so long as it produces g-force or a change in g-force), vibration, shock, and falling (a case where the proper acceleration changes, since it tends toward zero). Micromachined accelerometers are increasingly present in portable electronic devices and video game controllers, to detect the position of the device or provide for game input.

Pairs of accelerometers extended over a region of space can be used to detect differences (gradients) in the proper accelerations of frames of references associated with those points. These devices are called gradiometers, as they measure gradients in the gravitational field. Such pairs of accelerometers in theory may also be able to detect gravity waves.

Physical principles

An accelerometer measures proper acceleration, which is the acceleration it experiences relative to freefall and is the acceleration felt by people and objects. Put another way, at any point in spacetime the equivalence principle guarantees the existence of a local inertial frame, and an accelerometer measures the acceleration relative to that frame.[1] Such accelerations are popularly measured in terms of g-force.

An accelerometer at rest relative to the Earth's surface will indicate approximately 1 g *upwards*, because any point on the Earth's surface is accelerating upwards relative to the local inertial frame (the frame of a freely falling object near the surface). To obtain the acceleration due to motion with respect to the Earth, this "gravity offset" must be subtracted and corrections for effects caused by the Earth's rotation relative to the inertial frame.

The reason for the appearance of a gravitational offset is Einstein's equivalence principle,[2] which states that the effects of gravity on an object are indistinguishable from acceleration. When held fixed in a gravitational field by, for example, applying a ground reaction force or an equivalent upward thrust, the reference frame for an accelerometer (its own casing) accelerates upwards with respect to a free-falling reference frame. The effects of this acceleration are indistinguishable from any other acceleration experienced by the instrument, so that an accelerometer cannot detect the difference between sitting in a rocket on the launch pad, and being in the same rocket in deep space while it uses its engines to accelerate at 1 g. For similar reasons, an accelerometer will read *zero* during any type of free fall. This includes use in a coasting spaceship in deep space far from any mass, a spaceship orbiting the Earth, an airplane in a parabolic "zero-g" arc, or any free-fall in vacuum. Another example is free-fall at a sufficiently high altitude that atmospheric effects can be neglected.

However this does not include a (non-free) fall in which air resistance produces drag forces that reduce the acceleration, until constant terminal velocity is reached. At terminal velocity the accelerometer will indicate 1 g acceleration upwards. For the same reason a skydiver, upon reaching terminal velocity, does not feel as though he or she were in "free-fall", but rather experiences a feeling similar to being supported (at 1 g) on a "bed" of uprushing air.

Acceleration is quantified in the SI unit metres per second per second (m/s^2), in the cgs unit gal (Gal), or popularly in terms of g-force (*g*).

For the practical purpose of finding the acceleration of objects with respect to the Earth, such as for use in an inertial navigation system, a knowledge of local gravity is required. This can be obtained either by calibrating the device at rest,[3] or from a known model of gravity at the approximate current position.

Structure

Conceptually, an accelerometer behaves as a damped mass on a spring. When the accelerometer experiences an acceleration, the mass is displaced to the point that the spring is able to accelerate the mass at the same rate as the casing. The displacement is then measured to give the acceleration.

In commercial devices, piezoelectric, piezoresistive and capacitive components are commonly used to convert the mechanical motion into an electrical signal. Piezoelectric accelerometers rely on piezoceramics (e.g. lead zirconate titanate) or single crystals (e.g. quartz, tourmaline). They are unmatched in terms of their upper frequency range, low packaged weight and high temperature range. Piezoresistive accelerometers are preferred in high shock applications. Capacitive accelerometers typically use a silicon micro-machined sensing element. Their performance is superior in the low frequency range and they can be operated in servo mode to achieve high stability and linearity.

Modern accelerometers are often small *micro electro-mechanical systems* (MEMS), and are indeed the simplest MEMS devices possible, consisting of little more than a cantilever beam with a proof mass (also known as seismic mass). Damping results from the residual gas sealed in the device. As long as the Q-factor is not too low, damping does not result in a lower sensitivity.

Under the influence of external accelerations the proof mass deflects from its neutral position. This deflection is measured in an analog or digital manner. Most commonly, the capacitance between a set of fixed beams and a set of beams attached to the proof mass is measured. This method is simple, reliable, and inexpensive. Integrating piezoresistors in the springs to detect spring deformation, and thus deflection, is a good alternative, although a few more process steps are needed during the fabrication sequence. For very high sensitivities quantum tunneling is also used; this requires a dedicated process making it very expensive. Optical measurement has been demonstrated on laboratory scale.

Another, far less common, type of MEMS-based accelerometer contains a small heater at the bottom of a very small dome, which heats the air inside the dome to cause it to rise. A thermocouple on the dome determines where the heated air reaches the dome and the deflection off the center is a measure of the acceleration applied to the sensor.

Most micromechanical accelerometers operate *in-plane*, that is, they are designed to be sensitive only to a direction in the plane of the die. By integrating two devices perpendicularly on a single die a two-axis accelerometer can be made. By adding an additional *out-of-plane* device three axes can be measured. Such a combination always has a much lower misalignment error than three discrete models combined after packaging.

Micromechanical accelerometers are available in a wide variety of measuring ranges, reaching up to thousands of *g*'s. The designer must make a compromise between sensitivity and the maximum acceleration that can be measured.

Applications

Engineering

Accelerometers can be used to measure vehicle acceleration. They allow for performance evaluation of both the engine/drive train and the braking systems.

Accelerometers can be used to measure vibration on cars, machines, buildings, process control systems and safety installations. They can also be used to measure seismic activity, inclination, machine vibration, dynamic distance and speed with or without the influence of gravity. Applications for accelerometers that measure gravity, wherein an accelerometer is specifically configured for use in gravimetry, are called gravimeters.

Notebook computers equipped with accelerometers can contribute to the *Quake-Catcher Network* (QCN), a BOINC project aimed at scientific research of earthquakes.[4]

Biology

Accelerometers are also increasingly used in the biological sciences. High frequency recordings of bi-axial[5] or tri-axial acceleration[6] (>10 Hz) allows the discrimination of behavioral patterns while animals are out of sight. Furthermore, recordings of acceleration allow researchers to quantify the rate at which an animal is expending energy in the wild, by either determination of limb-stroke frequency[7] or measures such as overall dynamic body acceleration[8] Such approaches have mostly been adopted by marine scientists due to an inability to study animals in the wild using visual observations, however an increasing number of terrestrial biologists are adopting similar approaches. This device can be connected to an amplifier to amplify the signal.

Industry

Accelerometers are also used for machinery health monitoring of rotating equipment such as pumps,[9] fans,[10] rollers,[11] compressors,[12] and cooling towers,.[13] Vibration monitoring programs are proven to save money, reduce downtime, and improve safety in plants worldwide by detecting conditions such as shaft misalignment, rotor imbalance, gear failure[14] or bearing fault[15] which can lead to costly repairs. Accelerometer vibration data allows the user to monitor machines and detect these faults before the rotating equipment fails. Vibration monitoring programs are utilized in industries such as automotive manufacturing,[16] machine tool applications,[17] pharmaceutical production,[18] power generation[19] and power plants,[20] pulp and paper,[21] food and beverage production, water and wastewater, hydropower, petrochemical and steel manufacturing.

Building and structural monitoring

Accelerometers are used to measure the motion and vibration of a structure that is exposed to dynamic loads.[22] Dynamic loads originate from a variety of sources including:

- Human activities - walking, running, dancing or skipping
- Working machines - inside a building or in the surrounding area
- Construction work - driving piles, demolition, drilling and excavating
- Moving loads on bridges
- Vehicle collisions
- Impact loads - falling debris
- Concussion loads - internal and external explosions
- Collapse of structural elements
- Wind loads and wind gusts
- Air blast pressure
- Loss of support because of ground failure
- Earthquakes and aftershocks

Measuring and recording how a structure responds to these inputs is critical for assessing the safety and viability of a structure. This type of monitoring is called Dynamic Monitoring.

Medical applications

Zoll's AED Plus uses CPR-D•padz which contain an accelerometer to measure the depth of CPR chest compressions.

Within the last several years, Nike, Polar and other companies have produced and marketed sports watches for runners that include footpods, containing accelerometers to help determine the speed and distance for the runner wearing the unit.

In Belgium, accelerometer-based step counters are promoted by the government to encourage people to walk a few thousand steps each day.

Herman Digital Trainer uses accelerometers to measure strike force in physical training.[23] [24]

Navigation

An **Inertial Navigation System** (INS) is a navigation aid that uses a computer and motion sensors (accelerometers) to continuously calculate via dead reckoning the position, orientation, and velocity (direction and speed of movement) of a moving object without the need for external references. Other terms used to refer to inertial navigation systems or closely related devices include **inertial guidance system**, **inertial reference platform**, and many other variations.

An accelerometer alone is unsuitable to determine changes in altitude over distances where the vertical decrease of gravity is significant, such as for aircraft and rockets. In the presence of a gravitational gradient, the calibration and data reduction process is numerically unstable.[25] [26]

Transport

Accelerometers are used to detect apogee in both professional[27] and in amateur[28] rocketry.

Accelerometers are also being used in Intelligent Compaction rollers. Accelerometers are used alongside gyroscopes in inertial guidance systems.[29]

One of the most common uses for MEMS accelerometers is in airbag deployment systems for modern automobiles. In this case the accelerometers are used to detect the rapid negative acceleration of the vehicle to determine when a collision has occurred and the severity of the collision. Another common automotive use is in electronic stability control systems, which use a lateral accelerometer to measure cornering forces. The widespread use of accelerometers in the automotive industry has pushed their cost down dramatically.[30] Another automotive application is the monitoring of noise, vibration and harshness (NVH), conditions that cause discomfort for drivers and passengers and may also be indicators of mechanical faults.

Tilting trains use accelerometers and gyroscopes to calculate the required tilt.[31]

Vulcanology

Modern electronic accelerometers are used in remote sensing devices intended for the monitoring of active volcanos to detect the motion of magma[32]

Consumer electronics

Accelerometers are increasingly being incorporated into personal electronic devices.

Motion input

Some smartphones, digital audio players and personal digital assistants contain accelerometers for user interface control; often the accelerometer is used to present landscape or portrait views of the device's screen, based on the way the device is being held.

Automatic Collision Notification (ACN) systems also use accelerometers in a system to call for help in event of a vehicle crash. Prominent ACN systems include Onstar AACN service, Ford Link's 911 Assist, Toyota's Safety Connect, Lexus Link, or BMW Assist. Many accelerometer-equipped smartphones also have ACN software available for download. ACN systems are activated by detecting crash-strength G-forces.

Nintendo's Wii video game console uses a controller called a Wii Remote that contains a three-axis accelerometer and was designed primarily for motion input. Users also have the option of buying an additional motion-sensitive attachment, the Nunchuk, so that motion input could be recorded from both of the user's hands independently. Is also used on the Nintendo 3DS system.

The Sony PlayStation 3 uses the DualShock 3 remote which uses a three axis accelerometer that can be used to make steering more realistic in racing games, such as Motorstorm and Burnout Paradise.

The Nokia 5500 sport features a 3D accelerometer that can be accessed from software. It is used for step recognition (counting) in a sport application, and for tap gesture recognition in the user interface. Tap gestures can be used for controlling the music player and the sport application, for example to change to next song by tapping through clothing when the device is in a pocket. Other uses for accelerometer in Nokia phones include Pedometer functionality in Nokia Sports Tracker. Some other devices provide the tilt sensing feature with a cheaper component, which is not a true accelerometer.

Sleep phase alarm clocks use accelerometric sensors to detect movement of a sleeper, so that it can wake the person when he/she is not in REM phase, therefore awakes more easily.

Orientation sensing

A number of 21st century devices use accelerometers to align the screen depending on the direction the device is held, for example switching between portrait and landscape modes. Such devices include many tablet PCs and some smartphones and digital cameras.

For example, Apple uses an LIS302DL accelerometer in the iPhone, iPod Touch and the 4th and 5th generation iPod Nano allowing the device to know when it is tilted on its side. Third-party developers have expanded its use with fanciful applications such as electronic bobbleheads.[33] The BlackBerry Storm phone was also an early user of this orientation sensing feature.

The Nokia N95 and Nokia N82 have accelerometers embedded inside them. It was primarily used as a tilt sensor for tagging the orientation to photos taken with the built-in camera, later thanks to a firmware update it became available to other applications.

As of January 2009, almost all new mobile phones and digital cameras contain at least a tilt sensor and sometimes an accelerometer for the purpose of auto image rotation, motion-sensitive mini-games, and to correct shake when taking photographs.

Image stabilization

Camcorders use accelerometers for image stabilization. Still cameras use accelerometers for anti-blur capturing. The camera holds off snapping the CCD "shutter" when the camera is moving. When the camera is still (if only for a millisecond, as could be the case for vibration), the CCD is "snapped". An example application which has used such technology is the Glogger VS2,[34] a phone application which runs on Symbian OS based phone with accelerometer such as Nokia N96. Some digital cameras, contain accelerometers to determine the orientation of the photo being taken and also for rotating the current picture when viewing.

Device integrity

Many laptops feature an accelerometer which is used to detect drops. If a drop is detected, the heads of the hard disk are parked to avoid data loss and possible head or disk damage by the ensuing shock.

Gravimetry

A **gravimeter** or gravitometer, is an instrument used in gravimetry for measuring the local gravitational field. A gravimeter is a type of accelerometer, except that accelerometers are susceptible to all vibrations including noise, that cause oscillatory accelerations. This is counteracted in the gravimeter by integral vibration isolation and signal processing. Though the essential principle of design is the same as in accelerometers, gravimeters are typically designed to be much more sensitive than accelerometers in order to measure very tiny changes within the Earth's gravity, of 1 *g*. In contrast, other accelerometers are often designed to measure 1000 *g* or more, and many perform multi-axial measurements. The constraints on temporal resolution are usually less for gravimeters, so that resolution can be increased by processing the output with a longer "time constant".

Types of accelerometer

- Piezoelectric accelerometer
- Shear mode accelerometer
- Surface micromachined capacitive (MEMS)
- Thermal (submicrometre CMOS process)
- Bulk micromachined capacitive
- Bulk micromachined piezoelectric resistive
- Capacitive spring mass base
- Electromechanical servo (Servo Force Balance)
- Null-balance
- Strain gauge
- Resonance
- Magnetic induction
- Optical
- Surface acoustic wave (SAW)
- Laser accelerometer
- DC response
- High temperature
- Low frequency
- High gravity
- Triaxial
- Modally tuned impact hammers
- Seat pad accelerometers
- Pendulating integrating gyroscopic accelerometer

See also

- g-force
- Geophone
- Gyroscope
- Inertial navigation

References

[1] Einstein, Albert (1920). "20" (http://www.bartleby.com/173/20.html). *Relativity: The Special and General Theory*. New York: Henry Holt. p. 168. ISBN 1-58734-092-5. .
[2] Penrose, Roger (2005) [2004]. "17.4 The Principle of Equivalence". *The Road to Reality*. New York: Knopf. pp. 393–394. ISBN 0-470-08578-9.
[3] "Accelerometer Design and Applications" (http://www.analog.com/en/technical-library/faqs/design-center/faqs/CU_faq_MEMs/resources/fca.html). Analog Devices. . Retrieved 2008-12-23.
[4] "Quake-Catcher Network - Downloads" (http://qcn.stanford.edu/downloads/index.php). Quake-Catcher Network. . Retrieved 15 July 2009. "If you have a Mac laptop (2006 or later), a Thinkpad (2003 or later), or a desktop with a USB sensor, you can download software to turn your computer into a Quake-Catcher Sensor"
[5] Yoda et al. (2001) *Journal of Experimental Biology*204(4): 685-690
[6] Shepard et al. (2008) *Endangered Species Research* http://www.int-res.com/articles/esr2008/theme/Tracking/TMVpp1.pdf
[7] Kawabe et al. (2003) *Fisheries Science* 69 (5):959 - 965
[8] Wilson et al. (2006) *Journal of Animal Ecology*:75 (5):1081 - 1090
[9] http://www.wilcoxon.com/knowdesk/Know%20the%20health%20of%20your%20pumps.pdf
[10] http://www.wilcoxon.com/knowdesk/Guidance%20for%20mounting%204-20mA%20sensors%20on%20fans.pdf
[11] http://www.wilcoxon.com/knowdesk/Vibration%20monitoring%20of%20slow%20speed%20rollers.pdf
[12] http://www.wilcoxon.com/knowdesk/LF%20VM%20on%20compressor%20gear%20set.pdf

[13] http://www.wilcoxon.com/knowdesk/PT104%20VM%20of%20cooling%20towers%20and%20fans.pdf
[14] http://www.wilcoxon.com/knowdesk/gear.pdf
[15] http://www.wilcoxon.com/knowdesk/bearing.pdf
[16] http://www.wilcoxon.com/knowdesk/auto.pdf
[17] http://www.wilcoxon.com/knowdesk/rep11.pdf
[18] http://www.wilcoxon.com/knowdesk/pharmac.pdf
[19] http://www.wilcoxon.com/knowdesk/rep9.pdf
[20] http://www.wilcoxon.com/knowdesk/pwrplnt.pdf
[21] http://www.wilcoxon.com/knowdesk/pulp_pap.pdf
[22] O. Sircovich Saar "Dynamics in the Practice of Structural Design" 2006 WIT Press ISBN 1-84564-161-2
[23] The Contender 3 Episode 1 SPARQ testing ESPN
[24] Welcome to GoHerman.com innovator of interactive personal training for fitness, - MARTIAL ARTS & MMA (http://www.goherman.com/martialarts.aspx)
[25] *Vertical Speed Measurement*, by Ed Hahn in sci.aeronautics.airliners, 1996-11-22 (http://yarchive.net/air/airliners/ins_novert.html)
[26] US patent 6640165 (http://v3.espacenet.com/textdoc?DB=EPODOC&IDX=US6640165), Hayward, Kirk W. and Stephenson, Larry G., "Method and system of determining altitude of flying object", issued 2003-10-28
[27] Dual Deployment (http://westrocketry.com/articles/DualDeploy/DualDeployment.html)
[28] PICO altimeter (http://www.picoalt.com/)
[29] "Design of an integrated strapdown guidance and control system for a tactical missile" WILLIAMS, D. E.RICHMAN, J.FRIEDLAND, B. (Singer Co., Kearfott Div., Little Falls, NJ) AIAA-1983-2169 IN: Guidance and Control Conference, Gatlinburg, TN, August 15–17, 1983, Collection of Technical Papers (A83-41659 19-63). New York, American Institute of Aeronautics and Astronautics, 1983, p. 57-66.
[30] http://mafija.fmf.uni-lj.si/seminar/files/2007_2008/MEMS_accelerometers-koncna.pdf
[31] Tilting trains shorten transit time (http://www.memagazine.org/backissues/membersonly/june98/features/tilting/tilting.html)
[32] USGS - volcano monitoring (http://vulcan.wr.usgs.gov/Glossary/Seismicity/description_seismic_monitoring.html)
[33] Fun with the iPhone accelerometer (http://blog.medallia.com/2007/08/fun_with_the_iphone_accelerome.html)
[34] Glogger (http://m.eyetap.org)

External links

- Thinking About Accelerometers and Gravity by Dave Redell, LUNAR #322 (http://www.lunar.org/docs/LUNARclips/v5/v5n1/Accelerometers.html)
- Practical Guide to Accelerometers (http://www.sensr.com/pdf/practical-guide-to-accelerometers.pdf)
- How to Design an Accelerometer (http://www.memsuniverse.com/?page_id=1548)
- Different types of Accelerometer (http://www.sagem-ds.com/eng/site.php?spage=02010301)
- Considerations When Selecting an Accelerometer (http://www.pcb.com/techsupport/docs/vib/TN_17_VIB-0805.pdf)
- Introduction to Accelerometer Basics: Designs, Conditioning, and Mounting (http://www.pcb.com/techsupport/tech_accel.php)
- Database of acceleration data (http://www.opensignals.net/index.php?title=Accelerometry)

Secure Digital

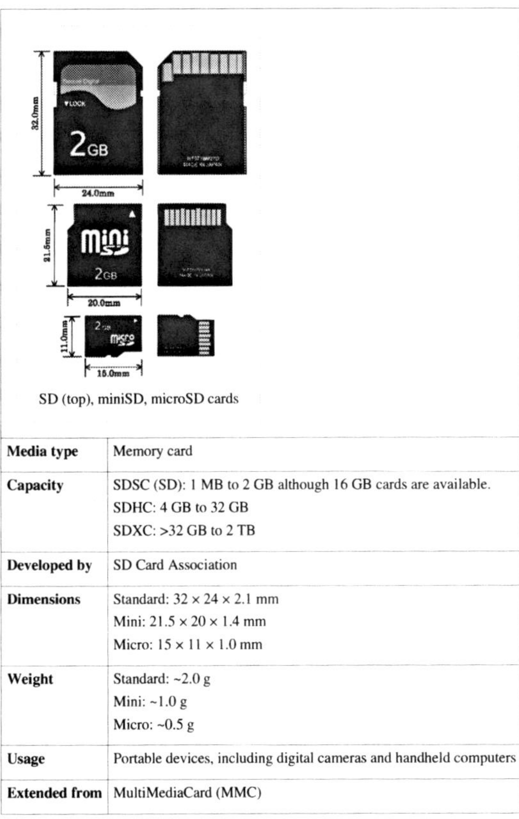

SD (top), miniSD, microSD cards

Media type	Memory card
Capacity	SDSC (SD): 1 MB to 2 GB although 16 GB cards are available. SDHC: 4 GB to 32 GB SDXC: >32 GB to 2 TB
Developed by	SD Card Association
Dimensions	Standard: 32 × 24 × 2.1 mm Mini: 21.5 × 20 × 1.4 mm Micro: 15 × 11 × 1.0 mm
Weight	Standard: ~2.0 g Mini: ~1.0 g Micro: ~0.5 g
Usage	Portable devices, including digital cameras and handheld computers
Extended from	MultiMediaCard (MMC)

Secure Digital (**SD**) is a non-volatile memory card format developed by the SD Card Association for use in portable devices. The SD technology is used by more than 400 brands across dozens of product categories and more than 8,000 models, and is considered the de-facto industry standard.[1]

The SDSC (standard-capacity) card family, commonly known as SD, has an official maximum capacity of 2 GB, though some are available up to 4 GB.[2] The SDHC (high-capacity) card family have a capacity of 4 GB to 32 GB.[3] SDXC (extended-capacity) card family have a capacity starting above 32 GB with a maximum capacity of 2 TB.[4] [5] The availability of 4 GB capacity in both the SD and SDHC families have caused much compatibility confusion with users since each has a slightly different communication protocol.

From a host device point of view, all cards within the same family appear the same to it. SD/miniSD/microSD are members of the SD family. SDHC/miniSDHC/microSDHC are members of the SDHC family. SDXC/microSDXC are members of the SDXC family. SDIO/miniSDIO are members of the special SDIO I/O family. SD adapters allow the physical conversion of smaller SD cards to work in a larger physical slot, and basically are passive devices that connect the pins from the smaller SD card to the pins of the larger SD adapter.

Since cards from all families have a similar physical size, it tends to cause confusion with consumers.[6] For example, microSD, microSDHC, and microSDXC are all the same physical size, but the capabilities for each is defined by its respective family.

The communication protocols for the SDHC/SDXC/SDIO families are slightly different from those of the established SD family, which has caused older host devices to not recognize the newer card families. When an SDHC or SDXC card is inserted into an older SD host device, it shouldn't cause any physical or electrical damage to either the card or host device, though the host device won't be able to recognize the card. Some older host devices don't correctly handle 2 GB and/or 4 GB SD cards since they use larger blocks. Most incompatibility issues can be resolved with a firmware update, but unfortunately vendors rarely correct issues in older host devices.

History

In 1999, SanDisk, Matsushita, and Toshiba first agreed to develop and market the SD (Secure Digital) Memory Card, which was a development of the **MMC** (MultiMediaCard). With a physical profile of 24×32×2.1 mm, the new card provided both DRM up to the SDMI standard, and a high memory density for the time.

8-GB microSDHC card on top of 8-Bytes of magnetic-core memory (1 core is 1 bit)

The new format was designed to compete with Sony's Memory Stick format, which was released the previous year, and featured MagicGate DRM. It was mistakenly predicted that DRM features[7] would be widely used due to pressure from music and other media suppliers to prevent piracy.

The signature *SD* logo was actually developed for another use entirely; it was originally used for the Super Density Disc, which was the unsuccessful Toshiba entry in the DVD format war. This is why the *D* resembles an optical disc.

At the 2000 CES trade show Matsushita, SanDisk, and Toshiba Corporation announced the creation of the SD Card Association to promote SD cards. It is headquartered in California and its executive membership includes some 30 world-leading high-tech companies and major content companies. Early samples of the SD Card were available in the first quarter of 2000, with production quantities of 32 and 64 MB cards available 3 months later.

In March 2003, SanDisk Corporation announced the introduction of the miniSD and demonstrated it at CeBIT 2003.[8] The miniSD card was adopted in 2003 by the SD Association [9] as a small form factor extension to the SD card standard. While the new cards were designed especially for use in mobile phones, they are usually packaged with a miniSD adapter which enables compatibility with all devices equipped with a standard SD Memory Card slot.

In April 2006, the SD Association released a detailed specification for the non-security related parts of the SD Memory Card standard. The organization also released specifications for the SDIO (Secure Digital Input Output) cards and the standard SD host controller. During the same year, specifications were finalized for the small-form-factor microSD (formerly known as TransFlash) and SDHC, with capacities in excess of 2 GB and a minimum sustained read/write speed of 17.6 Mbit/s

In September, 2006, SanDisk announced the 4GB miniSDHC.[9] Like the SD and SDHC, the miniSDHC card has the same form factor as the older miniSD card but the HC card requires HC support built into the host device. Devices that support miniSDHC will work with miniSD and miniSDHC, but devices without specific support for miniSDHC will work only with the older miniSD card.

In January 2009, the SD Association announced the SDXC family that will support cards up to 2 TB memory size and speeds up to 300 Mbyte/s.[10]

microSD

The microSD format was created by SanDisk. The concept was the brainchild of the CTO of SanDisk and CTO of Motorola, who believed current memory card formats were too large for phones. It was originally called T-Flash, however just prior to product launch T-Mobile sent a cease and desist order to SanDisk claiming they own T-(anything) and the name was then changed to TransFlash.[11] After pressure from Toshiba and Panasonic, SanDisks' partners in the 3C licensing group of the SDA, SanDisk negotiated to have the new format become a standard administered by the SDA (SD Card Association). The SDA announced the microSD format at CTIA Wireless 2005 on March 14, 2005, and approval of the final microSD specification was announced on July 13, 2005. At launch, the microSD format was available in capacities of 32, 64, and 128 MB. TransFlash and microSD cards are the same (each can be used in devices made for the other).

Design and implementation

SD cards are based on the older MultiMediaCard (MMC) format, but have a number of differences:

- The SD card is asymmetrically shaped in order not to be inserted upside down, while an MMC would go in most of the way but not make contact if inverted.
- SD cards are thicker than MMCs. SD cards generally measure 32 × 24 × 2.1 mm, but as with MMCs can be as slim as 1.4 mm if they lack a write-protect switch; such cards, called *Thin SD*, are described in the SD specification, but they are non-existent or rare in the market as most devices requiring a slimmer card use the smaller versions of SD: miniSD or microSD.
- The card's electrical contacts are recessed beneath the surface of the card, protecting them from contact with a user's fingers.
- SD cards typically have transfer rates in the range of 80–160 Mbit/s, but this is likely to grow, due to recent improvements to the MMC standard.[12]

Devices with SD slots can use the slimmer MMCs, but standard SD cards will not fit into the slimmer MMC slots. miniSD cards can be used directly in SD slots with a simple passive adapter, since the cards differ in size and shape but not electrical interface. With an active electronic adapter, SD cards can be used in CompactFlash or PC card slots. Some SD cards include a USB connector for compatibility with desktop and laptop computers, and card readers allow SD cards to be accessed via connectivity ports such as USB, FireWire, and the parallel printer port. SD cards can also be accessed via a floppy disk drive with a FlashPath adapter.

Physical size

Each SD card family is available in up to three physical sizes. The SD and SDHC families are available in all three sizes, but the SDXC family is not available in the mini size, and the SDIO family is not available in the micro size.

Size comparison of cards: SD, miniSD, microSD

Standard size

- SD, SDHC, SDXC, SDIO
- 32 mm × 24 mm × 2.1 mm. The MMC and rare *thin* SD cards are 1.4 mm thick.

Mini size

- miniSD, miniSDHC, miniSDIO
- 21.5 mm × 20 mm × 1.4 mm.

Micro size

- microSD, microSDHC, microSDXC
- 15 mm × 11 mm × 1.0 mm.

Optional write-protect tab

When looking at the card from the top (see pictures) there is one required notch on the right side (the side with the diagonal cut-off corner).

On the left side may be a write-protection notch. If this is present, the card cannot be written. If the notch is covered by a sliding write protection tab, or absent, then the card is writeable. Because the notch is detected only by the reader, the protection can be overridden if desired (and if supported by the reader). Not all devices support write protection, which is an optional feature of the SD standard.

Some SD cards have no write-protection notch,[13] and it is absent completely in the microSD and miniSD formats.

Some music and film media companies (e.g., Disney) have released limited catalogs of records and/or videos on SD. These usually contain DRM-encoded Windows Media files, making use of the SD format's DRM capabilities. Such media are usually permanently marked read-only by adding the notch with no tabs.

File system

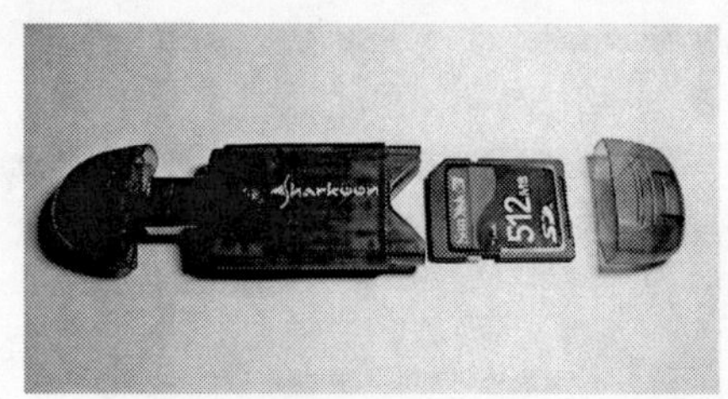

USB-based SD card reader

Like other flash memory card technologies, most SD cards ship preformatted with a file system on top of an MBR partition scheme. SD cards are typically formatted as FAT16, SDHC cards as FAT32, SDXC cards as exFAT. The ubiquity of FAT16 and FAT32 allows those cards to be accessed on virtually any host device with an SD reader. Also, standard FAT maintenance utilities (e.g., SCANDISK) can be used to repair or retrieve corrupted data, and some utilities can recover deleted files, providing that they have not been overwritten. However, because the card appears as a removable hard drive to the host system, the card can be reformatted to any file system supported by the operating system. Conversely, an SD card can contain an embedded operating system (such as a Live USB) to recover a corrupted host computer by natively booting from the flash media reader.

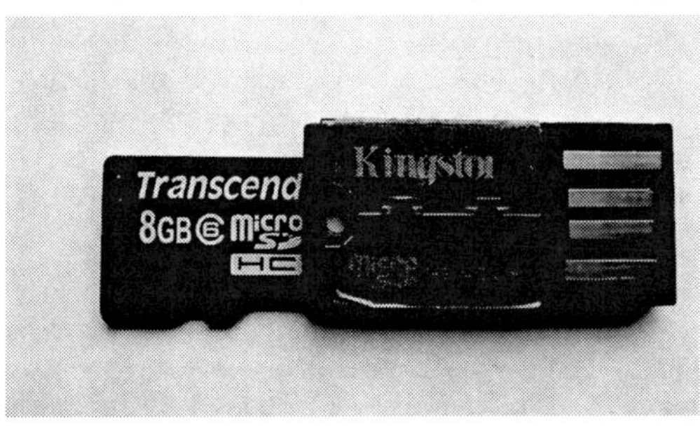

A Transcend Micro SD card being used in a Kingston Micro SD Reader device

SD cards with 4 GB and smaller capacities can be used with many systems by being formatted with FAT16 (4 GB only possible by using 64kiB clusters, and not widely supported) or FAT32 file system (common for file systems 4 GB and bigger). Cards 4 GB and bigger can only be formatted with a file system that can handle these storage sizes, such as FAT32.

SD cards are plain block devices and do not in any way imply any specific partition layout or file system thus partition schemes other than MBR partitioning and the FAT file systems can be used. Under Unix-like operating systems such as Linux or FreeBSD, SD cards can be formatted using, for example, the UFS, EXT3 or the ReiserFS file systems; under Mac OS X, SD cards can be partitioned as GUID devices and formatted with the HFS+ file system. Under MS-Windows and some unix systems, SD cards can be formatted using the NTFS and on later versions exFAT file system. However most consumer products will expect MBR partitioning and FAT16 / FAT32 / exFAT filesystem.

Fragmentation may slow down the effective write speed[14] but the effect is tiny compared with that of fragmentation on hard drives. Defragmentation tools may be used. However, it is unnecessary to use any disk optimization tool because on an SD card the time required to access any block is the same. Defragmenting an SD card will wear the card out and is not normally recommended, as the number of writes, before failure occurs, is limited (often as few as 100,000 times).

Transfer modes

Depending upon the capability of a specific SD card, it may support various combinations of the following bus types and transfer modes. The SPI bus and one-bit SD bus are mandatory for all SD families. See the electrical interface section for a more detailed description.

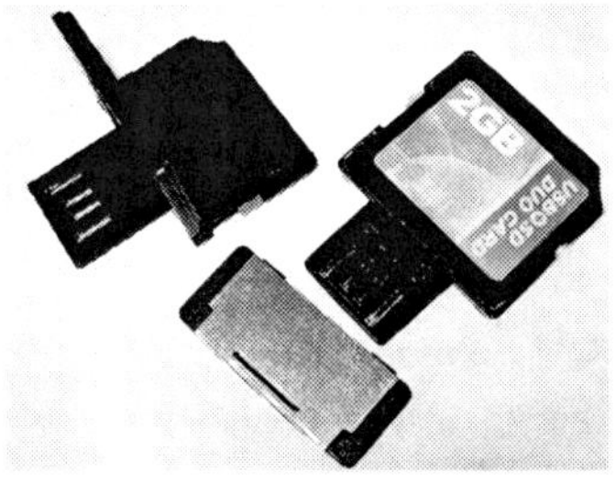

2GB SD card with dual-interface SD and USB connections

- **SPI:** Serial Peripheral Interface Bus is primarily used by embedded microcontrollers. This bus type supports only 3.3 volt power and communications.
- **One-bit SD:** Separate command and data channels and a proprietary transfer format.
- **Four-bit SD:** Uses extra pins plus some reassigned pins. UHS-I and UHS-II requires this bus type but after the card is reconfigured to communicate at 1.8 volts.
  - **UHS-I:** The Ultra High Speed mode is found exclusively on SDXC and SDHC products.[15] SDXC or SDHC products with the UHS-I symbol are capable of supporting data transfer speeds up to 104 MB/s. UHS-I quadruples the extant top speed of 25 MB/s. UHS bus interfaces are backwards compatible. SDXC UHS-I and SDHC UHS-I memory cards can achieve best performance when paired with a UHS-I device and are designed

to allow consumers to record HD resolution videos to tapeless camcorders, plus perform other simultaneous recording functions.

- **UHS-II:** Available exclusively on SDXC and SDHC products. The standard raises the data transfer speed to a theoretical maximum of 312 MB/s.[16]

- **USB:** Some SD cards may have an additional USB connector. Though not part of the SD electrical specification, this concept still meets the SD physical size specification.

Electrical interface

All SD card families must power-up at 3.3 volt and use 3.3 volt logic electrical interface, though SDHC and SDXC family cards can step down to 1.8 volt after receiving specific commands.[17]

All SD card families must support two signaling bus types at power-up: SPI bus and one-bit SD bus. Depending upon the card type, an additional four-bit SD bus type may be either optional or mandatory for the card.[17]

The host has the choice of selecting either SPI or SD bus type. After power-up of an SD card, the host will "tell" the card which bus type it wants to use for communications, either SPI or one-bit SD signaling. In one-bit SD bus mode, the host can send additional commands to change over to four-bit SD bus, 1.8 voltage, and higher transfer speeds.[17]

There is a special family of SD cards, called SDIO, of which there are two types: Low-Speed and Full-Speed. Both types of SDIO cards support SPI and one-bit SD bus types, but support for the four-bit SD bus type varies depending on the card. For Low-Speed SDIO cards, the four-bit SD bus is optional. For Full-Speed SDIO cards, the four-bit SD bus capability must exist. If a SDIO card is a "combo card", which means that it has memory and I/O, then it must be configured for four-bit SD bus before using both memory and I/O. The Low-Speed SDIO cards have an additional unique requirement of a maximum clock rate of 400 kHz for all communications. SDIO cards support another unique feature, which is an optional interrupt output pin.[18]

The signaling buses supports various clock rates, including a stopped clock. After power-up, the host must communicate with the SD card up to a maximum clock rate called the Default Speed (DS), which is a bus clock up to 400 kHz for Low-Speed SDIO cards, or up to 25 MHz for all other types of SD cards. Since Low-Speed SDIO cards are limited to 400 kHz, it is recommended this be the initial maximum clock rate until additional commands can be sent to determine the exact "flavor" of SD card.[17]

SD cards may support even higher clock rate modes, which require additional configuration prior to use, which are called: High Speed (HS), UHS-I, UHS-II. The High Speed (HS) mode supports a bus clock up to 50 MHz and supported by most SD cards. The UHS-I and UHS-II clock modes are available only by SDHC and SDXC family cards, and require a four-bit SD bus communicating at 1.8 volts.[17]

Though an SD card may be able to communicate at higher clock rates, the host is not required to communicate at high speeds. For low-power applications, it may be desirable to run the clock at slower speeds to consume less power.[17]

DRM features

The digital rights management scheme embedded in the SD cards is defined as the Content Protection for Recordable Media (CPRM) by the 4C Entity and is centered around use of the Cryptomeria cipher (also known as *C2*). The specification is kept secret and is accessible only to licensees. This DRM has not been seen "in the wild" and few, if any, devices appear to provide support for it. DVD-Audio uses a very similar scheme known as Content Protection for Prerecorded Media (CPPM).

Windows Phone 7 devices use SD that are designed to be accessed only by the phone manufacturer or mobile provider. An SD card inserted into phone underneath the battery compartment becomes locked "to the phone with an automatically generated key" so that "the SD card cannot be read by another phone, device, or PC".[19] Symbian devices, however, are some of the very few which can perform the necessary low-level format operations on locked

SD cards. It is therefore possible to use a device such as the Nokia N8 to reformat the card for subsequent use in other devices.[20]

Super*Talent, a manufacturer of computer memory, has created the *Super Digital* card. They are the same in appearance and function as regular Secure Digital cards, but they lack the CPRM code commonly found in Secure Digital cards.[21]

Power consumption

The power consumption of microSD cards varies by manufacturer, but appears to be in the range of 66-330 mW (20-100 mA at a supply voltage of 3.3 V). Specifications from TwinMos technologies list a maximum of 149 mW (45 mA) during transfer.[22] Toshiba, on the other hand, lists 264-330 mW (80-100 mA).[23]

Speeds

There are different speeds of SD card available. The official unit of measurement is the **Speed Class Rating**; an older unit of measurement is the × rating.

Inside a 512MB SD card. NAND flash chip that holds the data (bottom) and SD controller (top)

Speed Class Rating

The **Speed Class Rating** is the official unit of speed measurement for SD Cards, defined by the SD Association. The Class number represents a multiple of 8 Mbit/s (1 MB/s), the least sustained write speeds for a card in a fragmented state (Class 2, 4, 6) or the minimum non-fragmented sequential write speed (Class 10).[17]

These are the ratings of all currently available cards:[14] [24]

Class	Speed
Class 2	2 MB/s
Class 4	4 MB/s
Class 6	6 MB/s
Class 10	10 MB/s

Even though the class ratings are defined by a governing body, like "×" speed ratings, class speed ratings are quoted by the manufacturers and not verified by any independent evaluation process. In applications that require sustained write throughput, such as video recording, the device may not perform satisfactorily if the SD card's class rating falls below a particular speed. For example, a camcorder that is designed to record to class 6 media may suffer dropouts or corrupted video on slower media. On slower class cards, digital cameras may experience a lag of several seconds between photo-taking, while the camera writes the picture to the card.

Important differences between the Speed Class and the traditional CD-ROM drive speed measurement ("×" speed ratings) are that speed class:[25]

1. may be queried by the host device;
2. defines the *minimum* transfer speed.

Since the class rating is readable by devices, they can issue a warning to the user if the inserted card's reported rating falls below the application's minimum requirement.[25]

On 21 May 2009, Panasonic announced new *class 10* SDHC cards, claiming that this new class is "part of SD Card Specification Ver.3.0".[26] Toshiba also announced cards based on the new 3.0 spec.[27]

On 1 June 2010, Pretec announced the new Class-16 HD-video grade SDXC 64GB card at Computex Taipei 2010.[28]

× rating

The × rating is equal to 1.2 Mbit/s. It is derived from the standard CD-ROM drive speed of 1.2 Mbit/s (approximately 150 kB/s). Basic cards transfer data up to six times (6×) the data rate of the standard CD-ROM speed (7.2 Mbit/s vs 1.2 Mbit/s). The 2.0 specification defines speeds up to 200×, but unlike the class rating system, does not mandate that ×-ratings measure the card's least sustained write-speed. So, typically, manufacturers provide ×-ratings based on maximum read/write speeds. Furthermore, for most cards, the fastest *read* speed is typically swifter than its fastest *write* speed, leading some manufacturers to use read-speed as the ×-rating measurement. Other vendors, such as Transcend and Kingston, use write-speed.[29]

This table lists common ratings, the minimum transfer rates, and the corresponding Speed Class.

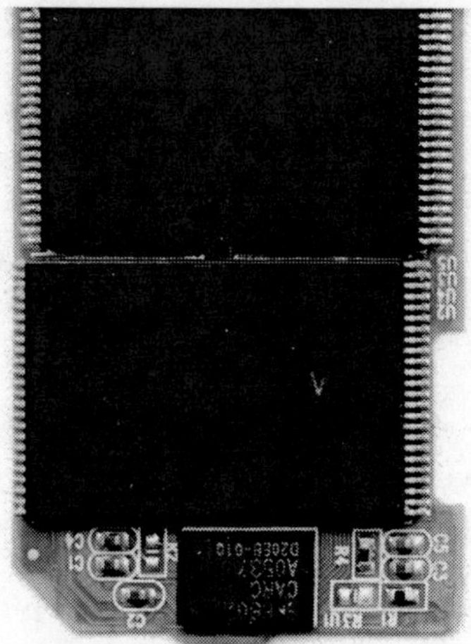

Inside a 2GB SD card. Two NAND flash chips (top and middle), SD controller chip (bottom)

Rating	Read Speed (Mbit/s)	Read Speed (MB/s)	Write Speed (Mbit/s)	Write Speed (MB/s)	Speed Class
6×	7.2	0.9			
10×	12.0	1.5			
13×	**16.0**	**2.0**	**16.0**	**2.0**	**2**
26×	**33.0**	**4.0**	**32.0**	**4.0**	**4**
32×	38.4	4.8	40.0	5.0	
40×	**48.0**	**6.0**	**48.0**	**6.0**	**6**
66×	**80.0**	**10.0**	**80.0**	**10.0**	**10**
100×	120.0	15.0	120.0	15.0	
133×	160.0	20.0	160.0	20.0	
150×	180.0	22.5	180.0	22.5	
200×	240.0	30.0	240.0	30.0	
266×	320.0	40.0	320.0	40.0	
300×	360.0	45.0	360.0	45.0	
400×	480.0	60.0	480.0	60.0	

600×	720.0	90.0	720.0	90.0	

UHS Speed Class

Requiring a new bus, the UHS Speed Class is intended for use in applications like real-time broadcasts and capturing large HD videos. The only currently available UHS SD cards are UHS Speed class 1.[30]

Types of cards

The SD card is not the only flash memory card standard ratified by the Secure Digital Card Association (SDCA). Other SD Card Association formats include miniSD, microSD (formerly known as TransFlash before ratification by the SD Card Association), and SDHC (Secure Digital High Capacity, for capacities above 4 GB–although, there are some card readers that cannot handle over 1 GB that are not SDHC). SDHC is not fully compatible with the format that it extends, in that SD devices that do not specifically support SDHC will not work with the newer cards.

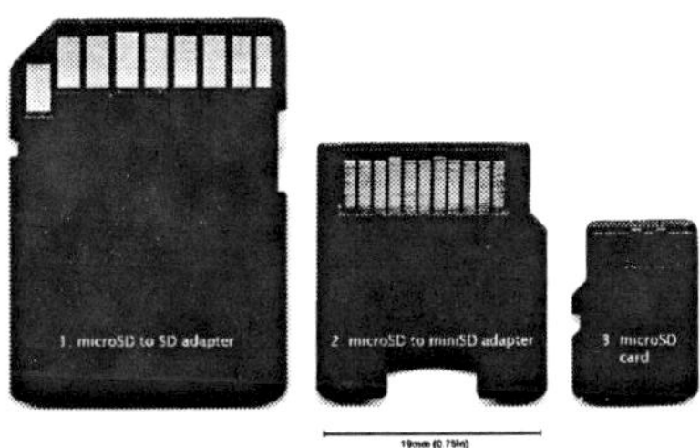

microSD to SD adapter (left), microSD to miniSD adapter (middle), microSD card (right)

The smaller miniSD and microSD cards are usable in full size MMC/SD/SDIO slots with an adapter (which must route the electrical connections as well as making physical contact). However, it is already difficult to create I/O devices in the SD form factor and this will be even more difficult in the smaller sizes.

microSD card is inserted into an SD adapter, which is inserted into an SD to USB reader.

As SD slots still support MMCs, the separately-evolved smaller MMC variants are also compatible with SD-supporting devices. Unlike miniSD and microSD (which are sufficiently different from SD to make mechanical adapters necessary), RS-MMC slots maintain backward compatibility with full-sized MMCs, because the RS-MMCs are simply shorter MMCs. More information on these variants can be found in the article about the MultiMediaCard standard.

It is also important to note that, unlike for data storage devices (which typically works everywhere an SD slot is present), an SDIO device must be supported and equipped with drivers and applications for the host system and usually does not work outside of the manufacturer's scope (which means, for example, that an HP SDIO camera usually does not work with PDAs for which it is not listed as an accessory). This behavior is often not expected by end users who typically expect that only the SD slot is required. Similar compatibility issues are sometimes seen with Bluetooth devices, although to a much lesser extent thanks to standardized Bluetooth profiles.

Most, possibly all, current MMC flash memory cards support SPI mode even if not officially required as failure to do so would severely affect compatibility. All cards currently made by SanDisk, Ritek/Ridata, and Kingmax digital appear to support SPI. Also, MMCs may be electrically identical to SD cards but in a thinner package and with an electronic fuse blown to disable SD functionality (so no SD royalties need to be paid).

MMC defined the SPI and one-bit MMC/SD protocols. The underlying SPI protocol has existed for years as a standard feature on many microcontrollers. The new protocol used open collector signaling to allow multiple cards on the same bus but this actually causes problems at higher clock rates. While SPI used three shared lines plus a separate chip select to each card, the new protocol allows up to 30 cards to be connected to the same three wires (with no chip select) at the expense of a much more complicated card initialization and the requirement that each card have a unique serial number for plug and play operation; this feature is rarely used and its use is actively discouraged in new standards (which recommend a completely separate channel to each card) because of speed and power consumption issues. The quasi-proprietary one-bit protocol was extended to support four bit wide (SD and MMC) and eight bit (MMC only) transfers for more speed while much of the rest of the computer industry is moving to higher speed narrower channels; standard SPI could simply have been clocked at higher data rates (such as 133 MHz) for higher performance than offered by four-bit SD — embedded CPUs that did not already have higher clock rates available would not have been fast enough to handle the higher data rates anyway. The SD card association dropped support for some of the old one-bit MMC protocol commands and added support for additional commands related to copy protection.

Storage capacity

SD cards (non-SDHC) with greater than 1 GB capacity

The SD Card Association's current specifications define how a standard SD (non-SDHC) card with more than 1 GB and up to 4 GB capacity should be designed. These cards should be readable in any SD 1.01 devices that take the block length data into account. Any 1 GB or lesser card should always work (so the key question is how one's reader handles block length).

According to the specification,[31] the maximum capacity of a standard SD card is defined by (BLOCKNR × BLOCK_LEN), where BLOCKNR may be (4,096 × 512) and BLOCK_LEN may be up to 2,048. This allows a capacity of 4 GB. The main problem is that some of the card readers support only a block (or, sector) size of 512 bytes, so greater than 1 GB non-SDHC cards may cause compatibility difficulties for users of such devices.

Compatibility issues with 4 GB and larger cards

Devices that use SD cards identify the card by requesting a 128-bit identification string from the card. For standard-capacity SD cards, 12 of the bits are used to identify the number of memory clusters (ranging from 1 to 4,096) and 3 of the bits are used to identify the number of blocks per cluster (which decode to 4, 8, 16, 32, 64, 128, 256, or 512 blocks per cluster).

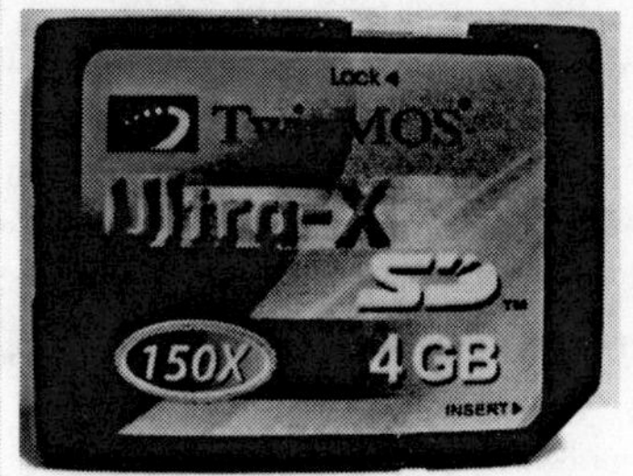

4 GB standard SD card (not SDHC)

In older 1.x implementations the standard capacity block was exactly 512 bytes. This gives 4,096 × 512 × 512 = 1 gigabyte of storage memory. A later revision of the 1.x standard allowed a 4-bit field to indicate 1,024 or 2,048 bytes per block instead, theoretically yielding up to 4 gigabytes of memory storage. However the specification specifies 2 gigabytes as the maximum capacity.

Host devices designed before this change may incorrectly identify such cards, usually by misidentifying a card with lower capacity than is the case by assuming 512 bytes per block rather than 1,024 or 2,048.

For the new SDHC (2.0) implementation, 32 bits of the identification string are used to indicate the memory size in increments of 512 bytes. The SDCA currently allows only 26 of the 32 bits to be used, giving a maximum size of

32 GB. All SD cards with a capacity larger than 4 GB must use the 2.0 implementation at minimum. Two bits that were previously reserved and fixed at 0, now called the "CSD Structure", are being used for identifying the type of card, 0 is standard capacity; 1 is high (SDHC) and extended (SDXC) capacity; 2 and 3 are reserved. Older host devices are not aware of this new field thus cannot correctly identify SDHC or SDXC cards.

All SDHC readers are able to use standard SD cards,[32] and all SDXC readers are able to use SD and SDHC cards.

Many older devices will not accept the 2 GB size even though it is in the revised standard. Some manufacturers have ignored the maximum size specification and manufactured cards with a 4 GB which have similar compatibility issues and also may not work in newer devices supporting the 2 GB size. The following statement is from the SD Card Association specification:

> To make 2 GByte card, the Maximum Block Length (READ_BL_LEN=WRITE_BL_LEN) shall be set to 1024 bytes. However, the Block Length, set by CMD16, shall be up to 512 bytes to keep consistency with 512 bytes Maximum Block Length cards (Less than and equal 2 Gbyte cards).
>
> —[33]

Storage capacity calculations

SD cards contain a Card-Specific Data (CSD) register which holds the card's capacity, among many other things. The format changed considerably between version 1.0 (SD) and version 2.0 (SDHC, SDXC), this is the cause of the incompatibility between SD and newer cards. CSD v2.0 expanded the C_SIZE register, removed the C_SIZE_MULT register, and no longer uses READ_BL_LEN for capacity calculation.[34] Capacity is calculated thus:

CSD Version 1.0:

```
Capacity=(C_SIZE+1)<<(C_SIZE_MULT+2)<<READ_BL_LEN        2GiB max.
Where 0<=C_SIZE<=4095, 0<=C_SIZE_MULT<=7, READ_BL_LEN==9 || READ_BL_LEN==10
```

CSD Version 2.0:

```
Capacity=(C_SIZE+1)*524288
where for SDHC       4112<=C_SIZE<=65375       (approx. 2 GB) < capacity < 32GiB
      for SDXC      65535<=C_SIZE                   32GiB <= capacity <= 2TiB max.
```

SDHC cards with greater than 32 GB capacity

Similarly to the above, as of version 2.00 of the specification,[31] the capacity of an SDHC card is limited to 32 GB. However, while not strictly adhering to that standard, it is in principle possible to create SDHC-like cards of up to 2 TB capacity. Some SDHC devices will accept SDXC cards with capacities greater than 32GB and recognize the full capacity, however compatibility is not guaranteed in all cases. SDHC cards have a fixed sector size of 512 bytes.

SDHC

8GB SDHC Card (top and bottom)

SDHC (Secure Digital High Capacity, SD 2.0) is an extension of the SD standard which increases card's storage capacity up to 32 GB. SDHC cards share the same physical and electrical form factor as older (SD 1.x) cards, allowing SDHC-devices to support both newer SDHC cards and older SD-cards. To increase addressable storage, SDHC uses sector addressing instead of byte addressing as in the previous SD standard. Byte addressing supported card capacities up to 4 GB, whereas sector addressing can theoretically support capacities up to 2 TB (2048 GB). The current standard limits the maximum capacity of an SDHC card to 32 GB[35] (it is expected that the SDHC specification will be revised in the future to allow card capacities greater than 32 GB[25]). SDHC cards will not work in devices designed to the older SD 1.x specification. The SDHC trademark is licensed to ensure compatibility.[36]

SD and SDHC compatibility issues

The SDHC specification was completed in June 2006,[37] but by that time, non-standard high-capacity (>1 GB) SD cards (based on the older 1.x specification) were already on the market. The two types of storage cards were not interchangeable, creating some confusion among customers. SD and SDHC cards and devices have these compatibility issues:

- Devices that do not specifically support SDHC do not recognize SDHC memory cards.[38] Some devices can support SDHC through a firmware upgrade.[31]
- SDHC devices are backward compatible with SD memory cards.[31]
- Some manufacturers have produced 4 GB SD cards that conform to neither the SD2.0/SDHC spec nor existing SD devices.[39]
- File System: SD cards are typically formatted with the FAT16 file system, while SDHC cards are typically formatted as FAT32.[] However, both types of cards can support other general-purpose file systems, such as UFS2, ext2 or the proprietary exFAT for example. Changing the filesystem used, or even reformatting may cause performance or life-span problems, as the card controllers frequently optimise a small area of the device for the access patterns typical of a FAT16, or FAT32 file allocation table (FAT) area.[40]
- Microsoft Windows may need a hotfix to support accessing SDHC cards.[41] [42] [43]

SDXC

The Secure Digital Extended Capacity (SDXC) format was unveiled at CES 2009 (January 7–10, 2009). The maximum capacity defined for SDXC cards is 2 TB (2048 GB). The older SDHC cards also have a maximum capacity of 2 TB based on the card data structures, but this is artificially limited to 32 GB by the SD 2.0 specification. The first SDXCs being released are governed by an SD 3.0 specification (which also still specifies FAT32 and thus lower capacities), whereas higher capacity and faster SDXCs are expected to follow an SD 4.0 specification, which was formally announced in January 2011.[44]

The maximum transfer rate of SDXCs which follow the SD 3.0 specification was announced as 832 Mbit/s (these are called *UHS104* speeds[44]), with plans that the SD 4.0 specification shall increase this to 2.4 Gbit/s.

The SDcard association selected Microsoft's proprietary exFAT file system in the official SDXC specification;[45] [46] [47] however, as with SD and SDHC, it is still a plain block device and thus arbitrary partitioning and other file systems can be used, such as btrFS, ext4, HFS Plus, NTFS, UFS, etc.

History

On January 7, 2009, SanDisk and Sony announced the joint development of the XC variant of the competing Memory Stick format, boasting the same 2 TB maximum capacity of SDXC.[48]

On January 8, 2009, Panasonic announced plans for production of 64 GB SDXC cards.[49]

On March 6, 2009, Pretec introduced the world's first SDXC card[50] with a capacity of 32 GB and a read/write speed of 400 Mbit/s. At the introduction, there were no products compatible with the new memory card.

On August 3, 2009, Toshiba announced it will launch the world's first 64 GB SDXC Memory Card[51] with a read speed of 480 Mbit/s. The 64 GB card (THNSU064GAA2BC) was planned to be available in the spring of 2010.[52][53] Toshiba card was available from April 13.

On January 6, 2010, Panasonic announced its first SDXC cards with 64 GB and 48 GB to be available in February[54] (RP-SDW64GE1K and RP-SDW48GE1K).

On January 6, 2010, Sony announced the launch of Handycam HDR-CX55V with SDXC support.

On February 8, 2010, Canon announced the launch of the new EOS Rebel T2i Digital SLR camera, the first EOS model to support SDXC memory cards.[55]

On February 19, 2010, Panasonic launched in Japan World's first available for consumers SDXC memory cards with 64 GB and 48 GB (RP-SDW64GE1K and RP-SDW48GE1K) together with USB card readers compatible with SDXC format.

On February 22, 2010, SanDisk launched its 64 GB SanDisk Ultra SDXC card.[56]

The first integrated SDXC card readers are available from JMicron[57] and are expected to be used in laptops in 2010.[58]

In January, 2011, Centon Electronics, Inc. began shipping its 64 GB and 128 GB Class 10 SDXC card.

In March, 2011, Lexar began shipping its 128 GB Class 10 SDXC card.[59]

SDHC and SDXC compatibility issues

In the 3.0 specification, the electronic interface of SDHC and SDXC cards is the same. This means that SDHC hosts that have drivers that recognize the newly used capability bits, and have operating system software that understands the exFAT filesystem, are compatible with SDXC cards. The decision to label cards with a capacity greater than 32GB as SDXC and to use a different filesystem is due solely to the limitations in creating larger filesystems in certain versions of Microsoft Windows. Other operating system kernels, such as Linux, make no distinction between SDHC and SDXC cards, as long as the card contains a compatible filesystem.

SDHC and SDXC cards and hosts have these compatibility issues:

- Existing SDHC hosts will only support the SDXC cards at up to UHS104 speeds;[44]
- SDXC hosts are backward compatible with SD and SDHC memory cards.[31]
- The operating systems that currently support SDXC are: Linux (with a proprietary driver for the exFAT filesystem[60]), Microsoft Windows 7, Windows Vista SP1+,[31] Windows XP SP2 or SP3 with KB955704,[61] Windows Server 2008 SP1+, Windows Server 2003 SP2 or SP3 with KB955704, Windows CE 6+, and Mac OS X Snow Leopard (Intel-based)[62]

SDIO

A SDIO (Secure Digital Input Output) card is a combination of an SD card and an I/O device. This kind of combination is increasingly found in portable electronics devices.

Hosts that support SDIO (typically PDAs like the Palm Treo, but occasionally laptops or mobile phones) can use small hosts designed for the SD form factor, like GPS receivers, Wi-Fi or Bluetooth adapters, modems, Ethernet adapters, barcode readers, IrDA adapters, FM radio tuners, TV tuners, RFID readers, digital cameras, or other mass storage media such as hard drives.

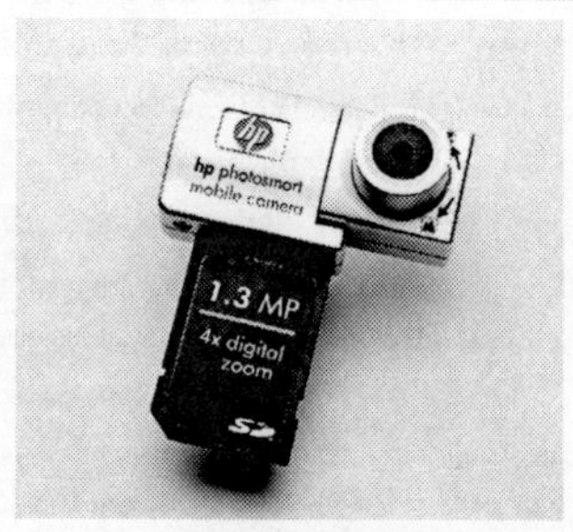

A camera that uses the SDIO interface to connect to some HP iPAQ devices.

A number of other devices have been proposed but not yet implemented, including RS-232 serial adapters, fingerprint scanners, SDIO to USB host/slave adapters (which would allow an SDIO-equipped handheld device to use USB peripherals and/or interface to PCs), magnetic strip readers, combination Bluetooth/Wi-Fi/GPS transceivers, cellular modems (PCS, CDPD, GSM, etc.), and APRS/TNC adapters.

SDIO cards are fully compatible with the SD Memory Card host controller (including mechanical, electrical, power, signaling, and software). When an SDIO card is inserted into a non SDIO-aware host, it will cause no physical damage or disruption to device or host controller. Most of the SD Memory commands are supported in SDIO. SDIO cards can contain 8 separate logical cards, although currently, this is at most a memory and IO function. SD slots will take SD cards only. SDIO slots will take SD cards and SDIO cards.

SDIO typical pin out is: CLK (clock), CMD (command), DAT0 (data0), DAT1 (data1), DAT2 (data2), DAT3 (data3)

SD cards with extra features

Various manufacturers have tried to make their SD cards stand out from the crowd in different ways

- **SD Plus** - A type of SD card made by Sandisk that has an integrated USB connector so it can be plugged directly into a USB port without needing any special card reader.[63] This concept has proven successful and other companies started introducing similar designs branded as *duo SD* or *3 Way* in the case of A-DATA's microSDHC to SDHC and USB all-in-one product, which was available in 2008 only.
- **Capacity Display** - In 2006, A-DATA announced an SD card with its own digital display that would show how much free space is left on the card.[64]
- **Eye-Fi**, Inc. - Produces an SD card with Wi-Fi capability built in for 802.11g, 802.11b, and backwards-compatible 802.11n wireless networks and supporting static WEP 40; 104; and 128, WPA-PSK, and WPA2-PSK security standards. The card works with any digital camera with an SD slot and can transmit captured images over a wireless network. When not in range of a wireless network connection, the card makes use of its 2 GB capacity (EYE-FI-2 GB model) until the images can be transferred.[65] Some models geotag their pictures.
- **Gruvi** - A rare type of microSD card with extra DRM features

Pre-loaded content

Towards the end of 2000s many manufacturers saw the need to distinguish their SD cards from one another. One idea was to introduce pre-loaded content onto new SD cards.

SanDisk introduced their SlotMusic which enabled users to buy digital music files already loaded onto their cards.[66]

Market penetration

Secure Digital cards are ubiquitous in consumer electronic devices, and have become the dominant means of storing several gigabytes of data in a small size.

Devices such as netbooks, digital cameras, camcorders, PDAs, mobile phones, video game consoles and digital audio players as well as many others use them.

Smaller devices tend to use microSD or miniSD rather than full sized SD cards.

SD cards are not generally used in mass produced devices where only a small amount of storage is needed due to economic reasons, or where a very large amount of storage is required.

A camcorder with a 4 GB SDHC card

Digital cameras

SD/MMC cards replaced Toshiba's SmartMedia as the dominant memory card format used in digital cameras. In 2001, SmartMedia had achieved nearly 50% use, but by 2005 SD/MMC had achieved over 40% of the digital camera market and SmartMedia's share had plummeted, with cards not being easily available in 2007.

At this time all the leading digital camera manufacturers use SD in their consumer product lines, including Canon, Casio, Fujifilm, Kodak, Nikon, Olympus, Panasonic, Pentax, Ricoh, Samsung, and Sony. Previously, Olympus and Fujifilm used xD cards exclusively, while Sony only used Memory Stick; however as of January 2010, all three support SD.

Some prosumer and professional digital camera models continue to offer CompactFlash, either on a second card slot or as the only storage, as it has historically offered a better price/capacity ratio and faster transfer rates.

Secure Digital memory cards can be used in Sony XDCAM EX camcorders via the MEAD-SD01 adapter.[67]

Embedded systems

Unlike CompactFlash, none of the SD card variants supports ATA signaling, limiting their use as solid state drives unless a separate converter chip is used. Although embedded systems exist that use SD cards as their main storage mechanism, a special SD controller chip is often used.[68] In September 2008, the SD Card Association announced the Embedded SD standard to be released in November.[69]

A homebrew hardware hack has brought SD card support to the popular Linksys WRT54G router by utilizing spare GPIO pins on the router's processor and the Linux kernel's MMC module. Transfer speeds of 1.6 Mbit/s can be achieved with this setup.[70]

Openness of standards

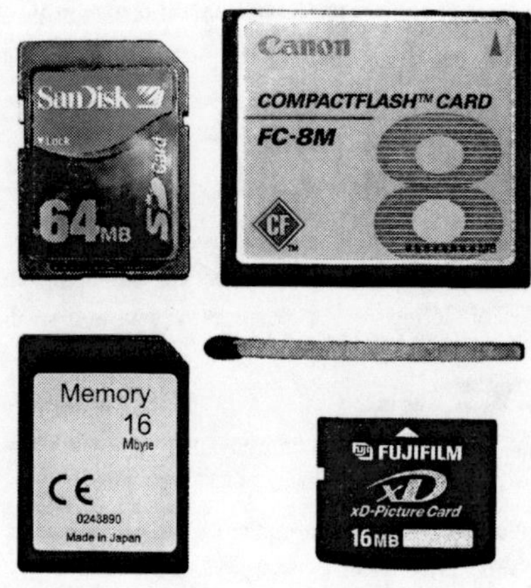

Size comparison of various flash cards: SD, CompactFlash, MMC, xD

Like most memory card formats, SD is covered by numerous patents and trademarks. Three versions of the SD specification have been set: 1.0, 1.1 and 2.0. These were originally available only after agreeing to a non-disclosure agreement (NDA) that prohibited development of an open source driver, which generated consternation in the open-source and free software communities. However, the system was eventually reverse-engineered, and the non-DRMed sections of the memory cards could be accessed by free software drivers. Since then, the SD Card Association (SDA) has made access to a simplified version of the specification available under a less restrictive license.[71] Although most open-source drivers were written before this, it has helped them to solve some compatibility issues.

In 2006, the SD Card Association also released a simplified version of their host controller interface specification (not to be confused with the physical specification, which covers the actual cards and their protocol) and later also for physical layer, ASSD extensions, SDIO and SDIO Bluetooth Type-A specifications under a disclaimers agreement.[72] Like the physical specification, most of the information had already been discovered before the public release[73] and at least Linux had a fully free driver for it. Still, building a chip conforming to this specification caused the One Laptop per Child project to claim "the first truly Open Source SD implementation, with no need to obtain an SDI license or sign NDAs to create SD drivers or applications."[74]

For the most part, the lack of a complete, open SD specification mainly affects embedded systems and laptop systems, since desktop users generally read SD cards via USB-based card readers. These card readers present a standard USB mass storage interface to memory cards, thus separating the operating system from the details of the underlying SD interface. However, embedded systems (such as portable music players) usually access SD cards directly, and therefore complete programming information is necessary. Desktop card readers are themselves examples of such embedded systems; the manufacturers of these readers have usually paid the SDCA for complete access to the SD specifications. Many notebook computers now include SD card readers *not* based on USB; device drivers for these essentially access the SD card directly, as in embedded systems.

Royalties for SD card licences are imposed for manufacture and sale of memory cards and host adapters (USD$1,000/year plus membership at USD$1,500/year) but SDIO cards can be made without royalties and MMC host adapters do not require a royalty. MMCs have a seven-pin interface; SD and SDIO have expanded this to nine pins and MMC Plus expands this even further with thirteen pins.

Compared to other flash memory formats

Overall, SD is less open than CompactFlash or USB flash memory drives; these are open standards which can be implemented free of payment for licensing, royalties, or documentation. (CompactFlash and USB flash drives may, however, require licensing fees for the use of associated logos and trademarks.)

However, SD is much more open than Memory Stick, for which no public documentation nor any documented legacy implementation is available. All SD cards can be accessed freely using the well-documented SPI bus.

xD cards are simply 18-pin NAND flash chips in a special package and support the standard command set for raw NAND flash access. Although the raw hardware interface to xD cards is well understood, the layout of its memory contents—necessary for interoperability with xD card readers and digital cameras—is totally undocumented. The consortium that licenses xD cards has not released any technical information to the public.

Type	MMC	RS-MMC	MMC Plus	SecureMMC	SD	SDIO	miniSD	microSD
SD Socket	Yes	Mechanical adapter	Yes	Yes	Yes	Yes	Electro-mechanical adapter	Electro-mechanical adapter
Pins	7	7	13	7	9	9	11	8
Form factor	shallow	shallow/narrow	shallow	shallow	deep (some)	deep	narrow/slim/shallow	narrow/slim/extra shallow
Breadth	24 mm	24 mm	24 mm	24 mm	24 mm	24 mm	20 mm	11 mm
Width	32 mm	18 mm	32 mm	32 mm	32 mm	32 mm+	21.5 mm	15 mm
Depth	1.4 mm	1.4 mm	1.4 mm	1.4 mm	2.1 mm (some)	2.1 mm	1.4 mm	1 mm
SPI mode	Optional	Optional	Optional	Yes	Yes	Yes	Yes	Yes
1-bit mode	Yes	Yes	Yes	Yes	Yes	Yes	Yes	Yes
4-bit mode	No	No	Yes	?	Optional	Optional	Optional	Optional
8-bit mode	No	No	Yes	No	No	No	No	No
Interrupts	No	No	No	No	No	Optional	No	No
Max clock rate	20 MHz	20 MHz	52 MHz	20 MHz?	208 MHz	50 MHz	208 MHz	208 MHz
Max transfer	20 Mbit/s	20 Mbit/s	416 Mbit/s	20 Mbit/s?	832 Mbit/s	200 Mbit/s	832 Mbit/s	832 Mbit/s
Max SPI transfer	20 Mbit/s	20 Mbit/s	52 Mbit/s	20 Mbit/s	50 Mbit/s	50 Mbit/s	50 Mbit/s	50 Mbit/s
DRM	No	No	No	Yes	Yes	N/A	Yes	Yes
User encrypt	No	No	No	Yes	No	No	No	No
Simplified spec	Yes	Yes	No	Not yet?	Yes	Yes	No	No
Membership cost	JEDEC $4400/yr (not required)				SD Card Association $2000/yr (General), $4500/yr (Executive)			
Specification cost	Free			?	Simplified Spec: Free. Full Spec: Free for members, $1000/yr for R&D non-members.			
Host license	No	No	No	No	Yes: $1000/yr			
Card royalties	Yes	Yes	Yes	Yes	Yes	Yes + $1000/yr	Yes	Yes

Open source compatible	Yes	Yes	Yes?	Yes?	Yes	Yes	Yes	Yes
Nominal operating voltage	3.3V	1.8V/3.3V	1.8V/3.3V[75][76]	1.8V/3.3V	3.3V	3.3V	3.3V	3.3V
Type	**MMC**	**RS-MMC**	**MMC Plus**	**SecureMMC**	**SD**	**SDIO**	**miniSD**	**microSD**

Table data compiled mostly from simplified versions of MMC and SDIO specifications and other data on SD card and MMC association web sites. Data for other card variations is interpolated.

Capacity limit in all SD/MMC formats appears to be 128 GB in LBA mode (28-bit sector address).

See also

- SD Card Association
- Comparison of memory cards
- Serial Peripheral Interface Bus (SPI)
- File Allocation Table (FAT16, FAT32) and exFAT
- Flash memory
- slotMusic
- MultiMediaCard
- USB FlashCard
- Universal Flash Storage

References

[1] About - SD Card Association (http://www.sdcard.org/developers/about/)

[2] "SD Card - SD Card Association" (http://www.sdcard.org/developers/tech/sdcard/). .

[3] SDHC Card - SD Card Association (http://www.sdcard.org/developers/tech/sdhc/)

[4] SDXC Card - SD Card Association (http://www.sdcard.org/developers/tech/sdxc/)

[5] Before Using your SDXC Memory Card - SD Card Association (http://www.sdcard.org/developers/tech/sdxc/using_sdxc/)

[6] "Using SD Memory Cards is Easy" (video on YouTube) - SD Card Association (http://www.youtube.com/watch?v=wX6NwBa1csY)

[7] "Press Releases 17 July 2003" (http://www.toshiba.co.jp/about/press/2003_07/pr1701.htm). Toshiba. 2003-07-17. . Retrieved 2010-08-22.

[8] SanDisk Introduces The World's Smallest Removable Flash Card For Mobile Phones-The miniSD Card (http://www.sandisk.com/Corporate/PressRoom/PressReleases/PressRelease.aspx?ID=1536) SanDisk.com

[9] SanDisk Introduces 4GB miniSDHC Flash Card for Mobile Phones (http://www.sandisk.com/Corporate/PressRoom/PressReleases/PressRelease.aspx?ID=3530) SanDisk.com

[10] SD Association - Press Release - Announced SDXC. (http://www.sdcard.org/press/SD_Association_Announces_SDXC_Revised_1-7-09.pdf)

[11] PhoneScoop - Sandisk T-Flash announcement. (http://www.phonescoop.com/news/item.php?n=801)

[12] See Comparison of memory cards.

[13] kingmaxdigi.com, Kingmax FAQ 2006 (http://www.kingmaxdigi.com/support/faq.htm)

[14] Fragmentation and Speed (http://www.sdcard.org/developers/tech/speed_class/) SDCard.org

[15] "SD cards branded with an upper-case 'I' are faster, yo" (http://www.engadget.com/2010/06/24/sd-cards-branded-with-an-upper-case-i-are-faster-yo/). Engadget. . Retrieved 2010-08-22.

[16] "SD Association announces UHS-II, ultra high-speed SD card specification" (http://www.robgalbraith.com/bins/content_page.asp?cid=7-11133-11156). Rob Galbraith. 2011-01-05. . Retrieved 2011-01-05.

[17] SD Card Simplified Specification, Part 1 - Physical Layer, v3.01, 2010 (http://www.sdcard.org/developers/tech/sdcard/pls/simplified_specs/Part_1_Physical_Layer_Simplified_Specification_Ver3.01_Final_100518.pdf)

[18] SDIO Card Simplified Specification, Part E1, v2.00, 2007 (http://www.sdcard.org/developers/tech/sdcard/pls/simplified_specs/Part_E1_SDIO_Simplified_Specification_Ver2.00.pdf)

[19] "Windows Phone 7 Secure Digital Card Limitations" (http://support.microsoft.com/kb/2450831). .

[20] "Windows Phone 7's microSD mess: the full story (and how Nokia can help you out of it)" (http://www.engadget.com/2010/11/17/windows-phone-7s-microsd-mess-the-full-story-and-how-nokia-ca). .

[21] "Super Talent Technology - DDR and DDR2 Memory" (http://www.supertalent.com/products/sd.php). Supertalent.com. . Retrieved 2010-08-22.

[22] http://www.twinmos.com.tw

[23] http://www.toshiba-memory.com/en/micro_sd_cards.html

[24] What are the applications for Speed Class? (http://www.sdcard.org/developers/tech/speed_class/) - SDCard.org

[25] "Simplified Physical Layer Specification" (http://www.sdcard.org/developers/tech/sdcard/pls/Simplified_Physical_Layer_Spec.pdf) (PDF). . Retrieved 2010-08-22.

[26] Thursday, 21 May 2009 10:15 GMT (2009-05-21). "Panasonic launches worlds first Class 10 SDHC cards: Digital Photography Review" (http://www.dpreview.com/news/0905/09052102panasonicclass10sdhc.asp). Dpreview.com. . Retrieved 2010-08-22.

[27] "Toshiba Plans Faster SD Cards for Early 2010" (http://www.pcworld.com/article/169547/toshiba_plans_faster_sd_cards_for_early_2010.html). PCWorld. 2009-08-04. . Retrieved 2010-08-22.

[28] "Press Release 2010 Vol. 8" (http://www.pretec.com/news-event/press-room/item/press-room/press-release-2010-vol-8). Pretec. 2010-06-01. . Retrieved 2010-08-22.

[29] "Kingston Technology Company - Flash Memory Cards and X-Speed Ratings" (http://www.kingston.com/flash/x/default.asp). Kingston.com. . Retrieved 2010-08-22.

[30] "SD Speed Class/UHS Speed Class" (http://www.sdcard.org/developers/tech/speed_class/). . Retrieved 11 May 2011.

[31] "Simplified Physical Layer Specification v2.00" (http://www.sdcard.org/developers/tech/sdcard/pls/Simplified_Physical_Layer_Spec.pdf). SD Card Association Website. 2006-09-25. p. 129. . Retrieved 2010-06-16.

[32] SD Compatibility (http://www.hjreggel.net/cardspeed/special-sd.html), CARDSPEED - Card Readers and Memory Cards, December 1, 2006

[33] SD Group Technical Committee (September 25, 2006). "Section 4: SD Memory Card Functional Description; 4.3.2: 2 Gbyte Card" (http://www.sdcard.org/developers/tech/sdcard/pls/Simplified_Physical_Layer_Spec.pdf) (PDF, HTML (http://72.14.209.104/search?q=cache:lVMIQpGALuUJ:www.sdcard.org/sd_memorycard/Simplified%20Physical%20Layer%20Specification.PDF+"Physical+Layer+Simplified+Specification"&hl=en&ct=clnk&cd=1&gl=us&client=firefox-a)). *SD Specifications, Part 1: Physical Layer Simplified Specification* (Version 2.00 ed.). SD Card Association. p. 19. . Retrieved 2007-02-23.

[34] "SD Specifications Part 1: Physical Layer Simplified Specification" (http://www.sdcard.org/developers/tech/sdcard/pls/simplified_specs/Part_1_Physical_Layer_Simplified_Specification_Ver3.01_Final_100518.pdf) (PDF). SD Card Association. 2010-05-18. . Retrieved 2011-01-22.

[35] "SDHC simplified specifications" (http://www.sdcard.org/developers/tech/sdhc/). Sdcard.org. . Retrieved 2010-08-22.

[36] What are SDHC, miniSDHC, and microSDHC? (http://www.sandisk.com/Assets/File/pdf/retail/SDHC1.pdf) SanDisk.com

[37] A look into how SDHC will affect the future Nand Flash market (http://www.dramexchange.com/WeeklyResearch/Post/1/492.aspx). DRAMeXchange, December 2006

[38] "WinXP SP3 can't read 4GB SD card in multicard reader" (http://www.eggheadcafe.com/software/aspnet/33338344/winxp-sp3-cant-read-4gb.aspx). Eggheadcafe.com. . Retrieved 2010-08-22.

[39] Techgage review (http://techgage.com/article/sd_card_roundup), including an OCZ 4 GBan OCZ 4 GB SD (non-SDHC) card

[40] "Optimizing Linux with cheap flash drives" (http://lwn.net/Articles/428584/). Linux Weekly News. . Retrieved 2011-04-11.

[41] "Microsoft Support 934428 - Hotfix for Windows XP that adds support for SDHC cards that have a capacity of more than 4 GB" (http://support.microsoft.com/kb/934428). Support.microsoft.com. 2008-02-15. . Retrieved 2010-08-22.

[42] "Microsoft Support 939772 - Some Secure Digital (SD) cards may not be recognized in Windows Vista" (http://support.microsoft.com/kb/939772). Support.microsoft.com. 2008-05-15. . Retrieved 2010-08-22.

[43] "Microsoft Support 949126 - A Secure Digital High Capacity (SDHC) card is not recognized on a Windows Vista Service Pack 1-based computer" (http://support.microsoft.com/kb/949126). Support.microsoft.com. 2008-02-21. . Retrieved 2010-08-22.

[44] "SD Association Triples Speeds with UHS-II" (https://www.sdcard.org/home/SD_Association_Announces_UHS-II_eBOOK_Jan_5_2011_ENGLISH.PDF). . Retrieved 2011-08-09.

[45] "SDXC memory cards promise 2TB of storage, 300MBps transfer" (http://www.engadget.com/2009/01/07/sdxc-memory-cards-promise-2tb-of-storage-300mbps-transfer/). Engadget.com. . Retrieved 2010-08-22.

[46] "SDXC on the official website" (http://www.sdcard.org/developers/tech/sdxc/). Sdcard.org. . Retrieved 2010-08-22.

[47] "SDXC signals new generation of removable memory with up to 2 terabytes of storage" (http://www.sdcard.org/press/SD_Association_Announces_SDXC_FINAL_1-6-2009.pdf) (PDF). . Retrieved 2010-08-22.

[48] "SanDisk and Sony to expand Memory Stick Pro and Memory Stick Micro formats" (http://www.sandisk.com/about-sandisk/press-room/press-releases/2009/2009-01-07-sandisk-and-sony-to-expand-âmemory-stick-proâ-and-âmemory-stick-microâ-formats). Sandisk.com. . Retrieved 2010-08-22.

[49] "SD Card, Memory Stick formats to reach 2 terabytes, but when? - Betanews" (http://www.betanews.com/article/SD_Card_Memory_Stick_formats_to_reach_2_terabytes_but_when/1231453659). . 090108 betanews.com

[50] "Pretec introduces world's first SDXC card: Digital Photography Review" (http://www.dpreview.com/news/0903/09030601pretecsdxc.asp). Dpreview.com. 2009-03-06. . Retrieved 2010-08-22.

[51] "TOSHIBA TO LAUNCH WORLD'S FIRST 64 GB SDXC CARD" (http://www.toshiba.com/taec/news/press_releases/2009/memy_09_572.jsp). Toshiba.com. . Retrieved 2010-08-22.
[52] Ng, Jansen (2009-12-22). "Toshiba Sampling First SDXC Flash Memory Cards" (http://www.dailytech.com/Toshiba+Sampling+First+SDXC+Flash+Memory+Cards/article16972.htm). DailyTech. . Retrieved 2009-12-22.
[53] "Toshiba's 64 GB SDXC card to finally go on sale (in Japan)" (http://www.crunchgear.com/2010/04/15/toshibas-64gb-sdxc-card-to-finally-go-on-sale-in-japan/). CrunchGear. . Retrieved 2010-08-09.
[54] "PANASONIC INTRODUCES NEW 64 GB* AND 48 GB* SDXC MEMORY CARDS, AVAILABLE GLOBALLY IN FEBRUARY 2010" (http://www2.panasonic.com/webapp/wcs/stores/servlet/prModelDetail?storeId=11301&catalogId=13251&itemId=389511&modelNo=Content01052010041118461&surfModel=Content01052010041118461). Panasonic. . Retrieved 2010-08-09.
[55] "Canon EOS Rebel T2i / 550D Digital SLR Camera Review" (http://www.the-digital-picture.com/Press-Release/Canon-EOS-Rebel-T2i-550D-Digital-SLR-Camera-Press-Release.aspx). . The-Digital-Picture.com
[56] "Sandisk ships its highest capacity sd card ever" (http://sandisk.com/about-sandisk/press-room/press-releases/2010/2010-02-22-sandisk-ships-its-highest-capacity-sd-card-ever,-the-64gb-sandisk-ultra-sdxc-card). SanDisk. . Retrieved 2010-08-09.
[57] Ng, Jansen (2009-11-24). "Lack of Card Readers Holding Back SDXC Flash Memory Adoption" (http://www.dailytech.com/Lack+of+Card+Readers+Holding+Back+SDXC+Flash+Memory+Adoption/article16915.htm). DailyTech. . Retrieved 2009-12-22.
[58] Ng, Jansen (2009-11-30). "Lenovo, HP, Dell Integrating SDXC Readers in New 32nm Intel "Arrandale" Laptops" (http://www.dailytech.com/Lenovo+HP+Dell+Integrating+SDXC+Readers+in+New+32nm+Intel+Arrandale+Laptops/article16937.htm). DailyTech. . Retrieved 2009-12-22.
[59] Lexar ships 128 GB Class 10 SDXC card; March 2011. (http://www.betanews.com/article/Lexar-ships-first-128GB-SDXC-cards/1300305310)
[60] "Tuxera exFAT Embedded" (http://www.tuxera.com/products/tuxera-exfat-embedded/). Tuxera.com. 2010-06-01. . Retrieved 2011-07-11.
[61] http://www.microsoft.com/downloads/details.aspx?FamilyID=1cbe3906-ddd1-4ca2-b727-c2dff5e30f61&displaylang=en
[62] "Mac mini (Mid 2010): External ports and connectors" (http://support.apple.com/kb/HT4210). Support.apple.com. 2010-07-08. . Retrieved 2010-08-22.
[63] http://www.theregister.co.uk/2005/07/25/review_sandisk_ultra_ii_sd_plus/
[64] "I4U News - A DATA Announces SD Card w/ Bi-stable Capacity Display" (http://www.i4u.com/article7106.html). I4u.com. 2006-11-14. . Retrieved 2010-08-22.
[65] "Home" (http://www.eye.fi). Eye-Fi. . Retrieved 2010-08-22.
[66] AudioHolics (http://www.audioholics.com/news/industry-news/sandisk-slotmusic)
[67] MEAD-SD01 SDHC card adapter (Sony) (http://pro.sony.com/bbsc/ssr/micro-xdcamexsite/cat-accessories/product-MEADSD01/)
[68] "TS-7800 Embedded" (http://www.embeddedarm.com/products/board-detail.php?product=TS-7800). Embeddedarm.com. . Retrieved 2010-08-22.
[69] SD Card Association (2008-09-11). "SD Card Association introduces embedded SD for mobile phones, consumer devices" (http://www.sdcard.org/press/2008_09_11_embedded_sd.pdf) (PDF). Press release. . Retrieved 2009-06-22.
[70] "Linksys WRT54G-TM SD/MMC mod - DD-WRT Wiki" (http://www.dd-wrt.com/wiki/index.php/Linksys_WRT54G-TM_SD/MMC_mod). Dd-wrt.com. 2010-02-22. . Retrieved 2010-08-22.
[71] "Sharp Linux PDA promotes the use of proprietary SD card, but more open MMC works just fine" (http://www.linux.com/archive/feed/20060). Linux.com. . Retrieved 2010-08-22.
[72] Simplified Specification Agreement (http://www.sdcard.org/developers/tech/sdcard/pls/) from the SDA's website
[73] Reverse-engineered register information for the standard host controller (http://mmc.drzeus.cx/wiki/Controllers/SDHCI)
[74] "OLPC mailing list archive" (http://mailman.laptop.org/pipermail/community-news/2006-September/000023.html). Mailman.laptop.org. . Retrieved 2010-08-22.
[75] JEDEC MMC 4.4 Standard Pg.7 (http://www.jedec.org/download/search/JESD84-A44.pdf), http://www.jedec.org 2008
[76] Transcend v4.0 Card Does not support 1.8V (http://www.transcendusa.com/support/dlcenter/datasheet/TSxxMMC4.pdf), http://www.transcendusa.com 2009

External links

Organizations

- SD Association (http://www.sdcard.org/), sdcard.org
  - Membership: $2000/yr for General, $4500/yr for Executive.
  - Full Specification: Free for members, $1000/yr for R&D non-members.

8 GB microSDHC card, shown on a USA dime coin for reference

Specifications

- SD Simplified Specifications (http://www.sdcard.org/developers/tech/sdcard/pls/simplified_specs/), sdcard.org, Free
  - SD Card Simplified Specification, Part 1 - Physical Layer, v3.01, 2010 (http://www.sdcard.org/developers/tech/sdcard/pls/simplified_specs/Part_1_Physical_Layer_Simplified_Specification_Ver3.01_Final_100518.pdf)
  - SDIO Card Simplified Specification, Part E1, v2.00, 2007 (http://www.sdcard.org/developers/tech/sdcard/pls/simplified_specs/Part_E1_SDIO_Simplified_Specification_Ver2.00.pdf)
- Microsoft Extensible Firmware Initiative FAT32 File System Specification, 2000 (http://download.microsoft.com/download/1/6/1/161ba512-40e2-4cc9-843a-923143f3456c/fatgen103.doc), Microsoft

Software

- SD Formatter for SD / SDHC / SDXC cards (Windows) (http://www.sdcard.org/consumers/formatter_3/), sdcard.org

Comparisons

- Comparison of numerous memory cards and readers, plus technical information (http://www.hjreggel.net/cardspeed/index.html#special-sd.html), hjreggel.net
- SDHC Card comparison (german) (http://www.hardware-infos.com/tests.php?test=81), hardware-infos.com
- Speed Testing of UHS-1 Cards in prosumer Nikon D7000 Camera (http://glamourphotography.co/gear/uhs-speed-class-1-sdhc-memory-cards-tested-delkin-8gb-elite-633x-secure-digital-uhs-i-95-mbsec-vs-sandisk-extreme-pro-32gb-
)
- Nikon D7000 Memory speed tests, SDHC Memory Cards: including Sandisk Extreme Pro UHS Speed Class 1 45 Mbyte/s and Several Popular Class 10 SDHC Cards (http://glamourphotography.co/gear/nikon-d7000-memory-speed-tests-sdhc-memory-cards-including-sandisk-extreme-pro-uhs-speed-class-1-45mbsec-and-several-po
)

Interfacing

- Interfacing to SD cards, great technical details (http://elm-chan.org/docs/mmc/mmc_e.html)
- Interfacing AVR (Arduino) to SD cards, C source code (http://www.dharmanitech.com/2009/01/sd-card-interfacing-with-atmega8-fat32.html)
- Interfacing ARM to SD cards, C source code (http://gandalf.arubi.uni-kl.de/avr_projects/arm_projects/arm_memcards/index.html)
- Interfacing MSP430 to SD cards, C source code (http://www.cs.ucr.edu/~amitra/sdcard/Additional/sdcard_appnote_foust.pdf), Michigan State University
- Interfacing MAXQ2000 to SD cards, good technical descriptions, C source code (http://www.maxim-ic.com/appnotes.cfm/an_pk/3969), maxim-ic.com
- SD card controller, Verilog source code (http://www.opencores.org/project,sdcard_mass_storage_controller), opencores.org

USB

Original logo	
Type	Computer Hardware Bus
Production history	
Designer	Compaq, DEC, IBM, Intel, Microsoft, NEC and Nortel
Designed	1994
Manufacturer	Intel, Compaq, Microsoft, NEC, Digital Equipment Corporation, IBM, Nortel
Superseded	serial port, parallel port, game port, Apple Desktop Bus, PS/2 connector
General specifications	
Length	5 metres (maximum)
Width	11.5 mm (A-plug), 8.45 mm (B-plug),
Height	4.5 mm (A-plug), 7.78 mm (B-plug, pre-v3.0)
Hot pluggable	Yes
External	Yes
Cable	4 wires (or 8 wires in USB 3.0 version)
Pins	4 (or 8 in USB 3.0 version) (1 supply, 2 data, 1 ground) (plus additional 4 for SuperSpeed technology in USB 3.0 version)
Connector	Unique
Electrical	
Signal	5 volt DC
Max. voltage	5 V(±5%)
Max. current	500–900 mA @ 5 V (depending on version)
Data	
Data signal	Packet data, defined by specifications
Width	1 bit
Bitrate	1.5/12/480/4,000 Mbit/s (depending on version)
Max. devices	127
Protocol	Serial
Pin out	
The standard USB A plug (left) and B plug (right)	
Pin 1	V_{CC} (+5 V)

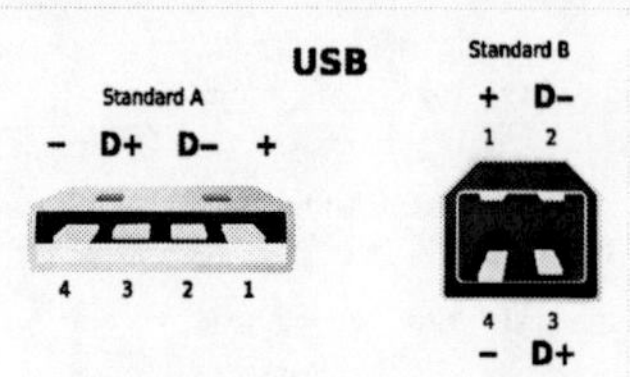

Pin 2		Data-	
Pin 3		Data+	
Pin 4		Ground	

USB (**Universal Serial Bus**) is an industry standard developed in the mid-1990s that defines the cables, connectors and protocols used for connection, communication and power supply between computers and electronic devices.

USB was designed to standardise the connection of computer peripherals, such as keyboards, pointing devices, digital cameras, printers, portable media players, disk drives and network adapters to personal computers, both to communicate and to supply electric power. It has become commonplace on other devices, such as smartphones, PDAs and video game consoles. USB has effectively replaced a variety of earlier interfaces, such as serial and parallel ports, as well as separate power chargers for portable devices.

As of 2008, about 2 billion USB devices were sold each year, and approximately 6 billion devices have been sold in total.[1]

History

The basic USB *trident* logo; each released version has a specific logo variant

A group of seven companies began development on USB in 1994: Compaq, DEC, IBM, Intel, Microsoft, NEC and Nortel. The goal was to make it fundamentally easier to connect external devices to PCs by replacing the multitude of connectors at the back of PCs, addressing the usability issues of existing interfaces, and simplifying software configuration of all devices connected to USB, as well as permitting greater data rates for external devices. The first silicon for USB was made by Intel in 1995.[2]

The original USB 1.0 specification, which was introduced in January 1996, defined data transfer rates of 1.5 Mbit/s "Low Speed" and 12 Mbit/s "Full Speed".[2] The first widely used version of USB was 1.1, which was released in September 1998. The 12 Mbit/s data rate was intended for higher-speed devices such as disk drives, and the lower 1.5 Mbit/s rate for low data rate devices such as joysticks.[3]

The USB 2.0 specification was released in April 2000 and was standardized by the USB Implementers Forum (USB-IF) at the end of 2001. Hewlett-Packard, Intel, Lucent Technologies (now Alcatel-Lucent), NEC and Philips jointly led the initiative to develop a higher data transfer rate, with the resulting specification achieving 480 Mbit/s, a fortyfold increase over the original USB 1.1 specification.

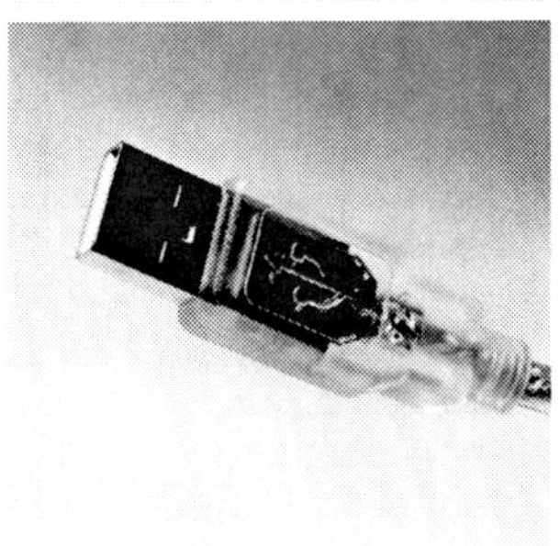
A USB Standard Type A plug, the most common USB plug

The USB 3.0 specification was published on 12 November 2008. Its main goals were to increase the data transfer rate (up to 5 Gbit/s), to decrease power consumption, to increase power output, and to be backwards-compatible with USB 2.0.[4] USB 3.0 includes a new, higher speed bus called SuperSpeed in parallel with the USB 2.0 bus.[5] For this reason, the new version is also called SuperSpeed.[6] The first USB 3.0 equipped devices were presented in January 2010.[6] [7]

Version history

Prereleases

- *USB 0.7*: Released in November 1994.
- *USB 0.8*: Released in December 1994.
- *USB 0.9*: Released in April 1995.
- *USB 0.99*: Released in August 1995.
- *USB 1.0 Release Candidate*: Released in November 1995.

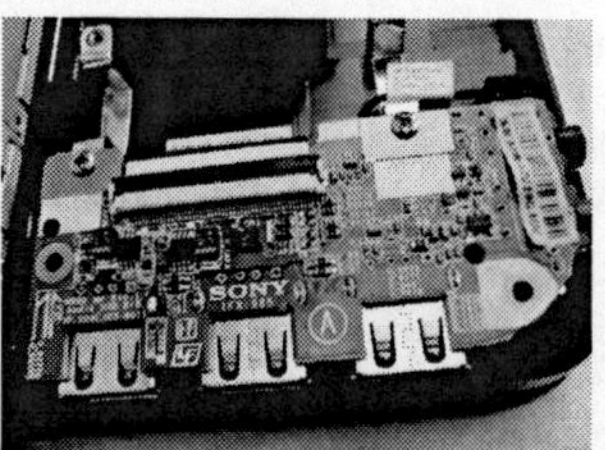

In-built USB female sockets on a Sony Vaio E series laptop

USB 1.0

- *USB 1.0*: Released in January 1996.
  Specified data rates of *1.5 Mbit/s* (*Low-Bandwidth*) and *12 Mbit/s* (*Full-Bandwidth*). Does not allow for extension cables or pass-through monitors (due to timing and power limitations). Few such devices actually made it to market.
- *USB 1.1*: Released in August 1998.
  Fixed problems identified in 1.0, mostly relating to hubs. Earliest revision to be widely adopted.

USB 2.0

- *USB 2.0*: Released in April 2000.
  Added higher maximum bandwidth of *480 Mbit/s* (60 MB/s) (now called *"Hi-Speed"*). Further modifications to the USB specification have been done via Engineering Change Notices (ECN). The most important of these ECNs are included into the USB 2.0 specification package available from USB.org [8]:

  HI-SPEED CERTIFIED USB TM

  The Hi-Speed USB Logo

  - *Mini-A and Mini-B Connector ECN*: Released in October 2000.
    Specifications for Mini-A and B plug and receptacle. Also receptacle that accepts both plugs for On-The-Go. These should not be confused with Micro-B plug and receptacle.
  - *Errata as of December 2000*: Released in December 2000.
  - *Pull-up/Pull-down Resistors ECN*: Released in May 2002.
  - *Errata as of May 2002*: Released in May 2002.
  - *Interface Associations ECN*: Released in May 2003.
    New standard descriptor was added that allows multiple interfaces to be associated with a single device function.
  - *Rounded Chamfer ECN*: Released in October 2003.
    A recommended, compatible change to Mini-B plugs that results in longer lasting connectors.
  - *Unicode ECN*: Released in February 2005.
    This ECN specifies that strings are encoded using UTF-16LE. USB 2.0 did specify that Unicode is to be used but it did not specify the encoding.
  - *Inter-Chip USB Supplement*: Released in March 2006.
  - *On-The-Go Supplement 1.3*: Released in December 2006.
    USB On-The-Go makes it possible for two USB devices to communicate with each other without requiring a separate USB host. In practice, one of the USB devices acts as a host for the other device.
  - *Battery Charging Specification 1.1*: Released in March 2007 (Updated 15 Apr 2009).
    Adds support for dedicated chargers (power supplies with USB connectors), host chargers (USB hosts that can act as chargers) and the No Dead Battery provision which allows devices to temporarily draw 100 mA current after they have been attached. If a USB device is connected to dedicated charger, maximum current drawn by

the device may be as high as 1.8 A. (Note that this document is not distributed with USB 2.0 specification package only USB 3.0 and USB On-The-Go.)

- *Micro-USB Cables and Connectors Specification 1.01*: Released in April 2007.
- *Link Power Management Addendum ECN*: Released in July 2007.
  This adds a new power state between enabled and suspended states. Device in this state is not required to reduce its power consumption. However, switching between enabled and sleep states is much faster than switching between enabled and suspended states, which allows devices to sleep while idle.

USB 3.0

USB 3.0 has transmission speeds of up to 5 Gbit/s, which is 10 times faster than USB2.0 (480 Mbit/s). USB 3.0 significantly reduces the time required for data transmission, reduces power consumption, and is backward compatible with USB 2.0. The USB 3.0 Promoter Group announced on 17 November 2008 that the specification of version 3.0 had been completed and had made the transition to the USB Implementers Forum (USB-IF), the managing body of USB specifications.[8] This move effectively opened the specification to hardware developers for implementation in future products.

The Super-Speed USB Logo

System design

A USB system has an asymmetric design, consisting of a host, a multitude of downstream USB ports, and multiple peripheral devices connected in a tiered-star topology. Additional USB hubs may be included in the tiers, allowing branching into a tree structure with up to five tier levels. A USB host may have multiple host controllers and each host controller may provide one or more USB ports. Up to 127 devices, including hub devices if present, may be connected to a single host controller.[9] [10]

USB devices are linked in series through *hubs*. There always exists one hub known as the root hub, which is built into the host controller.

A physical USB device may consist of several logical sub-devices that are referred to as *device functions*. A single device may provide several functions, for example, a webcam (video device function) with a built-in microphone (audio device function). Such a device is called a *compound device* in which each logical device is assigned a distinctive address by the host and all logical devices are connected to a built-in hub to which the physical USB wire is connected. A host assigns one and only one device address to a function.

USB device communication is based on *pipes* (logical channels). A pipe is a connection from the host controller to a logical entity, found on a device, and named an *endpoint*. Because pipes correspond 1-to-1 to endpoints, the terms are sometimes used interchangeably. A USB device can have up to 32 endpoints: 16 into the host controller and 16 out of the host controller. The USB standard reserves one endpoint of each type, leaving a theoretical maximum of 30 for normal use. USB devices seldom have this many endpoints.

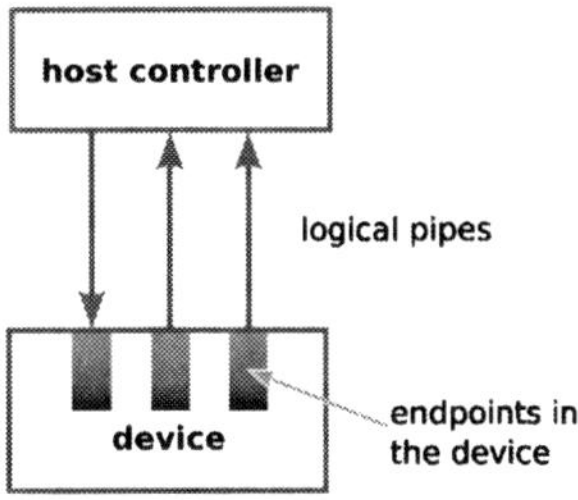

USB endpoints actually reside on the connected device: the channels to the host are referred to as pipes

There are two types of pipes: stream and message pipes depending on the type of data transfer.

- *isochronous transfers*: at some guaranteed data rate (often, but not necessarily, as fast as possible) but with possible data loss (e.g., realtime audio or video).

- *interrupt transfers*: devices that need guaranteed quick responses (bounded latency) (e.g., pointing devices and keyboards).
- *bulk transfers*: large sporadic transfers using all remaining available bandwidth, but with no guarantees on bandwidth or latency (e.g., file transfers).
- *control transfers*: typically used for short, simple commands to the device, and a status response, used, for example, by the bus control pipe number 0.

A stream pipe is a uni-directional pipe connected to a uni-directional endpoint that transfers data using an *isochronous*, *interrupt*, or *bulk* transfer. A message pipe is a bi-directional pipe connected to a bi-directional endpoint that is exclusively used for *control* data flow. An endpoint is built into the USB device by the manufacturer and therefore exists permanently. An endpoint of a pipe is addressable with a tuple *(device_address, endpoint_number)* as specified in a TOKEN packet that the host sends when it wants to start a data transfer session. If the direction of the data transfer is from the host to the endpoint, an OUT packet (a specialization of a TOKEN packet) having the desired device address and endpoint number is sent by the host. If the direction of the data transfer is from the device to the host, the host sends an IN packet instead. If the destination endpoint is a uni-directional endpoint whose manufacturer's designated direction does not match the TOKEN packet (e.g., the manufacturer's designated direction is IN while the TOKEN packet is an OUT packet), the TOKEN packet will be ignored. Otherwise, it will be accepted and the data transaction can start. A bi-directional endpoint, on the other hand, accepts both IN and OUT packets.

Endpoints are grouped into *interfaces* and each interface is associated with a single device function. An exception to this is endpoint zero, which is used for device configuration and which is not associated with any interface. A single device function composed of independently controlled interfaces is called a *composite device*. A composite device only has a single device address because the host only assigns a device address to a function.

Two USB receptacles on the front of a computer

When a USB device is first connected to a USB host, the USB device enumeration process is started. The enumeration starts by sending a reset signal to the USB device. The data rate of the USB device is determined during the reset signaling. After reset, the USB device's information is read by the host and the device is assigned a unique 7-bit address. If the device is supported by the host, the device drivers needed for communicating with the device are loaded and the device is set to a configured state. If the USB host is restarted, the enumeration process is repeated for all connected devices.

The host controller directs traffic flow to devices, so no USB device can transfer any data on the bus without an explicit request from the host controller. In USB 2.0, the host controller polls the bus for traffic, usually in a round-robin fashion. The slowest device connected to a controller sets the bandwidth of the interface. For *SuperSpeed USB* (defined since USB 3.0), connected devices can request service from host. Because there are two separate controllers in each USB 3.0 host, USB 3.0 devices will transmit and receive at USB 3.0 data rates regardless of USB 2.0 or earlier devices connected to that host. Operating data rates for them will be set in the legacy manner.

Device classes

USB defines class codes used to identify a device's functionality and to load a device driver based on that functionality. This enables every device driver writer to support devices from different manufacturers that comply with a given class code.

Device classes include:[11]

Class	Usage	Description	Examples, or exception
00h	Device	Unspecified[12]	Device class is unspecified, interface descriptors are used to determine needed drivers
01h	Interface	Audio	Speaker, microphone, sound card, MIDI
02h	Both	Communications and CDC Control	Modem, Ethernet adapter, Wi-Fi adapter
03h	Interface	Human interface device (HID)	Keyboard, mouse, joystick
05h	Interface	Physical Interface Device (PID)	Force feedback joystick
06h	Interface	Image	Webcam, scanner
07h	Interface	Printer	Laser printer, inkjet printer, CNC machine
08h	Interface	Mass storage	USB flash drive, memory card reader, digital audio player, digital camera, external drive
09h	Device	USB hub	Full bandwidth hub
0Ah	Interface	CDC-Data	Used together with class 02h: communications and CDC control
0Bh	Interface	Smart Card	USB smart card reader
0Dh	Interface	Content security	Fingerprint reader
0Eh	Interface	Video	Webcam
0Fh	Interface	Personal Healthcare	Pulse monitor (watch)
DCh	Both	Diagnostic Device	USB compliance testing device
E0h	Interface	Wireless Controller	Bluetooth adapter, Microsoft RNDIS
EFh	Both	Miscellaneous	ActiveSync device
FEh	Interface	Application-specific	IrDA Bridge, Test & Measurement Class (USBTMC),[13] USB DFU (Direct Firmware update)[14]
FFh	Both	Vendor-specific	Indicates that a device needs vendor specific drivers

USB mass storage

USB implements connections to storage devices using a set of standards called the *USB mass storage device class* (referred to as MSC or UMS). This was initially intended for traditional magnetic and optical drives, but has been extended to support a wide variety of devices, particularly flash drives. This generality is because many systems can be controlled with the familiar metaphor of file manipulation within directories (the process of making a novel device look like a familiar device is also known as extension). The ability to boot a write-locked SD card with a USB adapter is particularly advantageous for maintaining the integrity and non-corruptible, pristine state of the booting medium.

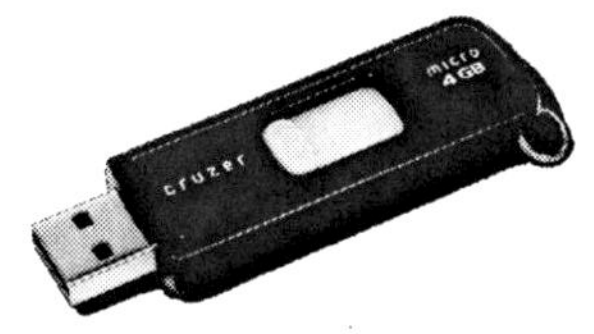

A flash drive, a typical USB mass-storage device

Though most newer computers are capable of booting off USB mass storage devices, USB is not intended to be a primary bus for a computer's internal storage: buses such as Parallel ATA (PATA or IDE), Serial ATA (SATA), or SCSI fulfill that role in PC class computers. However, USB has one important advantage in that it is possible to install and remove devices without rebooting the computer (hot-swapping), making it useful for mobile peripherals, including drives of various kinds. Originally conceived and still used today for optical storage devices (CD-RW drives, DVD drives and so on), several manufacturers offer external portable USB hard disk drives, or empty enclosures for disk drives, which offer performance comparable to internal drives, limited by the current number and type of attached USB devices and by the upper limit of the USB interface (in practice about 40 MB/s for USB 2.0 and potentially 400 MB/s or more[15] for USB 3.0). These external drives have typically included a "translating device" that bridges between a drive's interface to a USB interface port. Functionally, the drive appears to the user much like an internal drive. Other competing standards for external drive connectivity include eSATA, ExpressCard (now at version 2.0), and FireWire (IEEE 1394).

Another use for USB mass storage devices is the portable execution of software applications (such as web browsers and VoIP clients) with no need to install them on the host computer.[16] [17]

Human interface devices (HIDs)

Mice and keyboards usually have USB connectors. These can be used with older computers that have PS/2 connectors with the aid of a small USB-to-PS/2 adapter. Such adaptors contain no logic circuitry: the hardware in the USB keyboard or mouse is designed to detect whether it is connected to a USB or PS/2 port, and communicate using the appropriate protocol. Converters also exist to allow PS/2 keyboards and mice (usually one of each) to be connected to a USB port. These devices present two HID endpoints to the system and use a microcontroller to perform bidirectional translation of data between the two standards.

Joysticks, keypads, tablets and other human-interface devices are also progressively migrating from MIDI, and PC game port connectors to USB.

Physical appearance

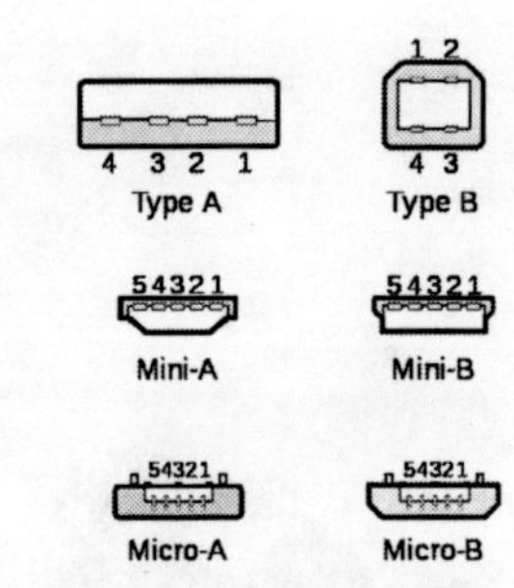

Pinouts of Standard, Mini, and Micro USB plugs. The USB logo is on the bottom of the two micro-USB plugs (as they are shown in this figure) but on the top of the other plugs[18]

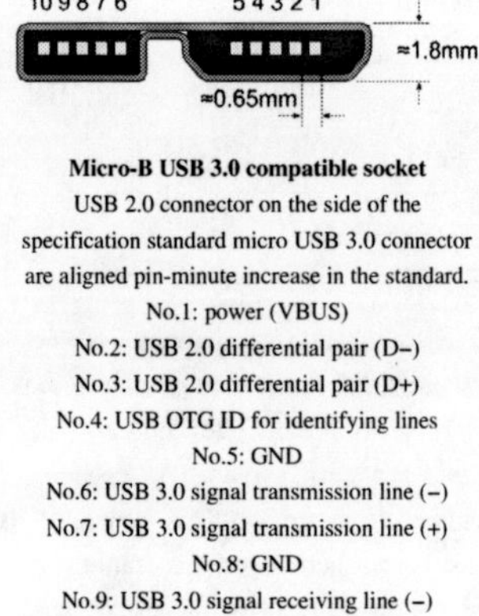

Micro-B USB 3.0 compatible socket

USB 2.0 connector on the side of the specification standard micro USB 3.0 connector are aligned pin-minute increase in the standard.

No.1: power (VBUS)

No.2: USB 2.0 differential pair (D–)

No.3: USB 2.0 differential pair (D+)

No.4: USB OTG ID for identifying lines

No.5: GND

No.6: USB 3.0 signal transmission line (–)

No.7: USB 3.0 signal transmission line (+)

No.8: GND

No.9: USB 3.0 signal receiving line (–)

No.10: USB 3.0 signal receiving line (+)

USB 1.x/2.0 standard pinout

Pin	Name	Cable color	Description
1	VBUS	Red	+5 V
2	D−	White	Data −
3	D+	Green	Data +
4	GND	Black	Ground

USB 1.x/2.0 Mini/Micro pinout

Pin	Name	Cable color	Description
1	VBUS	Red	+5 V
2	D−	White	Data −
3	D+	Green	Data +
4	ID	None	Permits distinction of A plug from B plug * A plug: connected to Signal ground * B plug: not connected
5	GND	Black	Signal ground

Connector properties

The connectors specified by the USB committee were designed to support a number of USB's underlying goals, and to reflect lessons learned from the menagerie of connectors which have been used in the computer industry. The connector mounted on the host or device is called the **receptacle**, and the connector attached to the cable is called the **plug**.[19] In the case of an extension cable, the connector on one end is a receptacle. The official USB specification documents periodically define the term **male** to represent the plug, and **female** to represent the receptacle.

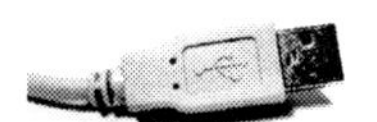

Standard type A plug and receptacle

Usability and "upside down" connectors

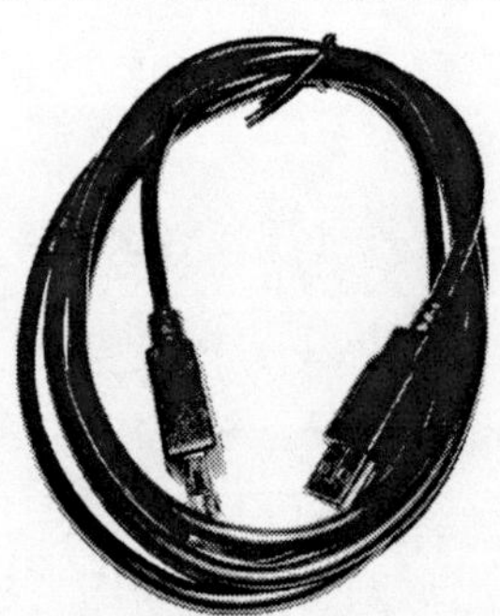
USB extension cord

By design, it is difficult to attach a USB connector incorrectly. Connectors cannot be plugged in upside down and it is clear from kinesthetic sensation of making a connection when the plug and receptacle are correctly mated. The USB specification states that the required USB Icon is to be "embossed" on the "topside" of the USB plug, which "provides easy user recognition and facilitates alignment during the mating process". The specification also shows that the "recommended" (optional) "Manufacturer's logo" ("engraved" on the diagram but not specified in the text) is on the opposite side of the USB Icon. The specification further states "the USB Icon is also located adjacent to each receptacle. Receptacles should be oriented to allow the Icon on the plug to be visible during the mating process". However, the specification does not consider the height of the device compared to the eye level height of the user, so the side of the cable that is "visible" when mated to a computer on a desk can depend on whether the user is standing or kneeling.[19]

- Only moderate insertion/removal force is needed. USB cables and small USB devices are held in place by the gripping force from the receptacle (without need of the screws, clips, or thumb-turns other connectors have required). The force needed to make or break a connection is modest, allowing connections to be made in awkward circumstances (i.e., behind a floor-mounted chassis, or from below) or by those with motor disabilities. This has the disadvantage of easily and unintentionally breaking connections that one has intended to be permanent in case of cable accident (e.g., tripping, or inadvertent tugging). Conversely, this prevents damage to the receptacle or device into which it is plugged allowing the cable to come free before pulling the device off a desk or shelf in the same accident above.
- The standard connectors were deliberately intended to enforce the directed topology of a USB network: type A connectors on host devices that supply power and type B connectors on target devices that receive power. This prevents users from accidentally connecting two USB power supplies to each other, which could lead to dangerously high currents, circuit failures, or even fire. USB does not support cyclical networks and the standard connectors from incompatible USB devices are themselves incompatible. Unlike other communications systems (e.g. network cabling) gender changers make little sense with USB and are almost never used, although cables with 2 standard type A plugs are commonly found in inexpensive retail outlets.

Durability

- The standard connectors were designed to be robust. Many previous connector designs were fragile, specifying embedded component pins or other delicate parts which proved vulnerable to bending or breakage, even with the application of modest force. The electrical contacts in a USB connector are protected by an adjacent plastic tongue, and the entire connecting assembly is usually protected by an enclosing metal sheath.
- The connector construction always ensures that the external sheath on the plug makes contact with its counterpart in the receptacle before any of the four connectors within make electrical contact. The external metallic sheath is typically connected to system ground, thus dissipating damaging static charges. This enclosure design also provides a degree of protection from electromagnetic interference to the USB signal while it travels through the mated connector pair (the only location when the otherwise twisted data pair travels in parallel). In addition, because of the required sizes of the power and common connections, they are made after the system ground but before the data connections. This type of staged make-break timing allows for electrically safe hot-swapping, a common practice in the design of connectors in the aerospace industry.

- The newer Micro-USB receptacles are designed for up to 10,000 cycles of insertion and removal between the receptacle and plug, compared to 1500 for the standard USB and 5000 for the Mini-USB receptacle. This is accomplished by adding a locking device and by moving the leaf-spring connector from the jack to the plug, so that the most-stressed part is on the cable side of the connection. This change was made so that the connector on the less expensive cable would bear the most wear instead of the more expensive micro-USB device.

Compatibility

- The USB standard specifies relatively loose tolerances for compliant USB connectors to minimize physical incompatibilities in connectors from different vendors. To address a weakness present in some other connector standards, the USB specification also defines limits to the size of a connecting device in the area around its plug. This was done to prevent a device from blocking adjacent ports due to the size of the cable strain relief mechanism (usually molding integral with the cable outer insulation) at the connector. Compliant devices must either fit within the size restrictions or support a compliant extension cable which does.

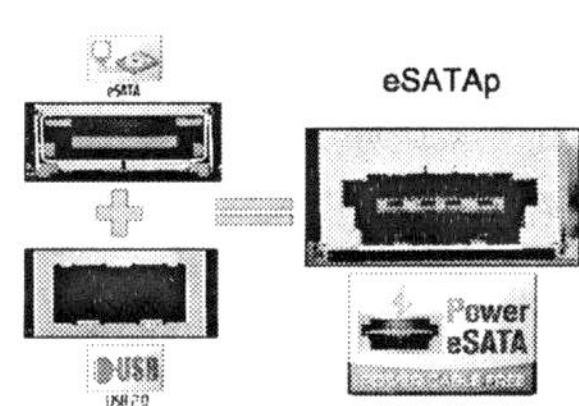

eSATAp (eSATA/USB) combo port is compatible with USB devices

- Two-way communication is also possible. In USB 3.0, full-duplex communications are done when using SuperSpeed (USB 3.0) transfer. In previous USB versions (i.e., 1.x or 2.0), all communication is half-duplex and directionally controlled by the host.

In general, cables have only plugs (very few have a receptacle on one end, although extension cables with a standard A plug and jack are sold), and hosts and devices have only receptacles. Hosts almost universally have type-A receptacles, and devices one or another type-B variety. Type-A plugs mate only with type-A receptacles, and type-B with type-B; they are deliberately physically incompatible. However, an extension to USB standard specification called USB On-The-Go allows a single port to act as either a host or a device—chosen by which end of the cable plugs into the receptacle on the unit. Even after the cable is hooked up and the units are communicating, the two units may "swap" ends under program control. This capability is meant for units such as PDAs in which the USB link might connect to a PC's host port as a device in one instance, yet connect as a host itself to a keyboard and mouse device in another instance.

- USB 3.0 receptacles are electrically compatible with USB Standard 2.0 device plugs if they physically match. USB 3.0 type-A plugs and receptacles are completely backward compatible, and USB 3.0 type-B receptacles will accept USB 2.0 and earlier plugs. However, USB 3.0 type-B plugs will not fit into USB 2.0 and earlier receptacles.
- eSATAp (eSATA/USB) port is also compatible with USB 2.0 devices.

Connector types

There are several types of USB connectors, including some that have been added while the specification progressed. The original USB specification detailed Standard-A and Standard-B plugs and receptacles. The first engineering change notice to the USB 2.0 specification added Mini-B plugs and receptacles.

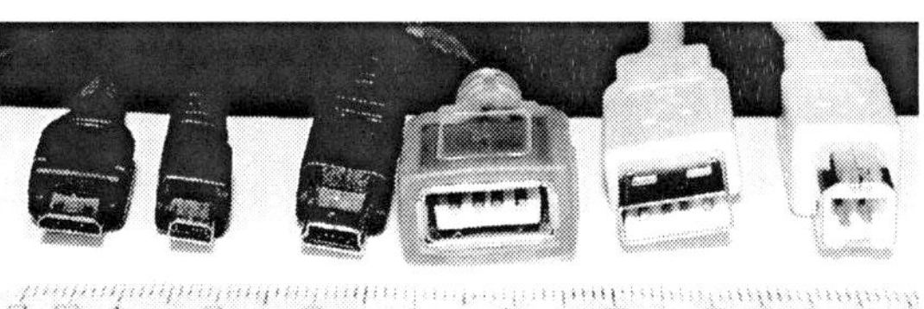
Types of USB connectors left to right (ruler in centimeters) (vertical reading):

The data connectors in the Standard-A plug are actually recessed in the plug as compared to the outside power connectors. This permits the power to connect first which prevents data errors by allowing the device to power up first and then transfer the data. Some devices will operate in different modes depending on whether the data connection is made. This difference in connection can be exploited by inserting the connector only partially. For example, some battery-powered MP3 players switch into file transfer mode and cannot play MP3 files while a USB plug is fully inserted, but can be operated in MP3 playback mode using USB power by inserting the plug only part way so that the power slots make contact while the data slots do not. This enables those devices to be operated in MP3 playback mode while getting power from the cable.

To reliably enable a charge-only feature, modern USB accessory peripherals now include charging cables that provide power connections to the host port but no data connections, and both home and vehicle charging docks are available that supply power from a converter device and do not include a host device and data pins, allowing any capable USB device to be charged and/or operated from a standard USB cable.

USB standard connectors

The USB 2.0 Standard-A type of USB plug is a flattened rectangle which inserts into a "downstream-port" receptacle on the USB host, or a hub, and carries both power and data. This plug is frequently seen on cables that are permanently attached to a device, such as one connecting a keyboard or mouse to the computer via usb connection.

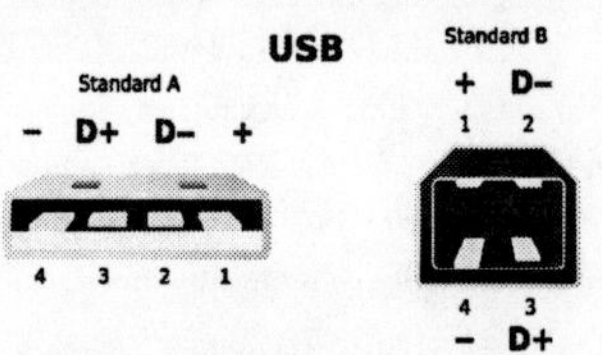

Pin configuration of the USB connectors Standard A/B, viewed looking into face/end of plug

USB connections eventually wear out as the connection loosens through repeated plugging and unplugging. The lifetime of a USB-A male connector is approximately 1,500 connect/disconnect cycles.[20]

A Standard-B plug—which has a square shape with bevelled exterior corners—typically plugs into an "upstream receptacle" on a device that uses a removable cable, e.g. a printer. A Type B plug delivers power in addition to carrying data. On some devices, the Type B receptacle has no data connections, being used solely for accepting power from the upstream device. This two-connector-type scheme (A/B) prevents a user from accidentally creating an electrical loop.[21]

Mini and Micro connectors

Various connectors have been used for smaller devices such as PDAs, mobile phones or digital cameras. These include the now-deprecated[22] (but standardized) Mini-A and the currently standard Mini-B,[23] Micro-A, and Micro-B connectors. The Mini-A and Mini-B plugs are approximately 3 by 7 mm.

Micro B USB

The micro-USB plugs have a similar width but approximately half the thickness, enabling their integration into thinner portable devices. The micro-A connector is 6.85 by 1.8 mm with a maximum overmold size of 11.7 by 8.5 mm. The micro-B connector is 6.85 by 1.8 mm with a maximum overmold size of 10.6 by 8.5 mm.[18]

The Micro-USB connector was announced by the USB-IF on 4 January 2007.[24] The Mini-A connector and the Mini-AB receptacle connector were deprecated on 23 May 2007.[25] As of February 2009, many currently available devices and cables still use Mini plugs, but the newer Micro connectors are being widely adopted and as of December 2010, the Micro connectors are the most widely used. The thinner micro connectors are intended to replace the Mini plugs in new devices including smartphones and personal digital assistants. The Micro plug design is rated for at least 10,000 connect-disconnect cycles which is significantly more than the Mini plug design.[26] The *Universal Serial Bus Micro-USB Cables and Connectors Specification*[26] details the mechanical characteristics of Micro-A plugs, Micro-AB receptacles, and Micro-B plugs and receptacles, along with a Standard-A receptacle to Micro-A plug adapter.

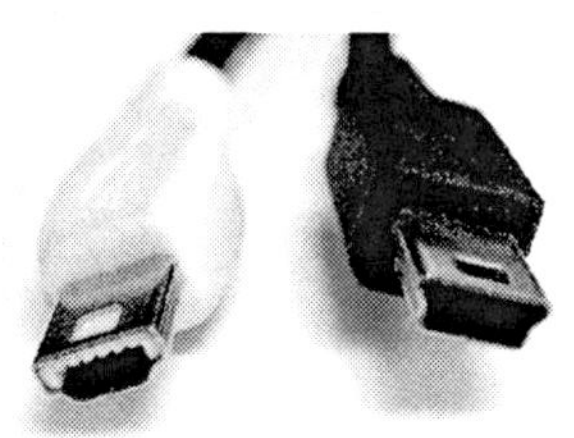

USB Mini A (left) and USB Mini B (right) plugs

The cellular phone carrier group, Open Mobile Terminal Platform (OMTP) in 2007 have endorsed Micro-USB as the standard connector for data and power on mobile devices.[27] These include various types of battery chargers, allowing Micro-USB to be the single external cable link needed by some devices.

As of 30 January 2009 Micro-USB has been accepted and is being used by almost all cell phone manufacturers as the standard charging port (including HTC, Motorola, Nokia, LG, Hewlett-Packard, Samsung, Sony Ericsson, Research In Motion) in most of the world.

On 29 June 2009, following a request from the European Commission and in close co-operation with the Commission services, major producers of mobile phones have agreed in a Memorandum of Understanding ("MoU") to harmonise chargers for data-enabled mobile phones sold in the European Union. Industry commits to provide charger compatibility on the basis of the Micro-USB connector. Consumers will be able to purchase mobile phones without a charger, thus logically reducing their cost.[28] Following a mandate from the European Commission, the European Standardisation Bodies CEN-CENELEC and ETSI have now made available the harmonised standards needed for the manufacture of data-enabled mobile phones compatible with the new common External Power Supply (EPS) based on micro-USB.[29]

In addition, on 22 October 2009 the International Telecommunication Union (ITU) has also announced that it had embraced micro-USB as the *Universal Charger Solution* its "energy-efficient one-charger-fits-all new mobile phone solution", and added: "Based on the Micro-USB interface, UCS chargers will also include a 4-star or higher efficiency rating—up to three times more energy-efficient than an unrated charger".[30]

A USB On-The-Go device is required to have one, and only one USB connector: a Mini-AB or Micro-AB receptacle. This receptacle is capable of accepting both Mini-A and Mini-B plugs, and alternatively, Micro-A and Micro-B plugs, attached to any of the legal cables and adapters as defined in Micro-USB1.01.

The OTG device with the A-plug inserted is called the A-device and is responsible for powering the USB interface when required and by default assumes the role of host. The OTG device with the B-plug inserted is called the B-device and by default assumes the role of peripheral. An OTG device with no plug inserted defaults to acting as a B-device. If an application on the B-device requires the role of host, then the HNP protocol is used to temporarily transfer the host role to the B-device.

OTG devices attached either to a peripheral-only B-device or a standard/embedded host will have their role fixed by the cable since in these scenarios it is only possible to attach the cable one way around.

Host interface receptacles

The following receptacles accept the following plugs:

Receptacle	Plug				
	Type A	Type B	Mini-B	Micro-A	Micro-B
Type A	Yes	No	No	No	No
Type B	No	Yes	No	No	No
Mini-B	No	No	Yes	No	No
Micro-AB	No	No	No	Yes	Yes
Micro-B	No	No	No	No	Yes

Cable plugs (USB 1.x/2.0)

Cables exist with pairs of plugs:

Plug	Plug				
	Micro-B	Micro-A	Mini-B	Type B	Type A
Type A	Yes	NS	Yes	Yes	NS
Type B	No	NS	No	No	
Mini-B	No	NS	No		
Micro-A	Yes	No			
Micro-B	No				

NS: non-standard, existing for specific proprietary purposes, and not interoperable with USB-IF compliant equipment.

In addition to the above cable assemblies comprising two plugs, an "adapter" cable with a Micro-A plug and a Standard-A receptacle is compliant with USB specifications.[18] Other combinations of connectors are not compliant. However, some older devices and cables with Mini-A connectors have been certified by USB-IF. The Mini-A connector has been deprecated: there will be no new certification of assemblies using Mini-A connector.[22]

Proprietary connectors and formats

- Microsoft's original Xbox game console uses standard USB 1.1 signalling in its controllers and memory cards, but uses proprietary connectors and ports. The Xbox 360 (pre Xbox 360 S) has two Memory Unit ports which are USB compliant with proprietary connectors.
- IBM UltraPort uses standard USB signalling, but via a proprietary connection format.
- American Power Conversion uses USB signalling and HID device class on its uninterruptible power supplies using 10P10C connectors.

HTC manufactured Windows Mobile and Android-based Communicators which have a proprietary connector called HTC ExtUSB (Extended USB). ExtUSB combines mini-USB (with which it is backwards-compatible) with audio input as well as audio and video output in an 11-pin connector.

HTC ExtUSB

Nokia included a USB connection as part of the Pop-Port connector on some older mobile phone models.

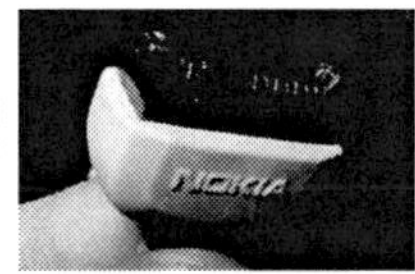

Nokia's discontinued Pop-Port connector

- Sony Ericsson used a proprietary connector called FastPort from 2005 to 2009.
- The second, third, and fourth generation iPod Shuffle uses a TRRS connector to carry USB, audio, or power signals.
- iriver added a fifth power pin within USB-A plugs for higher power and faster charging, used for the iriver U10 series. A mini-USB version contains a matching extra power pin for the cradle.
- Apple has shipped non-standard USB extension cables with some of their computers, for use with the included Apple USB keyboards. The extension cable's socket is keyed with a small protrusion to prevent the insertion of a standard USB plug, while the Apple USB keyboard's plug has a matching indentation. The indentation on the keyboard's plug does not interfere with insertion into a standard USB socket. Despite the keying, it is still possible to insert standard USB plugs into the extension cord. The protrusion can also be shaved off with an appropriate blade, or crushed with locking pliers.
- Apple also uses a proprietary USB 30-pin dock connector on its iPods, iPhones, and the iPad.
- HP Tablet computers use non-standard connectors to transmit the USB signals between the keyboard/mouse unit and the Computer Tablet Unit.
- PDMI (Portable Digital Media Interface) is a 30-pin docking connector for portable devices standardized by ANSI/CEA which includes USB 3.0 "SuperSpeed" and USB 2.0 "High/Standard Speed" with USB-on-the-go, as well as DisplayPort, HDMI CEC, 5 V power, and analog audio.
- Some digital cameras have their own USB connectors, like the Panasonic Lumix DMC-FT2.
- The United States Army's Land Warrior system uses standard USB signaling with 15.6 V power using a ruggedized connector from Glenair, Inc. [32]
- The ExpressCard interface includes a USB2 port as well as the express bus port.

Cable properties

Conductor configuration

A USB twisted pair, where the "Data +" and "Data -" conductors are twisted together in a double helix. The wires are enclosed in a further layer of shielding.

The data cables for USB 1.x and USB 2.x use a twisted pair to reduce noise and crosstalk. USB 3.0 cables are larger in diameter because there are twice as many wires than USB 2.x. This is to support the new **SuperSpeed** data transmission.[31]

Maximum cable length

For USB 2.0 or earlier, the maximum length of a standard cable is 5 metres (16.4 ft).[32] The primary reason for this limit is the maximum allowed round-trip delay of about 1.5 μs. If USB host commands are unanswered by the USB device within the allowed time, the host considers the command lost. When adding USB device response time, delays from the maximum number of hubs added to the delays from connecting cables, the maximum acceptable delay per cable amounts to 26 ns.[32] The USB 2.0 specification requires cable delay to be less than 5.2 ns per meter (192,000 km/s, which is close to the maximum achievable transmission speed for standard copper cable).[33] This allows for a five meter cable. The USB 3.0 standard does not directly specify a maximum cable length, requiring only that all cables meet an electrical specification. For copper wire cabling, some calculations have suggested a maximum length of perhaps 3 m.

Power

The USB 1.x and 2.0 specifications provide a 5 V supply on a single wire from which connected USB devices may draw power. The specification provides for no more than 5.25 V and no less than 4.75 V (5 V±5%) between the positive and negative bus power lines. For USB 3.0, the voltage supplied by low-powered hub ports is 4.45–5.25 V.[34]

A unit load is defined as 100 mA in USB 2.0, and was raised to 150 mA in USB 3.0. A maximum of 5 unit loads (500 mA) can be drawn from a port in USB 2.0, which was raised to 6 (900 mA) in USB 3.0. There are two types of devices: low-power and high-power. Low-power devices draw at most 1 unit load, with minimum operating voltage of 4.4 V in USB 2.0, and 4 V in USB 3.0. High-power devices draw the maximum number of unit loads supported by the standard. All devices default as low-power but the device's software may request high-power as long as the power is available on the providing bus.[35]

Some devices like high-speed external disk drives may require more than 500 mA of current[36] and therefore cannot be powered from one USB 2.0 port. Such devices usually come with Y-shaped cable that has two USB connectors to be inserted into a computer. With such a cable a device can draw power from two USB ports simultaneously.[37]

A bus-powered hub is initialized at 1 unit load and transitions to maximum unit loads after hub configuration is obtained. Any device connected to the hub will draw 1 unit load regardless of the current draw of devices connected to other ports of the hub (i.e. one device connected on a four-port hub will only draw 1 unit load despite the fact that all unit loads are being supplied to the hub).[35]

A self-powered hub will supply maximum supported unit loads to any device connected to it. An externally-powered hub (battery or DC converter) may supply maximum unit loads to ports. In addition, the V_{BUS} will supply 1 unit load upstream for communication if parts of the Hub are powered down.[35]

In *Battery Charging Specification*,[38] new powering modes are added to the USB specification. A host or hub Charging Downstream Port can supply a maximum of 1.5 A when communicating at low-bandwidth or full-bandwidth, a maximum of 900 mA when communicating at high-bandwidth, and as much current as the connector will safely handle when no communication is taking place; USB 2.0 standard-A connectors are rated at 1.5 A by default. A Dedicated Charging Port can supply a maximum of 1.8 A of current at 5.25 V. A portable device can draw up to 1.8 A from a Dedicated Charging Port. The Dedicated Charging Port shorts the D+ and D- pins with a resistance of at most 200 Ω. The short disables data transfer, but allows devices to detect the Dedicated Charging Port and allows very simple, high current chargers to be manufactured. The increased current (faster, 9 W charging) will occur once both the host/hub and devices support the new charging specification.

Sleep and Charge

Sleep-and-charge USB ports can be used to charge electronic devices even when the computer is switched off. Normally when a computer is powered off the USB ports are powered down. This prevents phones and other devices from being able to charge unless the computer is powered on. Sleep-and-charge USB ports remain powered even when the computer is off. On laptops, charging devices from the USB port when it is not being powered from AC will drain the laptop battery faster. Desktop machines need to remain plugged into AC power for Sleep-and-charge to work.[39]

Mobile device charger standards

As of 14 June 2007, all new mobile phones applying for a license in China are required to use the USB port as a power port.[40] [41] This was the first standard to use the convention of shorting D+ and D-.[42]

In September 2007, the Open Mobile Terminal Platform group (a forum of mobile network operators and manufacturers such as Nokia, Samsung, Motorola, Sony Ericsson and LG) announced that its members had agreed on micro-USB as the future common connector for mobile devices.[43] [44]

The Micro-USB interface is commonly found on chargers for mobile phones

On 17 February 2009, the GSM Association (GSMA) announced[45] that they had agreed on a standard charger for mobile phones. The standard connector to be adopted by 17 manufacturers including Nokia, Motorola and Samsung is to be the micro-USB connector (several media reports erroneously reported this as the mini-USB). The new chargers will be much more efficient than existing chargers.[45] Having a standard charger for all phones means that manufacturers will no longer have to supply a charger with every new phone. The basis of the GSMA's Universal Charger Solution (UCS) is the technical recommendation from OMTP and the USB-IF battery charging standard.[46] [47] [48]

On 22 April 2009, this was further endorsed by the CTIA – The Wireless Association.[49]

In June 2009, many of the world's largest mobile phone manufacturers signed a Memorandum of Understanding (MoU), agreeing to make most data-enabled mobile phones marketed in the European Union compatible with a common External Power Supply (EPS) based on the GSMA / OMTP Universal Charging Solution.[50] [51]

On 22 October 2009, the International Telecommunication Union (ITU) announced that it had embraced the Universal Charger Solution as its "energy-efficient one-charger-fits-all new mobile phone solution", and added: "Based on the Micro-USB interface, UCS chargers will also include a 4-star or higher efficiency rating—up to three times more energy-efficient than an unrated charger".[52]

Non-standard devices

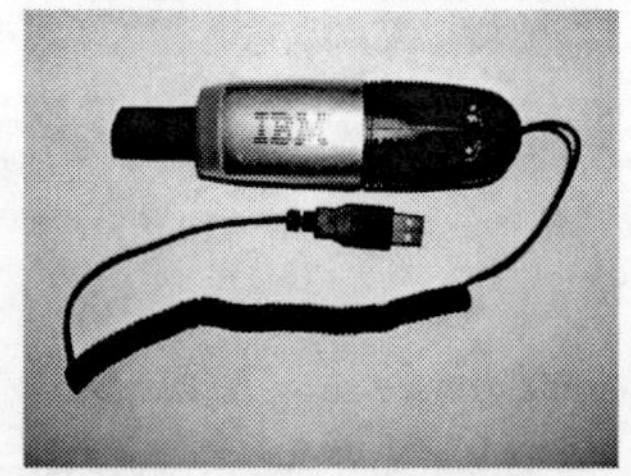

USB vacuum cleaner novelty device

Some USB devices require more power than is permitted by the specifications for a single port. This is common for external hard and optical disc drives, and generally for devices with motors or lamps. Such devices can use an external power supply, which is allowed by the standard, or use a dual-input USB cable, one input of which is used for power and data transfer, the other solely for power, which makes the device a non-standard USB device. Some external hubs may, in practice, supply more power to USB devices than required by the specification but a standard-compliant device may not depend on this.

Some non-standard USB devices use the 5 V power supply without participating in a proper USB network which negotiates power draws with the host interface. These are usually referred to as USB decorations. The typical example is a USB-powered keyboard light; fans, mug coolers and heaters, battery chargers, miniature vacuum cleaners, and even miniature lava lamps are available. In most cases, these items contain no digital circuitry, and thus are not Standard compliant USB devices at all. This can theoretically cause problems with some computers, such as drawing too much current and damaging circuitry; prior to the Battery Charging Specification, the USB specification required that devices connect in a low-power mode (100 mA maximum) and communicate their current requirements to the host, which would then permit the device to switch into high-power mode.

In addition to limiting the total average power used by the device, the USB specification limits the inrush current (i.e., that used to charge decoupling and filter capacitors) when the device is first connected. Otherwise, connecting a device could cause problems with the host's internal power. Also, USB devices are required to automatically enter ultra low-power suspend mode when the USB host is suspended. Nevertheless, many USB host interfaces do not cut off the power supply to USB devices when they are suspended since resuming from the suspended state would become a lot more complicated if they did.

There are also devices at the host end that do not support negotiation, such as battery packs that can power USB-powered devices; some provide power, while others pass through the data lines to a host PC. USB power adapters convert utility power and/or another power source (e.g., a car's electrical system) to run attached devices. Some of these devices can supply up to 1 A of current. Without negotiation, the powered USB device is unable to inquire if it is allowed to draw 100 mA, 500 mA, or 1 A.

Powered USB

Powered USB uses standard USB signaling with the addition of extra power lines. It uses four additional pins to supply up to 6 A at either 5 V, 12 V, or 24 V (depending on keying) to peripheral devices. The wires and contacts on the USB portion have been upgraded to support higher current on the 5 V line, as well. This is commonly used in retail systems and provides enough power to operate stationary barcode scanners, printers, PIN pads, signature capture devices, etc. This modification of the USB interface is proprietary and was developed by IBM, NCR, and FCI/Berg. It is essentially two connectors stacked such that the bottom connector accepts a standard USB plug and the top connector takes a power connector.

Signaling

USB supports the following signaling rates: The terms *speed* and *bandwidth* are used interchangeably. "high-" is alternatively written as "hi-".

- A *low-speed* rate of 1.5 Mbit/s (~183 kB/s) is defined by USB 1.0. It is very similar to full-bandwidth operation except each bit takes 8 times as long to transmit. It is intended primarily to save cost in low-bandwidth human interface devices (HID) such as keyboards, mice, and joysticks.
- The *full-speed* rate of 12 Mbit/s (~1.43 MB/s) is the basic USB data rate defined by USB 1.1. All USB hubs support full-bandwidth.
- A *high-speed* (USB 2.0) rate of 480 Mbit/s (~57 MB/s) was introduced in 2001. All hi-speed devices are capable of falling back to full-bandwidth operation if necessary; i.e., they are backward compatible with USB 1.1. Connectors are identical for USB 2.0 and USB 1.x.
- A *SuperSpeed* (USB 3.0) rate of 4.8 Gbit/s (~572 MB/s). The written USB 3.0 specification was released by Intel and partners in August 2008. The first USB 3 controller chips were sampled by NEC May 2009[53] and products using the 3.0 specification arrived beginning in January 2010.[54] USB 3.0 connectors are generally backwards compatible, but include new wiring and full duplex operation.

USB signals are transmitted on a twisted-pair data cable with 90Ω ±15% Characteristic impedance,[55] labeled D+ and D−. Prior to USB 3.0, these collectively use half-duplex differential signaling to reduce the effects of electromagnetic noise on longer lines. Transmitted signal levels are 0.0–0.3 volts for low and 2.8–3.6 volts for high in full-bandwidth and low-bandwidth modes, and −10–10 mV for low and 360–440 mV for high in hi-bandwidth mode. In FS mode, the cable wires are not terminated, but the HS mode has termination of 45 Ω to ground, or 90 Ω differential to match the data cable impedance, reducing interference due to signal reflections. USB 3.0 introduces two additional pairs of shielded twisted wire and new, mostly interoperable contacts in USB 3.0 cables, for them. They permit the higher data rate, and full duplex operation.

A USB connection is always between a host or hub at the "A" connector end, and a device or hub's "upstream" port at the other end. Originally, this was a "B' connector, preventing erroneous loop connections, but additional upstream connectors were specified, and some cable vendors designed and sold cables which permitted erroneous connections (and potential damage to the circuitry). USB interconnections are not as fool-proof or as simple as originally intended.

The host includes 15 kΩ pull-down resistors on each data line. When no device is connected, this pulls both data lines low into the so-called "single-ended zero" state (SE0 in the USB documentation), and indicates a reset or disconnected connection.

A USB device pulls one of the data lines high with a 1.5 kΩ resistor. This overpowers one of the pull-down resistors in the host and leaves the data lines in an idle state called "J". For USB 1.x, the choice of data line indicates a device's bandwidth support; full-bandwidth devices pull D+ high, while low-bandwidth devices pull D− high.

USB data is transmitted by toggling the data lines between the J state and the opposite K state. USB encodes data using the NRZI convention; a 0 bit is transmitted by toggling the data lines from J to K or vice-versa, while a 1 bit is transmitted by leaving the data lines as-is. To ensure a minimum density of signal transitions remains in the bitstream, USB uses bit stuffing; an extra 0 bit is inserted into the data stream after any appearance of six consecutive 1 bits. Seven consecutive received 1 bits is always an error. USB 3.0 has introduced additional data transmission encodings.

A USB packet begins with an 8-bit synchronization sequence '00000001'. That is, after the initial idle state J, the data lines toggle KJKJKJKK. The final 1 bit (repeated K state) marks the end of the sync pattern and the beginning of the USB frame. For high bandwidth USB, the packet begins with a 32-bit synchronization sequence.

A USB packet's end, called EOP (end-of-packet), is indicated by the transmitter driving 2 bit times of SE0 (D+ and D− both below max) and 1 bit time of J state. After this, the transmitter ceases to drive the D+/D− lines and the aforementioned pull up resistors hold it in the J (idle) state. Sometimes skew due to hubs can add as much as one bit time before the SE0 of the end of packet. This extra bit can also result in a "bit stuff violation" if the six bits before it in the CRC are '1's. This bit should be ignored by receiver.

A USB bus is reset using a prolonged (10 to 20 milliseconds) SE0 signal.

USB 2.0 devices use a special protocol during reset, called "chirping", to negotiate the high bandwidth mode with the host/hub. A device that is HS capable first connects as an FS device (D+ pulled high), but upon receiving a USB RESET (both D+ and D− driven LOW by host for 10 to 20 ms) it pulls the D− line high, known as chirp K. This indicates to the host that the device is high bandwidth. If the host/hub is also HS capable, it chirps (returns alternating J and K states on D− and D+ lines) letting the device know that the hub will operate at high bandwidth. The device has to receive at least 3 sets of KJ chirps before it changes to high bandwidth terminations and begins high bandwidth signaling. Because USB 3.0 uses wiring separate and additional to that used by USB 2.0 and USB 1.x, such bandwidth negotiation is not required.

Clock tolerance is 480.00 Mbit/s ±500 ppm, 12.000 Mbit/s ±2500 ppm, 1.50 Mbit/s ±15000 ppm.

Though high bandwidth devices are commonly referred to as "USB 2.0" and advertised as "up to 480 Mbit/s", not all USB 2.0 devices are high bandwidth. The USB-IF certifies devices and provides licenses to use special marketing logos for either "basic bandwidth" (low and full) or high bandwidth after passing a compliance test and paying a licensing fee. All devices are tested according to the latest specification, so recently compliant low bandwidth devices are also 2.0 devices.

USB 3 uses tinned copper stranded AWG-28 cables with 90 ± 7 Ω impedance for its high-speed differential pairs and linear feedback shift register and 8b/10b encoding sent with a voltage of 1 V nominal with a 100 mV receiver threshold; the receiver uses equalization.[56] SSC clock and 300 ppm precision is used. Packet headers are protected with CRC-16, while data payload is protected with CRC-32.[57] Power up to 3.6 W may be used. One unit load in superspeed mode is equal to 150 mA.[57]

Transfer rates

The theoretical maximum data rate in USB 2.0 is 480 Mbit/s (60 MB/s) per controller and is shared amongst all attached devices. Some chipset manufacturers overcome this bottleneck by providing multiple USB 2.0 controllers within the southbridge.

Typical hi-speed USB hard drives can be written to at rates around 25–30 MB/s, and read from at rates of 30–42 MB/s, according to routine testing done by CNet.[58] This is 70% of the total bandwidth available.

According to a USB-IF chairman, "at least 10 to 15 percent of the stated peak 60 MB/s (480 Mbit/s) of Hi-Speed USB goes to overhead—the communication protocol between the card and the peripheral. Overhead is a component of all connectivity standards".[59] Tables illustrating the transfer limits are shown in Chapter 5 of the USB spec.

For isochronous devices like audio streams, the bandwidth is constant, and reserved exclusively for a given device. The bus bandwidth therefore only has an effect on the number of channels that can be sent at a time, not the "speed" or latency of the transmission.

Communication

USB communication takes the form of packets. Initially, all packets are sent from the host, via the root hub and possibly more hubs, to devices. Some of those packets direct a device to send some packets in reply.

After the sync field, all packets are made of 8-bit bytes, transmitted least-significant bit first. The first byte is a packet identifier (PID) byte. The PID is actually 4 bits; the byte consists of the 4-bit PID followed by its bitwise complement. This redundancy helps detect errors. (Note also that a PID byte contains at most four consecutive 1 bits, and thus will never need bit-stuffing, even when combined with the final 1 bit in the sync byte. However, trailing 1 bits in the PID may require bit-stuffing within the first few bits of the payload.)

USB PID bytes

Type	PID value (msb-first)	Transmitted byte (lsb-first)	Name	Description
Reserved	0000	0000 1111		
Token	1000	0001 1110	**SPLIT**	High-bandwidth (USB 2.0) split transaction
	0100	0010 1101	**PING**	Check if endpoint can accept data (USB 2.0)
Special	1100	0011 1100	**PRE**	Low-bandwidth USB preamble
Handshake			**ERR**	Split transaction error (USB 2.0)
	0010	0100 1011	**ACK**	Data packet accepted
	1010	0101 1010	**NAK**	Data packet not accepted; please retransmit
	0110	0110 1001	**NYET**	Data not ready yet (USB 2.0)
	1110	0111 1000	**STALL**	Transfer impossible; do error recovery
Token	0001	1000 0111	**OUT**	Address for host-to-device transfer
	1001	1001 0110	**IN**	Address for device-to-host transfer
	0101	1010 0101	**SOF**	Start of frame marker (sent each ms)
	1101	1011 0100	**SETUP**	Address for host-to-device control transfer
Data	0011	1100 0011	**DATA0**	Even-numbered data packet
	1011	1101 0010	**DATA1**	Odd-numbered data packet
	0111	1110 0001	**DATA2**	Data packet for high-bandwidth isochronous transfer (USB 2.0)
	1111	1111 0000	**MDATA**	Data packet for high-bandwidth isochronous transfer (USB 2.0)

Packets come in three basic types, each with a different format and CRC (cyclic redundancy check):

Handshake packets

Handshake packets consist of nothing but a PID byte, and are generally sent in response to data packets. The three basic types are *ACK*, indicating that data was successfully received, *NAK*, indicating that the data cannot be received at this time and should be retried, and *STALL*, indicating that the device has an error and will never be able to successfully transfer data until some corrective action (such as device initialization) is performed.

USB 2.0 added two additional handshake packets, *NYET* which indicates that a split transaction is not yet complete. A NYET packet is also used to tell the host that the receiver has accepted a data packet, but cannot accept any more due to buffers being full. The host will then send PING packets and will continue with data packets once the device ACK's the PING. The other packet added was the *ERR* handshake to indicate that a split transaction failed.

The only handshake packet the USB host may generate is ACK; if it is not ready to receive data, it should not instruct a device to send any.

Token packets

Token packets consist of a PID byte followed by 2 payload bytes: 11 bits of address and a 5-bit CRC. Tokens are only sent by the host, never a device.

IN and *OUT* tokens contain a 7-bit device number and 4-bit function number (for multifunction devices) and command the device to transmit DATAx packets, or receive the following DATAx packets, respectively.

An IN token expects a response from a device. The response may be a NAK or STALL response, or a DATAx frame. In the latter case, the host issues an ACK handshake if appropriate.

An OUT token is followed immediately by a DATAx frame. The device responds with ACK, NAK, NYET, or STALL, as appropriate.

SETUP operates much like an OUT token, but is used for initial device setup. It is followed by an 8-byte DATA0 frame with a standardized format.

Every millisecond (12000 full-bandwidth bit times), the USB host transmits a special *SOF* (start of frame) token, containing an 11-bit incrementing frame number in place of a device address. This is used to synchronize isochronous data flows. High-bandwidth USB 2.0 devices receive 7 additional duplicate SOF tokens per frame, each introducing a 125 µs "microframe" (60000 high-bandwidth bit times each).

USB 2.0 added a *PING* token, which asks a device if it is ready to receive an OUT/DATA packet pair. The device responds with ACK, NAK, or STALL, as appropriate. This avoids the need to send the DATA packet if the device knows that it will just respond with NAK.

USB 2.0 also added a larger 3-byte *SPLIT* token with a 7-bit hub number, 12 bits of control flags, and a 5-bit CRC. This is used to perform split transactions. Rather than tie up the high-bandwidth USB bus sending data to a slower USB device, the nearest high-bandwidth capable hub receives a SPLIT token followed by one or two USB packets at high bandwidth, performs the data transfer at full or low bandwidth, and provides the response at high bandwidth when prompted by a second SPLIT token.

Data packets

A data packet consists of the PID followed by 0–1,023 bytes of data payload (up to 1,024 in high bandwidth, at most 8 at low bandwidth), and a 16-bit CRC.

There are two basic data packets, *DATA0* and *DATA1*. They must always be preceded by an address token, and are usually followed by a handshake token from the receiver back to the transmitter. The two packet types provide the 1-bit sequence number required by Stop-and-wait ARQ. If a USB host does not receive a response (such as an ACK) for data it has transmitted, it does not know if the data was received or not; the data might have been lost in transit, or it might have been received but the handshake response was lost.

To solve this problem, the device keeps track of the type of DATAx packet it last accepted. If it receives another DATAx packet of the same type, it is acknowledged but ignored as a duplicate. Only a DATAx packet of the opposite type is actually received.

When a device is reset with a SETUP packet, it expects an 8-byte DATA0 packet next.

USB 2.0 added *DATA2* and *MDATA* packet types as well. They are used only by high-bandwidth devices doing high-bandwidth isochronous transfers which need to transfer more than 1024 bytes per 125 µs microframe (8,192 kB/s).

PRE "packet"

Low-bandwidth devices are supported with a special PID value, *PRE*. This marks the beginning of a low-bandwidth packet, and is used by hubs which normally do not send full-bandwidth packets to low-bandwidth devices. Since all PID bytes include four 0 bits, they leave the bus in the full-bandwidth K state, which is the same as the low-bandwidth J state. It is followed by a brief pause during which hubs enable their low-bandwidth outputs, already idling in the J state, then a low-bandwidth packet follows, beginning with a sync sequence and PID byte, and ending with a brief period of SE0. Full-bandwidth devices other than hubs can simply ignore the PRE packet and its low-bandwidth contents, until the final SE0 indicates that a new packet follows.

Comparisons with other connection methods

FireWire

USB was originally seen as a complement to FireWire (IEEE 1394), which was designed as a high-bandwidth serial bus which could efficiently interconnect peripherals such as hard disks, audio interfaces, and video equipment. USB originally operated at a far lower data rate and used much simpler hardware, and was suitable for small peripherals such as keyboards and mice.

The most significant technical differences between FireWire and USB include the following:

- USB networks use a tiered-star topology, while FireWire networks use a tree topology.
- USB 1.0, 1.1 and 2.0 use a "speak-when-spoken-to" protocol; peripherals cannot communicate with the host unless the host specifically requests communication. USB 3.0 allows for device-initiated communications towards the host. A FireWire device can communicate with any other node at any time, subject to network conditions.
- A USB network relies on a single host at the top of the tree to control the network. In a FireWire network, any capable node can control the network.
- USB runs with a 5 V power line, while Firewire in current implementations supplies 12 V and theoretically can supply up to 30 V.
- Standard USB hub ports can provide from the typical 500 mA/2.5 W of current, only 100 mA from non-hub ports. USB 3.0 and USB On-The-Go supply 1.8 A/9.0 W (for dedicated battery charging, 1.5 A/7.5 W Full bandwidth or 900 mA/4.5 W High Bandwidth), while FireWire can in theory supply up to 60 watts of power, although 10 to 20 watts is more typical.

These and other differences reflect the differing design goals of the two buses: USB was designed for simplicity and low cost, while FireWire was designed for high performance, particularly in time-sensitive applications such as audio and video. Although similar in theoretical maximum transfer rate, FireWire 400 is faster than USB 2.0 Hi-Bandwidth in real-use,[60] especially in high-bandwidth use such as external hard-drives.[61] [62] [63] [64] The newer FireWire 800 standard is twice as fast as FireWire 400 and faster than USB 2.0 Hi-Bandwidth both theoretically and practically.[65] The chipset and drivers used to implement USB and Firewire have a crucial impact on how much of the bandwidth prescribed by the specification is achieved in the real world, along with compatibility with peripherals.[66]

Ethernet

The IEEE 802.3af Power over Ethernet (PoE) standard has a more elaborate power negotiation scheme than powered USB. It operates at 48 V DC and can supply more power (up to 12.95 W, PoE+ 25.5 W) over a cable up to 100 meters compared to USB 2.0 which provide 2.5 W with a maximum cable length of 5 meters. This has made PoE popular for VoIP telephones, security cameras, wireless access points and other networked devices within buildings. However, USB is cheaper than PoE provided that the distance is short, and power demand is low.

Ethernet standards requires electrical isolation between the networked device (computer, phone, etc.) and the network cable up to 1500 V AC or 2250 V DC for 60 seconds.[67] USB has no such requirement as it was designed for peripherals closely associated with a host computer, and in fact it connects the peripheral and host grounds. This gives Ethernet a significant safety advantage over USB with peripherals such as cable and DSL modems connected to external wiring that can assume hazardous voltages under certain fault conditions.[68]

Digital musical instruments

Digital musical instruments are another example of where USB is competitive for low-cost devices. However Power over Ethernet and the MIDI plug standard are preferred in high-end devices that must work with long cables. USB can cause ground loop problems in equipment because it connects the ground wires on both transceivers. By contrast, the MIDI plug standard and Ethernet have built-in isolation to 500 V or more.

eSATA/eSATAp

The eSATA connector is a more robust SATA connector, intended for connection to external hard drives and SSDs. It has a far higher transfer rate (3 Gbit/s or 6 Gbit/s, bi-directional) than USB 2.0. A device connected by eSATA appears as an ordinary SATA device, giving both full performance and full compatibility associated with internal drives.

eSATA does not supply power to external devices. This is an increasing disadvantage compared to USB. Even though USB's 2.5 W is sometimes insufficient to power external hard drives, technology is advancing and external drives gradually need less power, manifesting the eSATA disadvantage. eSATAp (power over eSATA; aka ESATA/USB) is a connector introduced in 2009 that supplies power to attached devices using a new, backwards-compatible, connector. On a notebook eSATAp usually supplies only 5 V to power a 2.5 in HDD/SSD; on a desktop workstation it can additionally supply 12 V to power larger devices including 3.5 in HDD/SSD and 5.25 in optical drives.

eSATAp support can be added to a desktop machine in the form of a bracket connecting to motherboard SATA, power, and USB resources.

eSATA, like USB, supports hot plugging, although this might be limited by OS drivers and device firmware.

Related standards

The PictBridge standard allows for interconnecting consumer imaging devices. It typically uses USB for its underlying communication layer.

The USB Implementers Forum is working on a wireless networking standard based on the USB protocol. Wireless USB is intended as a cable-replacement technology, and will use ultra-wideband wireless technology for data rates of up to 480 Mbit/s.

USB 2.0 High Speed Inter Chip (HSIC) is a chip-to-chip variant of USB 2.0 that eliminates the conventional analog transceivers found in normal USB. It was adopted as a standard by the USB Implementers Forum in 2007. The HSIC physical layer uses about 50% less power and 75% less board area compared to traditional USB 2.0. HSIC uses two signals at 1.2 V and has a throughput of 480 Mbit/sec using 240 MHz DDR signaling. Maximum PCB trace length for HSIC is 10 cm. It does not have low enough latency to support RAM memory sharing between two chips.[69] [70]

See also

- Computer bus
- List of computer peripheral bus bit rates

Further reading

- *USB Complete : The Developer's Guide*; 4th Ed; Jan Axelson; 506 pages; 2009; ISBN 9781931448086.
- *USB Design by Example : A Practical Guide to Building I/O Devices*; 2nd Ed; John Hyde; 510 pages; 2001; ISBN 9780970284655.
- *USB Mass Storage : Designing and Programming Devices and Embedded Hosts*; 1st Ed; Jan Axelson; 287 pages; 2006; ISBN 9781931448048.
- *Serial Port Complete : COM Ports, USB Virtual COM Ports, and Ports for Embedded Systems*; 2nd Ed; Jan Axelson; 380 pages; 2007; ISBN 9781931448062.
- *Debugging USB 2.0 for Compliance: It's Not Just a Digital World: Agilent Technologies Application Note 1382-3*

References

[1] "SuperSpeed USB 3.0: More Details Emerge" (http://www.pcworld.com/article/156494/superspeed_usb_30_more_details_emerge.html). 6 Jan 2009. .

[2] "Definition of Universal Serial Bus" (http://books.google.com/books?id=fRvbxgH4wmsC&pg=PA7). *1394 Newsletter* **2** (4): 7–9. April 1998. . Retrieved 2010-03-11.

[3] Seebach, Peter (April 26, 2005). "Standards and specs: The ins and outs of USB" (http://www.ibm.com/developerworks/power/library/pa-spec7.html). IBM. . Retrieved 2010-03-11.

[4] *Universal Serial Bus Specification Revision 3.0 : 3.1* (http://www.usb.org/developers/docs/usb_30_spec_020411.zip). 12 November 2008. p. 41 (3-1). . Retrieved 20 February 2011.

[5] *Universal Serial Bus Specification Revision 3.0 : 1.6* (http://www.usb.org/developers/docs/usb_30_spec_020411.zip). 12 November 2008. p. 31 (1–3). . Retrieved 20 February 2011.

[6] "USB 3.0 SuperSpeed gone wild at CES 2010, trumps even your new SSD" (http://www.engadget.com/2010/01/09/usb-3-0-superspeed-gone-wild-at-ces-2010-trumps-even-your-new-s/). January 9, 2010. . Retrieved 2011-02-20.

[7] "USB 3.0 Finally Arrives" (http://www.pcworld.com/article/186566/usb_30_finally_arrives.html). January 11, 2010. . Retrieved 2011-02-20.

[8] "Usb.org" (http://www.usb.org/press/USB-IF_Press_Releases/2008_11_17_USB_IF.pdf) (PDF). . Retrieved 2010-06-22.

[9] *Universal Serial Bus Specification Revision 2.0* (http://www.usb.org/developers/docs/usb_20_021411.zip). 27 April 2000. p. 13;30;256. . Retrieved 20 February 2011.

[10] *Universal Serial Bus Specification Revision 3.0 : 8.8* (http://www.usb.org/developers/docs/usb_30_spec_020411.zip). 12 November 2008. pp. 8–25. . Retrieved 20 February 2011.

[11] USB Class Codes (http://www.usb.org/developers/defined_class) at USB.org

[12] Use class information in the interface descriptors. This base class is defined to be used in device descriptors to indicate that class information should be determined from the Interface Descriptors in the device.

[13] *Universal Serial Bus Test and Measurement Class Specification (USBTMC), Revision 1.0, April 14, 2003*, USB Implementers Forum, Inc.

[14] "DFU_1.1.doc" (http://www.usb.org/developers/devclass_docs/DFU_1.1.pdf) (PDF). . Retrieved 2010-06-22.

[15] *Universal Serial Bus 3.0 Specification*,4.4.11 "Efficiency"

[16] "100 Portable Apps for your USB Stick (both for Mac and Win)" (http://www.makeuseof.com/tag/portable-software-usb/). . Retrieved 2008-10-30.

[17] "Skype VoIP USB Installation Guide" (http://www.VoIP-Download.com/Skype.htm#USB/). . Retrieved 2008-10-30.

[18] "Universal Serial Bus Micro-USB Cables and Connectors Specification" (http://193.219.66.80/datasheets/usb_20/Micro-USB_final/Micro-USB_1_01.pdf) (PDF). USB Implementers Forum. 2007-04-04. . Retrieved 2010-09-03.

[19] *Universal Serial Bus 3.0 Specification: Revision 1.0*. June 6, 2011. pp. 531.

[20] "What is the Life Cycle of a USB Flash Drive?" (http://www.getusb.info/what-is-the-life-cycle-of-a-usb-flash-drive/), GetUSB.info. Retrieved June 14, 2010.

[21] Quinnell, Richard A (1996). "USB: a neat package with a few loose ends" (http://www.edn.com/archives/1996/102496/df_01.htm#USB fundamentals). *USB Fundamentals*. EDN Magazine of Reed Properties Inc. . Retrieved 2008-08-06.

[22] USB Implementers Forum (2007-05-27). "Deprecation of the Mini-A and Mini-AB Connectors" (http://www.usb.org/developers/Deprecation_Announcement_052507.pdf) (PDF). Press release. . Retrieved 2009-01-13.

[23] "ID Pin Resistance on Mini B-plugs and Micro B-plugs Increased to 1 Mohm" (http://compliance.usb.org/index.asp?UpdateFile=Cables and Connectors&Format=Standard#63). USB IF Compliance Updates. December 2009. . Retrieved 2010-03-01.

[24] USB Implementers Forum (2007-01-04). "Mobile phones to adopt new, smaller USB connector" (http://www.usb.org/press/pressroom/2007_01_04_usbif.pdf) (PDF). Press release. . Retrieved 2007-01-08.

[25] USB Implementers Forum (2007-05-23). "Deprecation of the Mini-A and Mini-AB Connectors" (http://www.usb.org/developers/Deprecation_Announcement_052507.pdf) (PDF). Press release. . Retrieved 2010-12-23.

[26] *Universal Serial Bus Micro-USB Cables and Connectors Specification to the USB 2.0 Specification, Revision 1.01* (http://193.219.66.80/datasheets/usb_20/Micro-USB_final/Micro-USB_1_01.pdf), USB Implementers Forum, Inc., 2007-04-07, archived from the original (http://www.usb.org/developers/docs/usb_20_081810.zip) on 2007-04-08, , retrieved 2010-11-18, "Section 1.3: Additional requirements for a more rugged connector that will have durability past 10,000 cycles and still meet the USB 2.0 specification for mechanical and electrical performance was also a consideration. The Mini-USB could not be modified and remain backward compatible to the existingconnector as defined in the USB OTG specification"

[27] "OMTP Local Connectivity: Data Connectivity" (http://www.omtp.org/Publications/Display.aspx?Id=08d2e4e3-ebee-407c-a51b-94057e7f7b19). Open Mobile Terminal Platform. 17 September 2007. . Retrieved 2009-02-11.

[28] http://europa.eu/rapid/pressReleasesAction.do?reference=MEMO/09/301; The following 10 biggest mobile phone companies have signed the MoU: Apple, LG, Motorola, NEC, Nokia, Qualcomm, Research In Motion, Samsung, Sony Ericsson, Texas Instruments

[29] "Commission welcomes new EU standards for common mobile phone charger" (http://europa.eu/rapid/pressReleasesAction.do?reference=IP/10/1776&format=HTML&aged=0&language=EN&guiLanguage=en). *Press Releases*. EUROPA. 2010-12-29. . Retrieved 2011-05-22.

[30] pressinfo (2009-10-22). "Press Release: Universal phone charger standard approved—One-size-fits-all solution will dramatically cut waste and GHG emissions" (http://www.itu.int/newsroom/press_releases/2009/49.html). Itu.int. . Retrieved 2009-11-04.

[31] What is the USB 3.0 Cable Difference (http://hantat.com/News-Read-459-1.html)

[32] USB Frequently Asked Questions (http://www.usb.org/developers/usbfaq/#cab1) at USB.org. Retrieved 2010-12-10.

[33] "Propagation Delay" (http://www.wildpackets.com/support/compendium/ethernet/propagation_delay). . Retrieved 2008-10-31.

[34] "7.3.2 Bus Timing/Electrical Characteristics" (http://www.usb.org/developers/docs/). *Universal Serial Bus Specification*. USB.org. .

[35] "USB.org" (http://www.usb.org/developers/docs/). USB.org. . Retrieved 2010-06-22.

[36] "Roundup: 2.5-inch Hard Disk Drives with 500 GB, 640 GB and 750 GB Storage Capacities (page 17)" (http://www.xbitlabs.com/articles/storage/display/25inch-500-640-750gb-hdd-roundup_17.html#sect0). xbitlabs.com. 2010-06-16. . Retrieved 2010-07-09.

[37] "I have the drive plugged in but I cannot find the drive in "My Computer", why?" (http://www.simpletech.com/support/faq/portable_hard_disk_drives.php#1). simpletech.com. . Retrieved 2010-07-09.

[38] "Battery Charging Specification" (http://www.usb.org/developers/devclass_docs/batt_charging_1_1.zip). USB Implementers Forum, Inc. 15 April 2009. . Retrieved 23 September 2009.

[39] "Usb-core.co.uk" (http://web.archive.org/web/20080614031146/http://www.usb-core.co.uk/03-04-2008-toshiba-announces-sleep-and-charge-usb-ports.html). Usb-core.co.uk. 2008-04-03. Archived from the original (http://www.usb-core.co.uk/03-04-2008-toshiba-announces-sleep-and-charge-usb-ports.html) on June 14, 2008. . Retrieved 2010-06-22.

[40] Cai Yan (2007-05-31). "China to enforce universal cell phone charger" (http://www.eetimes.com/rss/showArticle.jhtml?articleID=199800238&cid=RSSfeed_eetimes_newsRSS). EETimes.com. . Retrieved 2007-08-25.

[41] The Chinese FCC's technical standard: YD/T 1591-2006, "Technical Requirements and Test Method of Charger and Interface for Mobile Telecommunication Terminal Equipment". (http://www.dianyuan.com/bbs/u/63/2015571206841181.pdf) (Chinese)

[42] Crystal LAM Yan Yan and Harry LIU Yao Hui, ON Semiconductor. "How to conform to China's new mobile phone interface standards" (http://www.wirelessnetdesignline.com/202800278?printableArticle=true). Wireless Net DesignLine. . Retrieved 2010-06-22.

[43] "Pros seem to outdo cons in new phone charger standard" (http://www.news.com/2100-1041_3-6209247.html). news.com. September 20, 2007. . Retrieved 2007-11-26.

[44] "Press Release: Broad Manufacturer Agreement Gives Universal Phone Cable Green Light" (http://www.omtp.org/News/Display.aspx?Id=4ec69ecb-0978-4df6-b045-34557aabbcbd). OTMP. September 17, 2007. . Retrieved 2007-11-26.

[45] "GSM World agreement on Mobile phone Standard Charger" (http://www.gsmworld.com/newsroom/press-releases/2009/2548.htm). .

[46] "Common Charging and Local Data Connectivity" (http://www.omtp.org/Publications/Display.aspx?Id=4dda105f-8472-4c12-ba04-75dd3c1d4ca6). Open Mobile Terminal Platform. 11 February 2009. . Retrieved 2009-02-11.

[47] "Universal Charging Solution ~ GSM World" (http://www.gsmworld.com/our-work/mobile_planet/universal_charging_solution.htm). Gsmworld.com. . Retrieved 2010-06-22.

[48] "Meeting the challenge of the universal charge standard in mobile phones" (http://www.planetanalog.com/article/printableArticle.jhtml?articleID=218501515). PlanetAnalog.com. . Retrieved 2010-06-22.

[49] "CTIA–The Wireless Association Announces One Universal Charger Solution to Celebrate Earth Day" (http://www.ctia.org/media/press/body.cfm/prid/1817). Ctia.org. 2009-04-22. . Retrieved 2010-06-22.

[50] "Ec.europa.eu" (http://ec.europa.eu/enterprise/rtte/chargers.htm). Ec.europa.eu. 2009-06-29. . Retrieved 2010-06-22.

[51] Previous post Next post (2009-06-13). "Wired.com" (http://www.wired.com/gadgetlab/2009/06/europe-gets-universal-cellphone-charger-in-2010/). Wired.com. . Retrieved 2010-06-22.

[52] pressinfo (2009-10-22). "Itu.int" (http://www.itu.int/newsroom/press_releases/2009/49.html). Itu.int. . Retrieved 2010-06-22.

[53] "NEC ready to sample 'world's first' USB 3.0 controller chip" (http://www.reghardware.co.uk/2009/05/19/nec_usb_3_host/). . Retrieved 2009-06-15.

[54] "When will USB 3.0 products hit the market?" (http://www.everythingusb.com/superspeed-usb.html#6). . Retrieved 2009-05-11.

[55] "USB in a NutShell—Chapter 2—Hardware" (http://www.beyondlogic.org/usbnutshell/usb2.htm). Beyond Logic.org. . Retrieved 2007-08-25.
[56] "Technical Specifications of the USB 3.0 SuperSpeed Cables" (http://www.usb3.com/images/usb_superspeed_cable_spec.jpg). . 100717 usb3.com
[57] "Universal Serial Bus 3.0 Specification, Rev 1.0 November 12, 2008" (http://www.usb3.com/whitepapers/USB 3 0 (11132008)-final. pdf). . 100717 usb3.com
[58] "Seagate FreeAgent GoFlex Ultra-portable Review" (http://reviews.cnet.com/external-hard-drives/seagate-freeagent-goflex-ultra/ 4505-3190_7-34183942-2.html). Reviews.cnet.com. . Retrieved 2011-05-22.
[59] Real Deal (http://www.pcworld.com/article/82005/news_and_trends_usb_20s_real_deal.html).
[60] "FireWire vs. USB 2.0" (http://www.qimaging.com/support/pdfs/firewire_usb_technote.pdf) (PDF). QImaging. . Retrieved 20 July 2010.
[61] "FireWire vs. USB 2.0 - Bandwidth Tests" (http://www.cwol.com/firewire/firewire-vs-usb.htm). . Retrieved 2007-08-25.
[62] "USB 2.0 vs FireWire" (http://www.digit-life.com/articles/usb20vsfirewire). Digit-Life. . Retrieved 2007-08-25.
[63] Metz, Cade. "The Great Interface-Off: FireWire Vs. USB 2.0" (http://www.pcmag.com/article2/0,4149,847716,00.asp). PC Magazine. . Retrieved 2007-08-25.
[64] Heron, Robert. "USB 2.0 Versus FireWire" (http://www.g4tv.com/techtvvault/features/39129/USB_20_Versus_FireWire_pg3.html). TechTV. . Retrieved 2007-08-25.
[65] "FireWire vs. USB 2.0" (http://www.usb-ware.com/firewire-vs-usb.htm). USB Ware. . Retrieved 2007-03-19.
[66] Key, Gary (2005-11-15). "Firewire and USB Performance" (http://www.anandtech.com/mb/showdoc.aspx?i=2602&p=15). . Retrieved 2008-02-01.
[67] "Ieee 802.3" (http://standards.ieee.org/getieee802/download/802.3-2008_section1.pdf). IEEE. .
[68] By consumerist.com on December 18, 2006 7:32 PM (2010-03-08). "Powerbook Explodes After Comcast Plugs In Wrong Cable" (http:// consumerist.com/2006/12/powerbook-explodes-after-comcast-plugs-in-wrong-cable.html). Consumerist.com. . Retrieved 2010-06-22.
[69] "Interchip Connectivity: HSIC, UniPro, HSI, C2C, LLI...oh my!" (http://info.arteris.com/blog/bid/59433/ Interchip-Connectivity-HSIC-UniPro-HSI-C2C-LLI-oh-my). . Retrieved 24 June 2011.
[70] "USB High Speed Inter-Chip Interface" (http://www.interfacebus.com/hsic-bus-high-speed-inter-chip-usb.html). . Retrieved 24 June 2011.

External links

- USB official website (USB Implementers Forum, Inc.) (http://www.usb.org/)
- Intel Universal Host Controller Interface (UHCI) (http://download.intel.com/technology/usb/UHCI11D.pdf)
- USB 3.0 Standard-A, Standard-B, Powered-B connectors pinouts (http://pinoutsguide.com/Slots/ usb_3_0_connector_pinout.shtml)
- Agilent characterization and compliance test (http://www.agilent.com/find/USB)

Article Sources and Contributors

HTC 7 Surround *Source*: http://en.wikipedia.org/w/index.php?title=HTC_7_Surround *Contributors*: Captain-tucker, Chris Ssk, CommonsDelinker, Eegorr, GoingBatty, HTCPHONE2010, Iamcool234, Illegal Operation, Imeriki al-Shimoni, JamalAlhabeil, McHale, MeInTheNewWorld, Ral725, The Seventh Taylor, Uturnaroun, ZebraheadCH, 6 anonymous edits

Windows Phone *Source*: http://en.wikipedia.org/w/index.php?title=Windows_Phone_7 *Contributors*: .:Alex:., 1mac4u, 1wolfblake, 4th-otaku, A Quest For Knowledge, AQFK, Aaaaplay, Abhishikt, Adityahbk, Airplaneman, Alan Liefting, AndrewHowse, Andries, Anthony Appleyard, Antonyh3, Appliance matt, Arghya139, Artifact2008, Attilios, BaldPark, Banej, Bardicunderlord, Barek, Basileias, Bazingamast007, BenBen1234, Bnkumar.k, Brianhama, Brianreading, Bryan.burgers, Btx40, C628, CalumCookable, Cameron Scott, CaptainStack, Casey boy, Chambo622, Chris Ssk, Chriscatto, ChromeFirst, Coilgunman222, CommonsDelinker, Computerwizkid, Coolaaron88, Coriolus, Crazynas, Crumb, Cumbiagermen, Curb Safe Charmer, Dainapeter, Darwin-rover, Dayewalker, December21st2012Freak, Diego Grez, Dogcatrabbit, Doniago, Dorsal Axe, Dr.K., EVula, Eb.eric, EdJohnston, Electricjolt, Enemenemu, Enterprise12, EoGuy, ErrantX, Eskimo.the, Fabsss, Fetchcomms, Ffooxx 2006, Finnrind, Fourthords, France64160, Frostedglcok, Gary King, Ghodannywahyudi99, Glenn, Gogo Dodo, Golf1052, Greendude33, Gregzeng, Haleme, Hay264, Hcaandersen, Heimis90, Hervegirod, Histrion, Hoseabrown, Hydrox, INTPnerd, IRWolfie-, Icairns, Iceman247, Illegal Operation, Intelati, Interframe, JDubman, JLaTondre, JamesNK, Jason24589, Jbreckenridge, Jerryobject, Jhripley, Jim.henderson, JohnJamesWIlson, Jolio81, Josephers, Jrkart99, KAMiKAZOW, Kasajian, Kellyselden, Kenny goo, Kethn, Kiranerys, Kixzer, Kkm010, Koman90, Kwiki, Kypr8, L daruwala, Lachliggity, Lesser hoo hoo, Lester, Leszek Jańczuk, LjL, Lkt1126, Lonaowna, Looie496, Loppyloplop7, LordArtemis, MER-C, MJF2000, Ma8thew, Manuelt15, Manway, Markbenecke, Martarius, MbdSeattle, Mernen, Minna Sora no Shita, Modamoda, Monzoone, Mortense, Mushroom9, My76Strat, Myscrnnm, N4931, NapoliRoma, Newbie82, Nezdek, Nick lovel04, Nickbedford, NoKiweatL2, NonStick, Norm mit, Nuujinn, Ohnoitsjamie, Okungnyo, Onyxqk, PPCInformer, PRRfan, Pak1standby, PeSHIr, PeterJohnson, Philg88, Philip Trueman, Pi, Pipodj, Plau, Pnm, Pointillist, Pol098, Pradeepviswav, Privateboz, Pushpinder86, Pyasin16, Quilnux, Racklever, Radear2, Rhoadrunner, Rixs, Rl, Robert Varga, RobertMfromLI, Rodwac, Rogerwt123, RomanySaad, Rps5, Ryan Norton, SENS11, SLBoy.Ivo, Sainath468, Salilshukla, Scottxbenson, Sebculture, Seefrank, Seifip, Shagna, Shamalyguy, Shangho, Shearonink, Silvergoat, Slavon37, Softdevusa, Solidsnake1211, Some jerk on the Internet, Soumyasch, Stevennic, SuperHamster, Superzohar, Surfo, Taz789, Tbhotch, Tenomk, TerraFrost, TheTechFan, TheWeirdMouse, Tomy9510, ToolSidOF3, Tragic romance, Turdburglar15, Usman956732, Utcursch, Uturnaroun, Venkatarangan, Vinokirk, ViperSnake151, Wgfinley, Woohookitty, Wpguru, Wreiad, Wysprgr2005, Xizer, Xpclient, Yamamoto114, Yworo, ZigZagZoug, ZirconiumTwice, 590 anonymous edits

AT&T Mobility *Source*: http://en.wikipedia.org/w/index.php?title=AT%26T_Mobility *Contributors*: 221br70a, 24 biggest fan, AEMoreira042281, Abdhiraj, Abhimat.gautam, Adamdavid85, Admrboltz, Adrian, Agoode, Aido2002, Aj4110lz, Akcarver, Alasdair, AlexanderHaas, AlistairMcMillan, Allen3, Aloughman, Alphachimp, Alpta, Amatulic, Andros 1337, Andy Marchbanks, Andyiou52, Angelo2525, Angr, Ann Stouter, Antandrus, Aomarks, Armbrust, Aspects, Athensoh, Audi152, AussieLegend, Aymatth2, BT14, Bammon, Banstaman, Bearcat, Beetstra, Beland, Benandorsqueaks, Big Oto, Big.P, Bingo ringo, Bjj07, Blackjack48, Blargh29, BloodInMySaltstream, BlueMint, Bobolon5, Boothy443, Boutitbenza 69 9, Bpg1968, BrandonR, Brim, BrotherFlounder, Brout8, Brownings, BruceDude, Bundas, CDMACORE, Cacophony, CalJW, Calwatch, Cameron789787, Can't sleep, clown will eat me, CaribDigita, CaseyPenk, Catgut, Centrx, CesarB, Cfergie, Ch Th Jo, Chambo622, Chayashida, Cherrydude, Chester Markel, Chowbok, Chris 73, Chris the speller, Chriswiki, Cingular hitman, Cingularlover, Cliffb, Cloud02, Cola2706, Colorvision, Cookiemonsta123, Coolcaesar, Cory Malik, Cpcheung, CrashingWave, CrazyElk, Cswardrep, Cuenca, D6, DMG413, Dale Arnett, Darkdigger, Darkfur93, Darth Panda, Darthdogbro, Dave6, Davewho2, David Haslam, Davodd, Dawnseeker2000, Dbalic, Dck7777, Dcooper, DeLarge, Desertsky85451, Desmond Hobson, Dgies, Dhaluza, Dialh, Dina, Discospinster, Dleav, DocWatson42, Don-Don, Dondilio, Dondondon, DowneyOcean, Drtimofey, DuKot, Duja, Durin, DylanW, E.aldelgir, EJDyksen, Edinborgarstefan, Eeekster, Eegorr, Elrocco1614, Elss, EnsRedShirt, Entrpy, Epbr123, Erik16, Escape Orbit, Estrategy, Evice, Evilhomer2300, Favonian, Fcx56, Ferdinand h2, Feydey, Firsfron, Flavious27, FlowerGirl, Fraziersmith92, Fred Bradstadt, Fruitloopeater, GGreeneVa, Gaius Cornelius, Gdo01, George100, GoldDragon, Googolme, Greenshed, Griffin5, Groink, Gu1dry, Guinness man, Gurch, Gus Polly, Gwernol, Hankbolito, Harmil, Hateless, Hblaney1, Hdt83, Hemidemisemiquaver, Highlander0012, Highlander1112, Hilary2u, Hollowman512, HoserHead, Hotgigs, Husond, Hypemick1980, ICberg7, IMac4ME, Iandiver, Iceberg3k, Igor Filippov, Ijedsigj, Ikescs, Immiphone, Inky, Insanity Incarnate, Irishguy, IronChef, IronWolve, Ithinkhelikesit, Ixfd64, J.delanoy, J450NH3, JForget, JLaTondre, JNW, James.pole, Japanese Searobin, Jauerback, Jcembree, Jdavidb, Jeff Fries, Jeffq, Jeffrey Mall, Jer v, Jerem43, Jerry, Jerryseinfeld, JesseW, Jgera5, JimXugle, Jmchuff, Jmoz2989, Jmrv75, Jnavas, Joe1997, Johnbelden, Johnbrownsbody, Jon32000, Jonajosh, Jonel, Jonnty, Jonpaulusa, Jonrev, Joolz, Josephf, Jstohler, Juanito925, Kadin2048, KansasCity, Kbdank71, Ke5crz, Keizers, Kesh, Keyser Söze, Khatru2, KillMJ132, Kilo-Lima, Kiranerys, Kitch, Kman618, Kmccoy, Knicholls, Koman90, Korifrank9922, Kukini, Kungfuazn, Kungming2, Kuru, Kwsn, KyleAndMelissa22, Lampython, Lasdlt, Lensovet, Lesbianadvocate, Lethe, Leuqarte, Lexicon, Lexlex, Lgeorgehsv, Libcub, Lightmouse, Linnell, Linuxerist, Locust43, Lola006, Loompyloompy313, Loren36, Lostchicken, M2Ys4U, MI canuck, MZMcBride, Mabdul, Magicalboy, Makeyouwork07, Maksdo, Manop, Marcus Finch, Mariod505, Mashford, Masterpjz9, Mathiastck, Matthewsoft, Melab-1, MementoVivere, Mendaliv, Mets501, Mfrancis87, Mgmirkin, Mhking, MiKESTERR, Minimac, Mintchocicecream, Mmccalpin, Momo san, Monkeyman, MonoManFom, Moonwick, Morio, MorrisS, Mphung, Mrherch89, Mroach, Mrsanitazier, Muriness, Mwyland, N328KF, Nana209, Naohiro19, Natalie Erin, Nate Silva, NeoChaosX, Neurolysis, Neutrality, Newyork4me, Nfg536, Nguerrero03, Nich01asx, Night Gyr, Ninja5624, Nintendude, Nishkid64, Nmz, Nollij, Notmicro, NovaFan8311, Oknazevad, Onopearls, Ouimetnick, PGWG, Pascal666, Patcat88, Pavel Vozenilek, Plainsong, Polenta3, Postdlf, Psantora, Puertorico.pr, QD4rmBAMA, Qwertyqazqaz, RBBrittain, RTG, RadicalBender, Radiosband, Radon210, RainbowCrane, RainbowOfLight, Raja99, RattleMan, Ravenhull, Rawmustard, Ray Radlein, Rbyrd8100, Realitycheckmate, Repetition, Rich Farmbrough, Richiekim, Rj, Rjd0060, Rjsteve34, Rjwilmsi, Rklawton, Rodhullandemu, Rodriguez9127, Roguegeek, Rrius, Rupertslander, Rwils, RxS, Ryulong, SCEhardt, SQFreak, ST47, Sailingtaz, Sakura Avalon, SandBoxTheVideoGame, Sansookid, Sardanaphalus, Saturday, Scepia, Schnell, Scorchus, Seabhcan, Sean D Martin, Search4Lancer, Serein (renamed because of SUL), Seth Nimbosa, Shake waves2001, Shankarnikhil88, Shirulashem, Shizane, Shoessss, Shoy, SilkTork, Skew-t, Skiasaurus, SkylineEvo, Slo-mo, Sloanlier, SmartestChild, Smash, Sneak n' love, Sohailstyle, Space toaster, SpacedOut, Speer320, Spinboy, Spitfire8520, SpongePedia WikiPants, Squiggleslash, Starionwolf, StarlitGlitter, Stemonitis, Stephen doctrin, Steven Weston, Stickguy, Stizz, Strunke, Sue Rangell, Sumsum2010, SuperJere, TEG24601, THEunique, TMC1982, TPM2006, TSO1D, Tabletop, Tacticality, Taneumann, Taral, Tbenzinger, Tbutler, Ted mcwilliams, The undertow, The.4thestate, The2ndflood, TheKMan, TheNewPhobia, This user has left wikipedia, Timneu22, Timouton, Tiptoety, Tjp1982, Tmuller2, Tngu77, Tony16, Totie, Trbmagic, Trevor MacInnis, Tsizzles55, USA300million, UncleBubba, Uvaduck, VCA, Vegaswikian, Verbalcontract, Viakenny, Videmus Omnia, Vincent.premysler, ViperSnake151, Viqsi, Vkmaxwell, Voyagerfan5761, Vroo, WJetChao, Warren, WatchingDragon, WestinPeachtree, Wheelboss, WhisperToMe, Whursey, Wibbble, Wikiklrsc, Wikiliki, Wikiman123321, Wikipedianinthehouse, Will Beback, William789, Wirelessman99, Woohookitty, X570, X958, Xnatedawgx, Xyqo, Yamamoto Ichiro, Yellowdesk, Yong, ZS, Zachary0220, Zachcoggin, Zimbabweed, Zztzed, Zzxc, , 1103 anonymous edits

HTC Corporation *Source*: http://en.wikipedia.org/w/index.php?title=HTC_Corporation *Contributors*: 5994995, 85Zed, Abriele93, Acanthopteroctetoidea, Accurimbono, Adrian Firth, Alanpierson, Alawadhi3000, Alexius08, Alexmok, AlistairMcMillan, Allen3, Armando, Aspects, Aviados, Avono, Azurepalm, Bandylack, Bayerischermann, Bearcat, Beetstra, Bender235, Benson85, Bobo192, Bongomatic, Bovineone, C 1, CZmarlin, CalumCook234, Cameron Scott, Carrlos, Caseybutt, Chenga, ChickenFalls, Chiu.co, Cinnamon42, Clubley2, Cocoaguy, Colenso, CommonsDelinker, Crabula, Crampedson, Crh66, Cromas, Curb Chain, Cyclonenim, Cyril, Daddygee, Dale Arnett, Dancter, Danski14, Dark-Fire, Darkinho, Darrenackers, Dawnseeker2000, Deepizza, Dequinix, Dicklyon, DireWolf, DmitryKo, DoingYourMom12321, DtD, Earthreach, Ed g2s, Ercolev, Erik9, Eyas Hajeh, FT2, Falcon9x5, Flubeca, Fudoreaper, Garryparton, Gary King, Geopgeop, Georgy90, Gogo Dodo, Goretsky, Gorinin, Grim Littlez, Gtoopuf, Gyrobo, HHHH, Haakon, Hanifbbz, Heiterheiter, Hiteshrajbhagat, Hos505, Htchien, Huangcjz, Hurhu, Hyins, I, Podius, Iadrian yu, IanVaughan, Ief, Illegal Operation, Indefatigable, IndianCorporates, Ingwar JR, IronGargoyle, Isnow, Itsme, J04n, JCDenton2052, JGXenite, JLaTondre, Jamcib, Jamie Kitson, Jbishop6660, Jcembree, Jeff G., Jerryobject, Jfruh, Jgw, Jim.henderson, Jjolsen, Jlin, Joej1985, Joelittlejohn, Johnteslade, JonHarder, Jonathen Skews, Joriki, Joseph Solis in Australia, Jpbowen, KAMiKAZOW, Kadoboy, Kingebrow, Kingofdetroit, Klushka, Kocio, Koman90, Kozuch, Kuru, Kylu, Kyng, L Kensington, Lambyuk, Laranand, LilHelpa, LorenzoB, Maball54, Madchester, MafiotuL, Manop, Mardus, Marek69, MasterMan, MasterOfTheXP, Mathiastck, McHale, MementoVivere, Meow, Mervyn, Miami33139, Michael2487, Mifter, Mmcminn2000, MrOllie, Multivariable, N2e, Nakon, Natalie indeed, Neerz, Netgarden, Nick Ottery, Nicolas1981, Nino63004, Noir, Notedgrant, Notmicro, Nvasi, Ohnoitsjamie, OlEnglish, Olivegarden10, Omegatron, Orangysb, Otduff, OwenBlacker, P.gobin, PJDiddy, Patiwat, Paulbrec, Payo, PermanentE, Petersam, PhilSchaffner, Philip Trueman, Piroroadkill, Plasmafire, Plau, Prof. Iain Scott, QG3618, QueBurro, Qwfp, R'n'B, RA0808, Racepacket, Ratarsed, Reflex Reaction, Rehnn83, Reliablesoft, RiV 2005, Rich Farmbrough, Richardgaywood, Richardlai, Ricky@36, Rileyfreeman, Rm20010, Roosterrulez, Rorydaredking, Rospaya, Rpop, Rshin, SEAL6, Saimhe, Sainath468, Samuel Curtis, Sandman30s, Sapwood2, Sarrus, Seneschal, Sertion, Shawnc, Shortride, SilkTork, SiobhanHansa, Slo-mo, Spacepotato, Speculatrix, Spunking, Strcat, Strunke, Suruena, Svgalbertian, THEunique, TMV943, Telepheedian, The Anome, The Seventh Taylor, The Thing That Should Not Be, Thegreatglobetrotter, Thegsrguy, Tpansky, Trentjohnson, Tsdek, Turf91, Turgan, UberMan5000, Vchao, Vchimpanzee, Vegarn, Veselin nedev, Viakenny, W3bbo, Werdna, WiZZLa, Wibbble, Wikipelli, Wikiuser100, Wirefree, Witchwooder, Woodsstock, Woohookitty, XboxLiveSlayer, Xecuterbox, Yatito, Yusufguleryuz, Zahnrad, Zanter, ZavuloN, 576 anonymous edits

HTC 7 Mozart *Source*: http://en.wikipedia.org/w/index.php?title=HTC_7_Mozart *Contributors*: Anjiro, Auntof6, Chobro, Chris Ssk, CommonsDelinker, DRS1973, FamilyGuy1998, Fokouli, Illegal Operation, JamalAlhabeil, Mikahuntington, Myscrnnm, Pnm, Roif456, Skudo900630, WissensDürster, ZebraheadCH, احمد دمح ىفطصم ىسيدلا, 8 anonymous edits

Snapdragon (system on chip) *Source*: http://en.wikipedia.org/w/index.php?title=Snapdragon_%28system_on_chip%29 *Contributors*: 1exec1, AABR, Abdull, Adrian-polglase, Allsunnydays, Arlo.Clauser, Artem-S-Tashkinov, BD2412, Bender235, Bpdlr, Brianski, CPGus511, Cecilyen, Coolbho3000, Cybercobra, DJTachyon, Dimawik, DmitryKo, Dominik78, Ehn, Electron9, Epsilonsa, Eugrus, Ewbrowning, Fram, Frap, Fullyrandomtandem, Garion96, Ged UK, GoingBatty, GreenAsJade, Gsarwa, Gu1dry, Guoguo12, Hi-Tone, Hkultala, Huangcjz, Illegal Operation, Imroy, Jantangring, Jeffdgr8, Jhay777, Joeinwap, Jonathan-Morris711, Jontintinjordan, Jt, Jwoodmansee, KAMiKAZOW, Kierant, Kozuch, Kushal one, Lazugod, Lester, Lexchandra, Little Professor, MadnessInside, Mardus, Marginoferror, Mariostache, MarkMLl, Matthew V Ball, MoreNet, Munemune, Mysdaao, Nanouk, Nathancac, Pierre5018, PizzaMan, Prcjac, Privatechef, R'n'B, RHaworth, Radaghast, Raysonho, Rudefyet, ScottHW, Sd7755, Shreddy, SidP, Signisia, Slacka123, Slavon37, Ssniper, Superxain, Syp, TMV943, TeKaBaKa, Ujainday, User931, Vvijayk, Wintermute314, Wreiad, Xcrivener, ZebraheadCH, Zouzzou, , 208 anonymous edits

Accelerometer *Source*: http://en.wikipedia.org/w/index.php?title=Accelerometer *Contributors*: Aayushg1991, Aceleo, AcoustiMax, Aido2002, Alex.g, Aliento, AlistairMcMillan, Aluvus, Andy Dingley, Antonbarabashov, Ariefwn, Ashlux, Ateachout, Auntof6, Axel.mulder, Baburaj kp, Beland, BigHairRef, Buechner, CalumCook234, Cambrant, Camw, CaptainG, CezarkennySeF,

Chadcarr, Chancek, Chances1, Charles Matthews, Chilichaz33, Chris the speller, Christopherjfoster, Chriswaterguy, ColinHelvensteijn, Dale Arnett, Dancter, Dane13, Daniel Olsen, Davwillev, Debresser, Decan tulahi, Demorphica, Denisarona, Dicklyon, Dmd, Dmn, Dontmentionit, Dr Gangrene, Dravick, Drbreznjev, Drunken Pirate, Duwem, E smith2000, Ed g2s, Edcolins, Edgar v. Hinüber, Editore99, Eh kia, Elangsto, Electric hits, Emerson7, Eridani, EugeneUngar, Ev, Evil saltine, Finfindiscotheque, Fixentries, Frederick Munster, Fredrik, FrummerThanThou, Fstanchina, Fuutott, Getsnoopy, Gioto, Giulianorock, Glaurung, Glengarry, Glenn, Greensoda, Greg L, Gufiak, Headbomb, Heron, Hillshum, Hipocrite, HiroJudgement, Hooperbloob, Ibbn, Icairns, Iluvcapra, Indigoanalysis, Iridescent, Irregular Shed, J04n, JJ Harrison, JamesBWatson, JanBurg, Jarus, Jayr168, Jhsounds, Jim.henderson, Jjmgoblue, Jmrowland, Jo Weber, JoaoRicardo, JohannVisagie, Jorgbrown, Jsherm2, Juan Fco. Araya, Jwigton, KKL, KSchmitt6755, KTo288, Katieh5584, Kelly Martin, Kenyon, Khommel, Khullah, Kku, Kokoo, Kwikwish, Kylegordon, Laderaranch, Leonard G., Linas, Lonelymiesarchie, Lumos3, Luotianci, Lwoodyiii, Maande10, Maclarcs, Mangogirl2, Marcmarroquin, Marklwil, Marshallsumter, Martarius, Mawich, Mbierman, Michael.poplawski, Mike1024, MikelZap, Mikemurphy, Mit-Mit, Mizouman, Mmarroquin, Mmkils, Motumboe, Mozzerati, Mtffm, NawlinWiki, Nicopipo2, Nneonneo, Nopetro, Nposs, Omegatron, Oneiros, Onion25, Oxwil, Pichote, Pietrow, Pinethicket, Pinkgothic, Primenay13, Pwnage97, Quintote, Qutezuce, Ramblinknight, Rated325, Referencellc, ReyBrujo, Rich Farmbrough, RichG, Richiekim, Rjwilmsi, Rlsheehan, Rmsuperstar99, Robin Johnson, Ronz, Rustyguts, Rwalker, Ryanrs, Salsb, Sasha5113, SatyrTN, Sbharris, Sbmehta, Scepia, Sebastiangarth, SecretDisc, Seldo, Serrano24, Shopingjs, Skimaniac, Smadidas, Socrates2008, Srleffler, Sternutator, Steve Pucci, Suihkulokki, Symmetric, Syrthiss, TestingInfo, Themfromspace, Timneu22, Timo Honkasalo, Tmcw, Topbanana, Tordail, Tushar.bhatnagar, UncleSamPatriot, Unwill, Vclaw, Vegaswikian, Viknesh1996, WLU, Waleswatcher, Wasell, WilcoxonResearch, Wkkm007, Wolfkeeper, Youaremyrefuge, Zaybertamer, Zazou25, Ztolstoy, Zunaid, 413 anonymous edits

Secure Digital *Source*: http://en.wikipedia.org/w/index.php?title=Secure_Digital *Contributors*: 24frames, 81120906713, 99bluefoxx, 9allenride9, A Man In Black, AVRS, Aab298347927384, Adam Schloss, Adam2288, Adsp, Aeons, Agateller, Aikenware, Airplaneman, Akaustav, Alansohn, Aldie, AlexJ, Alexbuster500, Alexthekiwi, Allaun, Alphaman, Alvis, Amoiwangjy, Amram99, Andrevan, Andrew sh, AndrewKepert, Andrewpmk, Andru nl, Angela, Angerdan, Animehawaii, Appraiser, Aqn, Aribronstein, Armando, Arrowcatcher, Asim18, AssetBurned, Atanasov, Atompowered, Austinmurphy, Autoandragogist, Axcelis555, AzaToth, BENNYSOFT, BPM, Bastique, Bdelisle, Bearcat, Beeline23, Beland, Bergsten, Bholstege, Billgordon1099, Binba, Bjdehut, Blanchardb, BlindWanderer, Blorg, Bobblewik, Bobianite, Boboangel, Bookandcoffee, Bostwickenator, Brer vole, Brian Patrie, Brian-L, Briandgregory, Brianski, Brouhaha, Buster2058, Buuneko, C 1, Calcprogrammer1, Caleson, Calor, Can't sleep, clown will eat me, Canrocks, CaseyPenk, Caspertheghost, Catskul, Cdrum, CesarB, Chandu15, CharlotteWebb, Chealer, ChrisCork, Chrisjj3, Christian75, Ckmac97, Climber22, Clorox, Cmdrjameson, Compellingelegance, Compuguy1088, Coneslayer, Consumed Crustacean, Cootiequits, Copysan, Corge, Coughinink, CrookedAsterisk, Csendesmark, Cyawman, Cybercobra, Cybertai, CyclePat, D0nj03, DMahalko, Dabomb87, Dah31, Dale Arnett, Damian Yerrick, Dan100, DanMS, Dancingonmice, Dancter, Dandv, Daniel Newby, Dankru, Darin-0, Darkxsun, Darrien, Daveswagon, David from Downunder, David spector, David.Monniaux, Dawd, Deineka, Dennbruce, DervishD, Dhanashekar, Djm1279, Doc glasgow, DocWatson42, Doctorno, Dogcow, Drabant, Draconiator, Dreadstar, Drmies, Dustin Howett, Długosz, EJSawyer, Echtner, Ed Poor, Eftpotrm, Electricnet, Electron9, ElementFire, Elemesh, Elwilke, EncMstr, Ente75, Erencexor, Ericzhang789, Esowteric, Eurleif, Evice, Excirial, Exearly, ExplicitImplicity, ExportRadical, FCartegnie, Fast healthy fish, Feedmecereal, Feydey, FlashSheridan, Flasher, Fleminra, Flowerflower, Fmillour, Freddyzdead, Fresheneesz, Fudoreaper, Fullerene, Funandtrvl, Furrykef, Fvw, Gadol87, Gaselvin, Ge0rge, Geekosaurus, Glockner, Ghaib, Glaw10, GodGell, Goosnarrggh, GraemeLeggett, Grafen, Graham87, GregorB, Grunt, HDCase, Haipa Doragon, Hankwang, Hansa11, Harlekeyn, Harvester, Hebrides, Henry W. Schmitt, Heron, Heybales, Hgrosser, Hoagg, Hooperbloob, HoserHead, IAmAI, IW.HG, IceHunter, Ichimonji10, IkonicDeath, Iliev, Impi, Intelliot, InternetMeme, Irayo, Ismouton, J.delanoy, JJLatWiki, Jachim, JackTinWNY, Jafeluv, James JK, JamesAM, JamesTeterenko, Jdowland, Jeffq, Jerryobject, Jhsounds, Jidanni, Jim McKeeth, Jim.henderson, Jj2235, Jlslspam, Jnavas, Joaoplim, Jocunddus, JohnAlexan, Johnteslade, JordoCo, Jory, JudyJohn, Justin Ormont, Jvr725, Jw21, Kartano, Kaszeta, Kazrak, Kbdank71, Kiimmyluff, Kinema, Kingpin13, Kjohna, Klkmiooo, KnowBuddy, Koolman2, Korj.by, Kozuch, KryptoCleric, KsprayDad, Kungfujoe, Kungming2, Kusunose, LM1987, Lamrock, Lavenderbunny, Lbecque, Le Déchaîné, LeoO3, Leszek Jańczuk, Liaocyed, Lightmouse, LilHelpa, Lindosland, Little Professor, Littleendian, Lord Nightmare, Lordsatri, LostLeviathan, LovesMacs, Lucasreddinger, MER-C, MMuzammils, Macrakis, MarXidad, Marianocecowski, Mark Renier, Martarius, Maury Markowitz, Maxim Leyenson, Maxí, Mboverload, Memorysuppliers, Metallica10, Michael L. Kaufman, MichaelJanich, Microsofkid, Mihai Capotă, Mikus, Misterkillboy, Mju7nhy6, Mmj, Mnts, Modster, Moreati, Moxfyre, MrBurns, Mram80, Mrdungx, Mrzaius, Mwarren us, Myke2020, N1truX, N5iln, NEMT, Nahuel.carvajal, Nasukaren, Neelix, Neilka, NerdyNSK, Neurolysis, Newzack, Nil Einne, Nintendude, Nixdorf, Nnan, Noir, Noq, Notmicro, Now3d, Ntsimp, Nulltransfer, Nurg, Nv8200p, OMA2k, Oahiyeel, Oe1kenobi, Offbeatcinema, Ojigiri, Oliverdl, Omegatron, Oxymoron83, Pabouk, Paranoid, PatrikR, Peace81, Peaceninja28, Peter Campbell, Peter S., Peterl, Peterrobbemond, Peyre, Photographerguy, Photoguy439, Phr, Pickmynose1999, PierreOssman, Pinkevin, Piper8, Placi1982, Plasmaroo, Pranjal87, ProhibitOnions, Psharrock, Psiddall, Quaeler, Queefycreatures, Ravedave, Ravenperch, Razor2988, Rcawsey, RealGrouchy, Reaperducer, Rebroad, RichardTector, Riddley, RingtailedFox, Rjc34, Rjquillin, Rjwilmsi, Rlcantwell, Rmsuperstar99, Rmunn, Rofl cawpters, Rohan Jayasekera, RoseTech, Rosenbluh, Rstoplabe14, Ruud Koot, SD Card Version 2.Wiki.0, SGBailey, SMD915, SPKirsch, SRG275, Saimhe, Saipraneethn, Saltmiser, Sam8, SanGatiche, Sandymac, Saravanants, Sasan.j, Saverworld2, Sbmeirow, SchnitzelMannGreek, Scotty jasper2000, SeanAhern, Seaphoto, Sebadee, Sedimin, Sergei, Shadowjams, Shanes, SidP, Sin-man, Skathol, Skierpage, Skyykj, Slakr, Slashme, Slicing, Smack, Smileyborg, Smyth, Snolygoster, Speedevil, Spikesagal, Stanleyivan, Starnestommy, Steinsomers, Stephan Leeds, Stevage, Stuston, Sunny house, Surf243, Suruena, Szzuk, TAC-3, TCav, Tacvek, Tarquin, The Giant Puffin, The Thing That Should Not Be, TheDoober, Themoment, ThevillagesmithE, Thewikipedian, Thunderbird2, Thunderpenguin, TimSE, Timharwoodx, Tintenfischlein, Tiredofscams, Tkgd2007, Tmansour, TobleRone, Todd Vierling, Toehead2001, Tomgibbons, Tone, Tony1, Tonyhawz, Totakeke423, Towel401, Tpbradbury, Triscal1990, Tristan Schmelcher, Twinmostech, UU, UberMan5000, UltraMagnus, Vdcappel, Versus22, Vexorg, Viggio, Viol8or, Vladsinger, VoxLuna, Waffle, Wammes Waggel, Wanderer099, Wbuch, Weezee, Wernher, WhiteDragon, Whitis, Wibbble, WikHead, WinTakeAll, Wine Guy, Wirbelwind, Wjejskenewr, Wjw0111, Wolfling, WriterHound, Wrlee, Wtshymanski, Wuhwuzdat, XP1, Xdddex, Xenon54, Xmhd, Xonicx, Xpclient, Yaniv Kunda, Yealout, Z hosen, Zarcillo, Zarenor, Zbrahead91, Zerpent, Ziga, Zodon, Zoicon5, Zurotai, Zviangi, 1101 anonymous edits

USB *Source*: http://en.wikipedia.org/w/index.php?title=Universal_Serial_Bus *Contributors*: 0612, 132qwerty, 1wolfblake, 223fms, 4176shelton, 5 albert square, A Train, A0183305, A5b, AJ6J, AMK1211, ANTMAN, AaronLLF, Aaronbrick, Aaweisen, Abce2, Abdul raja, Abune, Access Denied, Accounting4Taste, Accurizer, Acela Express, Achraf52, AdRock, Adambro, Addps4cat, AdeMiami, Adot, AdunaicLayman, Advantecheautomation, Aeons, Agateller, Agilent.Showard, Agitate, Ahivarn, Ahoerstemeier, Ahruman, Aido2002, Aidoor, Airplaneman, Airsplit, Ajfweb, Ajitesh Madai, Ajpvalente, Akasnakeyes, Alansohn, Aldie, Aleksandrit, Alex mayorga, Alexander.stohr, Alexei123, Algae, Algocu, Ali@gwc.org.uk, AlistairMcMillan, Allesbehalve, Alpha 4615, Alphathon, Altermike, Alvin-cs, Alyssa3467, Amdma2003, AmiAyalon1969, AnOddName, Andrew sh, Andrew19881123, AndrewLeeson, Andreweaton, Andrewpmk, Andy Marchbanks, Andyzweb, Angela, Anibius, Anonymi, Ant75, Antandrus, Antialias, Apoc2400, AppOnKey, Archer3, Arichnad, Aries21erika, Arkrishna, Arlie davis, Arm, Armando, ArnoldReinhold, Aronzak, Arthur Rubin, Asafoot, Asbjornu, Asetwofifty, Ashenai, Ashleypurdy, Asigler, Asim mahakul, Asim18, Asparagus, Atalsandip, Atamido, Atannen, Atenor1932, Atlant, Attilios, Audrius u, Avalyn, AxelBoldt, Axlq, Azhyd, B. van der Wee, BCG999, BZRatfink, Baoap, Baricom, Bcrscahh198987, BdON003, Bdesham, Beao, Becksguy, Beland, Belvdme, Bender2k14, Benhoyt, Benignbala, Benny45boy, BesigedB, Bestalex, Bgkwtnyqhzor, Big gun, Bitchbastardd, BjKa, Black Walnut, BlackWolf, Blacklife85, Blu3tooth, Blugill, Bo98, Bobbb53, Bobblewik, Bobo192, Bobrayner, Boijunk, Boing! said Zebedee, BorgQueen, Bratch, Brenbren92, Brewthatistrue, BrianRecchia, Brianpeiris, Brianski, BrickMcLargeHuge, Brighterorange, Brim, Brisvegas, BrockF5, Brouhaha, Brownsteve, Bruns, Bryan Derksen, Brycen, Bssasidhar, Btornado, Bullzeye, Bungle, Burnte, Burrin.p, Buxtehude, Bytencoder, Bz2, C0nanPayne, CALR, CAkira, CCFreak2K, CINCABF, CWenger, Cabe6403, Cactus.man, Cadre, Caiaffa, Calabraxthis, Calltech, Cambrant, CambridgeBayWeather, Can't sleep, clown will eat me, CannonR, Capbat, Capricorn42, CaptainClawz, CaptainVideoJW, Carmichael95, Casper2k3, Caspertheghost, Caulde, Ccradio, CecilWard, Ceros, CesarB, Cgumas, Charles Gaudette, Chealer, Chiefcoolbreeze, Chimin 07, Chipp C. Chovain, Chowbok, Chridd, Chris Chittleborough, Chris G, Chris53516, ChrisFAF, Christopher Parham, Chronulator, Chrumps, Chrylis, Chuunen Baka, Ciaranjns, Clam0p, Classical geographer, Cleared as filed, ClickRick, Closedmouth, Closenplay, Cmcqueen1975, Cmgross, Cobaltbluetony, Codemsan, Colenso, Colfer2, Colinkgl, Colonies Chris, Cometstyles, CommonsDelinker, Compellingelegance, Compilation finished successfully, Coneslayer, Conrad.Irwin, Conversion script, CoolFox, Coolstr24, Cootiequits, Coreywalters06, Coroboy, Corrosive.element, Corvus cornix, CountFlux, Courcelles, Crazy Fox, Crispmuncher, Crissov, Crywalt, Ctachme, Ctjf83, Cwalger, Cwolfsheep, Cybercobra, Cyferz, D zone, D0762, DKqwerty, DMahalko, DSRH, Da Vynci, Daft Creftsman, DaisyChainer, DaleDe, Dalziel 86, Damian Yerrick, Dan100, Daniel Pritchard, Danski14, DarkFalls, Darkdawn75, Darkknight512, Darkride, DarthShrine, Dave laird, Dave6, David Biddulph, DavidCary, DavidFarmbrough, DavidMarsh, Davidcx, Davidfstr, Davidgordon101, Dcook32p, De728631, Dead3y3, DeadEyeArrow, Deh, Dekisugi, Deletros, Den fjättrade ankan, DenisBlanchette, Depakote, Derek Ross, DerekMorr, Derepi, Devin6687, Diamondland, Diderot's dreams, Dirtyfrank10, Dispenser, Dittaeva, Djbyrne17, Djcapelis, Djmckee1, Dlother, DmitTrix, DmitryKo, Dnas, Doc Magnus, DocWatson42, Dolda2000, Don-vip, DopefishJustin, Doradus, Dori, Dougher, DragonHawk, Drdomestod, Drewdc90, Ds13, Dsgreat3, Duckbill, Dvelez1985, Dysprosia, E.boyer7, E090, EagleOne, Earle Martin, Ed Brey, Ed Poor, Ed g2s, EdLegend, Edgar181, Editore99, Edokter, Ee79, Efitu, Egil, Egmontaz, Ehn, Eighthave, Electron9, ElementFire, Elpincha, Elsendero, Elvey, Emerson7, Energyequation, Engineerism, Enochlau, Enquire, Enviroboy, Epbr123, EpiVictor, Epson291, Equendil, Eric Wester, Espertus, Eurleif, Eus Kevin, Evert Mouw, Everyking, Evice, Evil saltine, Excirial, Eyreland, Ezhuttukari, F l a n k e r, FT2, Fabulatech, Facts707, Fahidka, Failofbeaner, False vacuum, Falsifian, Favonian, Feedmecereal, FelisLeo, Ffgamera, Fibonacci, Fieldday-sunday, Filceolaire, Filelakeshoe, Filzstift, Finnegar, Fir0002, Fireaxe888, Fishnet37222, Flazh, Flightsoffancy, Floorwalker, FlyingToaster, Fox, Frammy7, Frap, Fredrik, Fromageestciel, Fudoreaper, Fumo7887, Func, Fustigate314159, Fuzzie, Fvw, G2M, GDonato, Gabbe, Gail, Gaius Cornelius, Gardar Rurak, Gauravsangwan, Geekstuff, Geniac, Georgy90, Gh5046, Ghartwig, Ghermann3, Giftlite, Gilliam, Ginsengbomb, GioCM, Giraffedata, Givemeornot, Glenn, Gogo Dodo, GoldKanga, Good Intentions, Goodone121, Gordeonbleu, Gosale, Gpearson2, Graglin, Grand Am, GrandMoffVixen, Grapetonix, Gregben, GregorB, Gregsea, Grendelkhan, Groink, Groogle, Gryffon5147, Gschizas, Gssq, Guaka, Gutza, Guyjohnston, Gyll, H2g2bob, H3llbringer, Ha runner, Hankwang, Hans Dunkelberg, Hargrimm, Harvester, Haseo9999, Hayabusa future, Hcaaman, Hcs, Hduckman, Hellgi, Heron, Hgrosser, Hideyuki, Hlandro77, Hoemaco, Hohohob, Homerjay, Honeycake, Hoof Hearted, Hooperbloob, Hopp, HorsePunchKid, Hughcharlesparker, Husky, Hydrargyrum, Hyins, I am a true NOS person, I dream of horses, IAMBATMANDEALWITHIT, INVERTED, ISquishy, Ian Pitchford, Ian01, IanGM, Iandiver, Icairns, IceSlicer, IcedNut, Icydid, Ilia Kr., Iloveandersoncooper, Immunize, Imotor, Impasse, Imperator3733, Imroy, Inclusivedisjunction, Intelligentsium, InternetMeme, Intersofia, Intgr, IntrigueBlue, Iridescent, Irishguy, Isaac, Ixfd64, J.delanoy, J.smith, JCLAWSON, JDX, JHP, JLaTondre, JLuna103, JR98664, JTN, JaGa, Jacob Poon, Jake Wartenberg, James Kemp, Janto, Jargoness, Jason One, Jasper Deng, Jaufrec, Jay-the-mad'n, Jcarroll, Jdthood, Jdwinx, Je007, Jean-Baptiste Catté, Jeffq, Jeffro77, Jeffthejiff, Jeltz, JeremyA, Jerryobject, Jesse Viviano, Jesslovesmeganandpie, Jesster79, Jezmck, Jhsounds, Jidanni, Jim A H, Jim-Bob Harris, Jim.henderson, Jimgawn, Jimmi Hugh, Jjjjooooeeee123, Jmayorga5, Jmrowland, Jmundo, Jnavas, Jnsears, JoanneB, Joaopaulo1511, JoeOnSunset, Joeinwap, Joel D. Reid, Johammer, John Fader, John Reaves, JohnCD, JohnSawyer, Johnteslade, Jon125, JonHarder, JonSangster, Jonathan Grynspan, Jonathunder, Jonel, Jonverve, Jordan Brown, JosephCampisi, Josh Parris, Joshua Scott, Jossi, Jpgordon, Jruderman, Jrvz, JtMinahan, Julesd, Julienrl, JustinRossi, Juux, Jwidjaja, Jwinius, Jwoodger, KJRehberg, KUsam, KVeil, Kajaco2, Kalan, Kaldosh, Karn, Katanada, Katyare, Kazvorpal, Kbh3rd, Kbolino, Kbrose, Keilana, Kelleheretic, KelleyCook, Kemiv, Kendal Ozzel, Kenny sh, Kenyon, KerryVeenstra, Kghose, Khalid hassani, Kia.Rahimi, Kilo-Lima, King of Hearts, Kiranerys, Kiteinthewind, Kittens-Pedro, Kjkolb, Kjohna, Kniesten, KnowledgeOfSelf, Knuckleskin, Kocio, Kooo, Koopa turtle, Kostmo, Kozuch, Kralljа, Krash, Krishvanth, Kristof vt, Ktr101, Kudret abi, Kuru, Kvng, L Kensington, LN2, La Pianista, Lab16, Lada103, Laefer, Lambtron, Landroo, Lankiveil, LarryLACa, Lawpjc, Leandrod, Letdorf, Lhopitalified, Lightmouse, Linas, Ling Kah Jai, Link83, Lipatden, Lithpiperpilot, Little Mountain 5, Livebird, LivingShadow, Lockoom, LodeRunner, Logan, Lonaowna, LorenzoB, Lotje, LouScheffer, Lovely Chris, Lowellian, Lowenddan, Lucasreddinger, Luna Santin, Lupo, M1ss1ontomars2k4, MCG, MER-C, MISTYFAN4EVER8887, MNAdam, MSR93,

MaGioZal, Maaf, Mabdul, Mac, Mad with power, Madison Alex, Manassehkatz, Mange01, Manishearth, Manuactive, Manuelt15, Margin1522, Mark Yen, Markhoney, Markstuart44, Marstronix, Martarius, Maschneider, Materialscientist, Matt Crypto, Matta33178, Maury Markowitz, MaxHund, Maximus Rex, Maxis ftw, Maxvip, Maxwellversion2, Maxí, Mayhemm, Mazin07, McGeddon, McSly, Mcarling, Mcorazao, Meaningful Username, Mendaliv, Mentifisto, Merlinsorca, Mewtu, Mgdunn, Michael Hardy, Michaelkourlas, MidMadWiki, Midlandstoday, MightyWarrior, Mike.lifeguard, Mike1024, Mikeblas, Mikus, Mild Bill Hiccup, Miquonranger03, Mirddes, Misocroft, Mj fan1995, Mjpieters, Mkdw, Mkouklis, Mlewis000, Mnw2000, Mobius, ModsRule, Modster, Mojo-chan, Morcheeba, Moreati, Mortense, Moxfyre, Mpa, Mr Minchin, Mr.Z-man, MrBurns, MrDolomite, MrFish, MrOllie, MrSomeone, MrStalker, Mrappleton, Mrschimpf, Mrtangent, Mschlindwein, Muad, Mugunth Kumar, Muhandes, Mulad, Mun206, Munge, Mushroom, Music Sorter, Mvjs, Mwarren us, Mwilso24, Mxjose, My man Friday, Mysekurity, Mysidia, N2e, N5iln, NHRHS2010, NZR, Nageh, Nahaj, Nanshu, Naohiro19, Narge, Nasukaren, NawlinWiki, Nchalada, Neil916, Neilm, NellieBly, Netkinetic, Niceter, Nick, NickVeys, Nikkibella21, Nikpapag, Nil Einne, Nishantjr, Nixdorf, Nk, Nlaporte, Nnetala, Noahspurrier, Nopetro, Norm, Nrbelex, Nsaa, Nubi78, Nullaman, Nurg, Nw15062, O18, Odam, Odatus, Oehoeboeroe, Ohnoitsjamie, OlEnglish, Old Moonraker, Olekrst, OllieFury, OllyH, Oman9978, Omegared23, Omegatron, Omicronpersei8, Oneiros, Oni Ookami Alfador, OpenToppedBus, Osarius, Osram, Ottawa4ever, Outlyer, OverlordQ, Owengibbins, Oxymoron83, PRRfan, Pabouk, Padillah, Paradoctor, Paranoid, Parmastew, Patriarch, PaulColby, PaulMcCulloh, Pavel.nps, Pbacina, Pchov, Pcuser42, Peak, Pedant17, Pedro, Pembers, Perardi, Perfectblue97, Perryizgr8, Persian Poet Gal, Peruvianllama, PeterGrecian, Peyre, Pgan002, Pgiii, Phantasee, Phantomsteve, Phatom87, Phgao, PhilKnight, Philip Trueman, Phip, Phobie, Phoenix314, Photographerguy, PiMaster3, PiaH, Pie4all88, Pietrow, Pinkadelica, Pinkcious, Pip2andahalf, Pivotto, PizzaMan, Pjrm, PlatinumX, PlayStation 69, Plugwash, PluniAlmoni, Pmc, Pne, Pointillist, Pol098, Polluks, Poppafuze, Prari, Praveentech, Preslethe, ProhibitOnions, Puchiko, Pugetbill, Pugglewuggle, Pushpinder86, Qasimnb, Qk, Quadell, Quentin Jones, Quinxorin, Quizzicus, Qxz, R!SC, R'n'B, R2D2 C3PO R2D2, RAMChYLD, RJHall, RadioactiveKiller1, Radiojon, Ragzouken, Ramu50, Randomperson666111, Raptor007, RasputinAXP, Ravenperch, Ravensfan5252, Raymond Hill, Raysonho, Rbellika, Rbrittner, Rchandra, Rcingham, Rdnetto, Reach Out to the Truth, Realist2, Rearden9, Rebroad, Red, RedWolf, Redsully, Reeceyyyy15, RegentsPark, Reisio, Remember the dot, Remove indian propaganda, Res2216firestar, Retodon8, Revera, Revrant, RexNL, Rexrodo, Rfc1394, Rfl, Rhindle, Rhobite, Rich Farmbrough, Richardcavell, Richardpitt, Ridge Runner, Rikonate, Ringbang, Rinix, Rip969, RitKill, Rjwilmsi, Rmhand, Rmsuperstar99, Rob Cranfill, Robert Loring, RobertG, Rocastelo, RockMaestro, Rodneyorpheus, Rohasnagpal, Romanm, Ronark, Ronhjones, RoninRVP, Rossheth, Rpkrawczyk, Rprpr, RufusThorne, Rupert Clayton, RussNelson, Russella, Rwestafer, Rwwww, Ryper, S. Neuman, S.K., SLi, SMC, Sadalmelik, Sadharan, SafariSunD, Saimhe, Salamurai, Salavat, Salvio giuliano, Sam Hocevar, Samarqandi, Samuel Grant, Sango123, Sanspeur, Sasuke Sarutobi, Saulo Paiva, Savant13, Sawyeriii, Sbmeirow, SchmuckyTheCat, Scollk, Scope creep, Scuac, Sdsds, Seidenstud, Semicolons, SentientSeven, Servel333, Sfoehner, Shamilton, Shayno, Sherool, Shirimasen, Shjacks45, Shniken1, Shop Bucuresti, SidP, Sietse Snel, Sigma 7, Silica-gel, Siliconov, Sillydragon, SimonEast, SimonP, Simulcra, Sintau.tayua, SivaKumar, Skylinerspeeder, Sleepy Sentry, Sleske, Sligocki, Smbp, Smjg, SmolderinCorpse, Smyth, Snafflekid, Snkcube, Snori, SnowRaptor, Soliloquial, Some jerk on the Internet, Someguy1221, Sonicsuns, Sonjaaa, Soren121, South Bay, SpadesSlick, Spamboy, Spartan117458, Spe88, Spik3balloon, Spike, Srijan89, Srleffler, Stacrd, Staffwaterboy, Stan Shebs, StarkRG, Ste.Ri, SteinbDJ, Stephan Leeds, Stephen Gilbert, Stephen Morley, Stephenchou0722, Steven Zhang, Steveprutz, Stimson, StoneGiant, Storm Rider, Strait, Strom, Stuart P. Bentley, StuffOfInterest, Sublastic, Sully76, Sumonbd, SuperBeav, Superway25, Suvituuli, Suwa, Sven Godin, Svick, Sweeet ann, T Arndt 40, T4bits, THEN WHO WAS PHONE?, Tacvek, Tagishsimon, Tarquin, Taw, Taxman, Tbolioli, Technopat, Techtonic, Tecknode, TedE, Tedder, Thaiio, The Pondermatic, The Rambling Man, The Thing That Should Not Be, The Wild Falcon, The guy who kleanz, The.Computer1, TheDoober, TheFearow, TheJosh, Theboss48506, Thebrains29, Thechuck, Thegreatestmoever3, Theodore Kloba, Thomas Blomberg, Thorpe, ThreeBlindMice, Threyon, Thumperward, Thunderboltz, Tiefighter, TiffaF, Tim Forcer, Timaru, Timbrowne, Timeshift9, Timhoppen, Timm123, Timwi, Titoxd, Tjpeople, Tkgd2007, Tkteun, TobyDZ, Tobz1000, Todd Vierling, Tollsjo, Tom.freeman, Tomashcu60, Tomaxer, Tomg1234, Tomlee1968, Tommy2010, Tony1, Tooki, Torturetyler, Toyotatundra, Tpbradbury, Transfinite, Traut, Traxs7, Treygdor, TrickyNik, Truerock2, Tsedit, Tsk, Turkeyphant, TutterMouse, Tweek17, Tweisbach, Twintop, Twocs, Tymothy, UdovdM, Ugnich Anton, Uisqebaugh, Undeference, UnicornTapestry, Unnyn, Unyoyega, Urhixidur, Usb3o, Useight, User5910, Utcursch, Utility Monster, Uwe Hermann, V Brian Zurita, Varnish, VasilievVV, Vaughan Pratt, Versus22, Vespristiano, Vhann, Victorgrigas, Vid, Viktor, Viljo Viitanen, Vippylaman, Voetsjoeba, Voidxor, Vuongfat, Wabernat, WackyBoots, Waiwai933, Walter Görlitz, Waltervulej, Wavelength, Wehe, Wesrick, Whitis, Whompage, WhosAsking, Whowhodilly, WikHead, Wiki alf, Wiki777777ikiw, Wikid77, Wikifan21century, Wikkrockiana, Wiknerd, Wimt, Windsok, Wizpig64, Wizzy, Wmahan, Wolbo, Wolfgang Kufner, Wonko, Woohookitty, WorldGentoo, Worm That Turned, Wtf305, Wtmitchell, Ww, WynnSmith, Wyveryx, X!, X1cygnus, Xavier86, Xezbeth, Xmm0, Xolom, Xorx, Y2kboy23, Yanayz, Yeastygoodness, Yellowdesk, Yetasoli, Yitzhak, Yosh3000, Yuckhil, Z hosen, Zac67, ZakuSage, Zalgo, Zebe, Zenlax, Zenotek, Zephyric, Zephyris, Zidane2k1, Zippanova, Zirconscot, Zlhappyone, Zntrip, Дарко Максимовић, පසිඳු කාවින්ද, , 2546 anonymous edits

Image Sources, Licenses and Contributors

File:HTC 7 Surround.jpg *Source*: http://en.wikipedia.org/w/index.php?title=File:HTC_7_Surround.jpg *License*: Creative Commons Attribution-Sharealike 2.0 *Contributors*: Kai - Christian

File:WindowsPhone7logo.png *Source*: http://en.wikipedia.org/w/index.php?title=File:WindowsPhone7logo.png *License*: unknown *Contributors*: Aaaaplay

File:Windows Phone 7 Start screen.png *Source*: http://en.wikipedia.org/w/index.php?title=File:Windows_Phone_7_Start_screen.png *License*: unknown *Contributors*: Chris Ssk, Illegal Operation, Koman90, Skier Dude, Soundvisions1, Sven Manguard

File:Windows Phone 7 Timeline.svg *Source*: http://en.wikipedia.org/w/index.php?title=File:Windows_Phone_7_Timeline.svg *License*: Creative Commons Attribution-Sharealike 3.0 *Contributors*: User:Modamoda

File:Nokia-windows-phone-7.jpg *Source*: http://en.wikipedia.org/w/index.php?title=File:Nokia-windows-phone-7.jpg *License*: unknown *Contributors*: Jason24589

File:Internet Explorer Mobile 9.png *Source*: http://en.wikipedia.org/w/index.php?title=File:Internet_Explorer_Mobile_9.png *License*: unknown *Contributors*: Illegal Operation

File:WPZuneHub.jpg *Source*: http://en.wikipedia.org/w/index.php?title=File:WPZuneHub.jpg *License*: unknown *Contributors*: Chris Ssk, Hugahoody, Illegal Operation, Koman90

File:WP7Bing.jpg *Source*: http://en.wikipedia.org/w/index.php?title=File:WP7Bing.jpg *License*: unknown *Contributors*: Bkell, Chris Ssk, Hugahoody, Illegal Operation, Koman90

File:Microsoft Office Mobile 2010 hub.png *Source*: http://en.wikipedia.org/w/index.php?title=File:Microsoft_Office_Mobile_2010_hub.png *License*: unknown *Contributors*: Calmer Waters, Illegal Operation, Sven Manguard

File:WinPhoneUpdate.jpg *Source*: http://en.wikipedia.org/w/index.php?title=File:WinPhoneUpdate.jpg *License*: unknown *Contributors*: Chris Ssk, Hugahoody, Illegal Operation, Interframe, Koman90, Skier Dude, Sven Manguard

File:Windows Phone Marketplace.png *Source*: http://en.wikipedia.org/w/index.php?title=File:Windows_Phone_Marketplace.png *License*: unknown *Contributors*: Chris Ssk, Illegal Operation, Koman90, Skier Dude, Sven Manguard

File:Samsung Omnia 7.jpg *Source*: http://en.wikipedia.org/w/index.php?title=File:Samsung_Omnia_7.jpg *License*: Creative Commons Attribution 3.0 *Contributors*: StevieBallz (http://www.pocketpc.ch/members/stevieballz.html)

Image:AT&T logo.svg *Source*: http://en.wikipedia.org/w/index.php?title=File:AT&T_logo.svg *License*: unknown *Contributors*: Alpta, Armbrust, Eastmain, Fæ, Henry W. Schmitt, Jeff G., KansasCity, Koman90, LAX, Mendaliv, Oxymoron83, Presidentman, Sfan00 IMG, TheNewPhobia, Videmus Omnia, Zigger, 10 anonymous edits

File:Increase2.svg *Source*: http://en.wikipedia.org/w/index.php?title=File:Increase2.svg *License*: unknown *Contributors*: Sarang

Image:ATT Mobility HQ De Kalb Co GA.JPG *Source*: http://en.wikipedia.org/w/index.php?title=File:ATT_Mobility_HQ_De_Kalb_Co_GA.JPG *License*: Creative Commons Attribution-Sharealike 3.0 *Contributors*: User:Keizers

Image:Cingular logo.svg *Source*: http://en.wikipedia.org/w/index.php?title=File:Cingular_logo.svg *License*: unknown *Contributors*: Neurolysis

Image:AT&TWirelessLogo.png *Source*: http://en.wikipedia.org/w/index.php?title=File:AT&TWirelessLogo.png *License*: unknown *Contributors*: Admrboltz, Alpta, KansasCity, MBisanz, Markhurd, RadicalBender, Sue Anne, Zzyzx11

Image:CingularLogoNew.svg *Source*: http://en.wikipedia.org/w/index.php?title=File:CingularLogoNew.svg *License*: unknown *Contributors*: Koman90

Image:Attdevicesupportcenter.jpg *Source*: http://en.wikipedia.org/w/index.php?title=File:Attdevicesupportcenter.jpg *License*: GNU Free Documentation License *Contributors*: Gusgus, Kastey, Tbsdy lives

Image:Dobson transition banner.png *Source*: http://en.wikipedia.org/w/index.php?title=File:Dobson_transition_banner.png *License*: unknown *Contributors*: Calmer Waters, Ninja5624, Sreejithk2000

Image:Dobson cellular.png *Source*: http://en.wikipedia.org/w/index.php?title=File:Dobson_cellular.png *License*: unknown *Contributors*: User:Admrboltz, User:Andros 1337, User:Cydebot, User:PNG crusade bot

Image:Dobson cellularone logo.png *Source*: http://en.wikipedia.org/w/index.php?title=File:Dobson_cellularone_logo.png *License*: unknown *Contributors*: Ninja5624, Sfan00 IMG

File:Htc new logo.svg *Source*: http://en.wikipedia.org/w/index.php?title=File:Htc_new_logo.svg *License*: Trademarked *Contributors*: Svgalbertian at en.wikipedia.

File:Qualcomm-SnapDragon.jpg *Source*: http://en.wikipedia.org/w/index.php?title=File:Qualcomm-SnapDragon.jpg *License*: unknown *Contributors*: Adrian-polglase, DJTachyon

Image:Accelerometer.png *Source*: http://en.wikipedia.org/w/index.php?title=File:Accelerometer.png *License*: Public Domain *Contributors*: Original uploader was SatyrTN at en.wikipedia

Image:SD Cards.svg *Source*: http://en.wikipedia.org/w/index.php?title=File:SD_Cards.svg *License*: GNU Free Documentation License *Contributors*: Tkgd2007,

Image:8 bytes vs. 8Gbytes.jpg *Source*: http://en.wikipedia.org/w/index.php?title=File:8_bytes_vs._8Gbytes.jpg *License*: Creative Commons Attribution 2.0 *Contributors*: Daniel Sancho from Málaga, Spain

Image:MicroSD MemoryCard 002.jpg *Source*: http://en.wikipedia.org/w/index.php?title=File:MicroSD_MemoryCard_002.jpg *License*: Creative Commons Attribution-Sharealike 2.1 *Contributors*: User:Kropsoq

Image:Secure digital card usb-adapter 3.jpg *Source*: http://en.wikipedia.org/w/index.php?title=File:Secure_digital_card_usb-adapter_3.jpg *License*: GNU Free Documentation License *Contributors*: User:Hundehalter

Image:MicroSDFDrive.JPG *Source*: http://en.wikipedia.org/w/index.php?title=File:MicroSDFDrive.JPG *License*: Creative Commons Attribution-Sharealike 3.0 *Contributors*: User:Ravenperch

Image:USB-SD-Cards.jpg *Source*: http://en.wikipedia.org/w/index.php?title=File:USB-SD-Cards.jpg *License*: Public Domain *Contributors*: User:AssetBurned

Image:Sd insides.png *Source*: http://en.wikipedia.org/w/index.php?title=File:Sd_insides.png *License*: Creative Commons Attribution-Sharealike 3.0 *Contributors*: User:Saltmiser

File:SDHC Speed Class 2.svg *Source*: http://en.wikipedia.org/w/index.php?title=File:SDHC_Speed_Class_2.svg *License*: Creative Commons Attribution-Sharealike 3.0 *Contributors*: User:Kizar

File:SDHC Speed Class 4.svg *Source*: http://en.wikipedia.org/w/index.php?title=File:SDHC_Speed_Class_4.svg *License*: Creative Commons Attribution-Sharealike 3.0 *Contributors*: User:Kizar

File:SDHC Speed Class 6.svg *Source*: http://en.wikipedia.org/w/index.php?title=File:SDHC_Speed_Class_6.svg *License*: Creative Commons Attribution-Sharealike 3.0 *Contributors*: User:Kizar

File:SDHC Speed Class 10.svg *Source*: http://en.wikipedia.org/w/index.php?title=File:SDHC_Speed_Class_10.svg *License*: Creative Commons Attribution-Sharealike 3.0 *Contributors*: User:Kizar

Image:SD-extreMEmory 2GB alt innen.jpg *Source*: http://en.wikipedia.org/w/index.php?title=File:SD-extreMEmory_2GB_alt_innen.jpg *License*: Creative Commons Attribution-Sharealike 3.0 *Contributors*: User:Manorainjan

File:Sdadaptersandcards.jpg *Source*: http://en.wikipedia.org/w/index.php?title=File:Sdadaptersandcards.jpg *License*: Creative Commons Attribution 3.0 *Contributors*: Original uploader was Atanasov at en.wikipedia Later version(s) were uploaded by Brybry26 at en.wikipedia.

File:Czytnik kart.jpg *Source*: http://en.wikipedia.org/w/index.php?title=File:Czytnik_kart.jpg *License*: GNU Free Documentation License *Contributors*: User:FxJ

File:Sd4gy crop.jpg *Source*: http://en.wikipedia.org/w/index.php?title=File:Sd4gy_crop.jpg *License*: Creative Commons Attribution-Sharealike 3.0 *Contributors*: User:Wirepath

Image:SanDisk SD Card 8GB.jpg *Source*: http://en.wikipedia.org/w/index.php?title=File:SanDisk_SD_Card_8GB.jpg *License*: Creative Commons Attribution-Sharealike 3.0 *Contributors*: User:Asim18

Image:HP PhotoSmart SDIO Kamera.jpg *Source*: http://en.wikipedia.org/w/index.php?title=File:HP_PhotoSmart_SDIO_Kamera.jpg *License*: Creative Commons Attribution-Sharealike 2.0 *Contributors*: User:Afrank99

Image:Canon hf100 with memory card.jpg *Source*: http://en.wikipedia.org/w/index.php?title=File:Canon_hf100_with_memory_card.jpg *License*: Creative Commons Attribution-Sharealike 3.0 *Contributors*: User:Mikus

Image:Flash memory cards size.jpg *Source*: http://en.wikipedia.org/w/index.php?title=File:Flash_memory_cards_size.jpg *License*: unknown *Contributors*: Afrank99, Ivob, MMuzammils, Moxfyre, Rhe br, Solomon203, Warden, Zxb, 1 anonymous edits

File:MSD68GB.jpg *Source*: http://en.wikipedia.org/w/index.php?title=File:MSD68GB.jpg *License*: Public Domain *Contributors*: User:Ittiz

file:Certified USB.svg *Source*: http://en.wikipedia.org/w/index.php?title=File:Certified_USB.svg *License*: unknown *Contributors*: KUsam, Zyxw, 1 anonymous edits

file:USB.svg *Source*: http://en.wikipedia.org/w/index.php?title=File:USB.svg *License*: Creative Commons Attribution-Sharealike 2.5 *Contributors*: User:LivingShadow

file:USB Icon.svg *Source*: http://en.wikipedia.org/w/index.php?title=File:USB_Icon.svg *License*: Public Domain *Contributors*: Mobius at en.wikipedia

file:USB TypeA Plug.JPG *Source*: http://en.wikipedia.org/w/index.php?title=File:USB_TypeA_Plug.JPG *License*: Creative Commons Attribution-Sharealike 2.0 *Contributors*: User:Afrank99

file:EBusb ports.JPG *Source*: http://en.wikipedia.org/w/index.php?title=File:EBusb_ports.JPG *License*: Creative Commons Attribution-Sharealike 3.0 *Contributors*: User:Ravenperch

file:Certified Hi-Speed USB.svg *Source*: http://en.wikipedia.org/w/index.php?title=File:Certified_Hi-Speed_USB.svg *License*: unknown *Contributors*: Frap, KUsam, Zyxw

file:SuperSpeed USB.svg *Source*: http://en.wikipedia.org/w/index.php?title=File:SuperSpeed_USB.svg *License*: unknown *Contributors*: Caspertheghost

file:USB pipes and endpoints (en).svg *Source*: http://en.wikipedia.org/w/index.php?title=File:USB_pipes_and_endpoints_(en).svg *License*: unknown *Contributors*: User:Bdesham

file:USB Front Port.jpg *Source*: http://en.wikipedia.org/w/index.php?title=File:USB_Front_Port.jpg *License*: Public Domain *Contributors*: User:Wyveryx

file:SanDisk Cruzer Micro.png *Source*: http://en.wikipedia.org/w/index.php?title=File:SanDisk_Cruzer_Micro.png *License*: Public Domain *Contributors*: User:Beao, User:Evan-Amos

file:Types-usb new.svg *Source*: http://en.wikipedia.org/w/index.php?title=File:Types-usb_new.svg *License*: GNU Free Documentation License *Contributors*: User:Darx

file:USB 3.0 Micro B plug.PNG *Source*: http://en.wikipedia.org/w/index.php?title=File:USB_3.0_Micro_B_plug.PNG *License*: Creative Commons Attribution 3.0 *Contributors*: User:Tosaka

file:Male and Female USB Connectors.jpg *Source*: http://en.wikipedia.org/w/index.php?title=File:Male_and_Female_USB_Connectors.jpg *License*: GNU Free Documentation License *Contributors*: Original uploader was Zephyris at en.wikipedia Later version(s) were uploaded by Osama bin dipesh at en.wikipedia.

file:Usb extension cable.jpg *Source*: http://en.wikipedia.org/w/index.php?title=File:Usb_extension_cable.jpg *License*: Creative Commons Attribution-Sharealike 2.5 *Contributors*: Original uploader was J.smith at en.wikipedia

file:esatap.jpg *Source*: http://en.wikipedia.org/w/index.php?title=File:Esatap.jpg *License*: Public Domain *Contributors*: User:Colinkgl

file:Usb connectors.JPG *Source*: http://en.wikipedia.org/w/index.php?title=File:Usb_connectors.JPG *License*: Public Domain *Contributors*: User:Viljo Viitanen

file:MicroB USB Plug.jpg *Source*: http://en.wikipedia.org/w/index.php?title=File:MicroB_USB_Plug.jpg *License*: Creative Commons Attribution-Sharealike 3.0 *Contributors*: User:masamic

file:Mini usb AB.jpg *Source*: http://en.wikipedia.org/w/index.php?title=File:Mini_usb_AB.jpg *License*: Creative Commons Attribution 2.5 *Contributors*: User Mgdunn on en.wikipedia

File:USB Std A.png *Source*: http://en.wikipedia.org/w/index.php?title=File:USB_Std_A.png *License*: Creative Commons Attribution-Sharealike 3.0 *Contributors*: User:Music Sorter

File:USB Std B.png *Source*: http://en.wikipedia.org/w/index.php?title=File:USB_Std_B.png *License*: Creative Commons Attribution-Sharealike 3.0 *Contributors*: User:Music Sorter

File:USB Mini B.png *Source*: http://en.wikipedia.org/w/index.php?title=File:USB_Mini_B.png *License*: Creative Commons Attribution-Sharealike 3.0 *Contributors*: User:Music Sorter

File:USB Micro A.png *Source*: http://en.wikipedia.org/w/index.php?title=File:USB_Micro_A.png *License*: Creative Commons Attribution-Sharealike 3.0 *Contributors*: User:Music Sorter

File:USB Micro B.png *Source*: http://en.wikipedia.org/w/index.php?title=File:USB_Micro_B.png *License*: Creative Commons Attribution-Sharealike 3.0 *Contributors*: User:Music Sorter

File:USB Mini-B receptacle.png *Source*: http://en.wikipedia.org/w/index.php?title=File:USB_Mini-B_receptacle.png *License*: Creative Commons Attribution-Sharealike 3.0 *Contributors*: User:Music Sorter

File:USB Micro-AB receptacle.jpg *Source*: http://en.wikipedia.org/w/index.php?title=File:USB_Micro-AB_receptacle.jpg *License*: Creative Commons Attribution-Sharealike 3.0 *Contributors*: User:Music Sorter

File:USB Micro-B receptacle.jpg *Source*: http://en.wikipedia.org/w/index.php?title=File:USB_Micro-B_receptacle.jpg *License*: Creative Commons Attribution-Sharealike 3.0 *Contributors*: User:Music Sorter

file:Ext usb.gif *Source*: http://en.wikipedia.org/w/index.php?title=File:Ext_usb.gif *License*: Attribution *Contributors*: Groink, Julienrl

file:Popport.jpg *Source*: http://en.wikipedia.org/w/index.php?title=File:Popport.jpg *License*: Public Domain *Contributors*: w:en:User:EiZeiEiZei

file:USB Twisted Pair.svg *Source*: http://en.wikipedia.org/w/index.php?title=File:USB_Twisted_Pair.svg *License*: Public Domain *Contributors*: User:Inductiveload, User:WolfWings

file:Micro USB phone charger.jpg *Source*: http://en.wikipedia.org/w/index.php?title=File:Micro_USB_phone_charger.jpg *License*: Public Domain *Contributors*: User:Reinraum

file:USBVacuumCleaner.jpg *Source*: http://en.wikipedia.org/w/index.php?title=File:USBVacuumCleaner.jpg *License*: Public Domain *Contributors*: User:Raysonho

License

Creative Commons Attribution-ShareAlike 3.0 Unported - Deed

This is a human-readable summary of the Creative Commons Attribution ShareAlike 3.0 Unported License (http://en.wikipedia.org/wiki/Wikipedia:Text_of_Creative_Commons_Attribution-ShareAlike_3.0_Unported_License)
You are free:

- to **Share**—to copy, distribute and transmit the work, and
- to **Remix**—to adapt the work

Under the following conditions:

- **Attribution**—You must attribute the work in the manner specified by the author or licensor (but not in any way that suggests that they endorse you or your use of the work.)
- **Share Alike**—If you alter, transform, or build upon this work, you may distribute the resulting work only under the same, similar or a compatible license.

With the understanding that:

- **Waiver**—Any of the above conditions can be waived if you get permission from the copyright holder.
- **Other Rights**—In no way are any of the following rights affected by the license:
  - your fair dealing or fair use rights;
  - the author's moral rights; and
  - rights other persons may have either in the work itself or in how the work is used, such as publicity or privacy rights.
- **Notice**—For any reuse or distribution, you must make clear to others the license terms of this work. The best way to do that is with a link to http://creativecommons.org/licenses/by-sa/3.0/

GNU Free Documentation License

As of July 15, 2009 Wikipedia has moved to a dual-licensing system that supersedes the previous GFDL only licensing. In short, this means that text licensed under the GFDL can no longer be imported to Wikipedia. Additionally, text contributed after that date can not be exported under the GFDL license. See Wikipedia:Licensing update for further information.

Version 1.3, 3 November 2008 Copyright (C) 2000, 2001, 2002, 2007, 2008 Free Software Foundation, Inc. <http://fsf.org/>
Everyone is permitted to copy and distribute verbatim copies of this license document, but changing it is not allowed.

0. PREAMBLE

The purpose of this License is to make a manual, textbook, or other functional and useful document "free" in the sense of freedom: to assure everyone the effective freedom to copy and redistribute it, with or without modifying it, either commercially or noncommercially. Secondarily, this License preserves for the author and publisher a way to get credit for their work, while not being considered responsible for modifications made by others.

This License is a kind of "copyleft", which means that derivative works of the document must themselves be free in the same sense. It complements the GNU General Public License, which is a copyleft license designed for free software.

We have designed this License in order to use it for manuals for free software, because free software needs free documentation: a free program should come with manuals providing the same freedoms that the software does. But this License is not limited to software manuals; it can be used for any textual work, regardless of subject matter or whether it is published as a printed book. We recommend this License principally for works whose purpose is instruction or reference.

1. APPLICABILITY AND DEFINITIONS

This License applies to any manual or other work, in any medium, that contains a notice placed by the copyright holder saying it can be distributed under the terms of this License. Such a notice grants a world-wide, royalty-free license, unlimited in duration, to use that work under the conditions stated herein. The "Document", below, refers to any such manual or work. Any member of the public is a licensee, and is addressed as "you". You accept the license if you copy, modify or distribute the work in a way requiring permission under copyright law.

A "Modified Version" of the Document means any work containing the Document or a portion of it, either copied verbatim, or with modifications and/or translated into another language.

A "Secondary Section" is a named appendix or a front-matter section of the Document that deals exclusively with the relationship of the publishers or authors of the Document to the Document's overall subject (or to related matters) and contains nothing that could fall directly within that overall subject. (Thus, if the Document is in part a textbook of mathematics, a Secondary Section may not explain any mathematics.) The relationship could be a matter of historical connection with the subject or with related matters, or of legal, commercial, philosophical, ethical or political position regarding them.

The "Invariant Sections" are certain Secondary Sections whose titles are designated, as being those of Invariant Sections, in the notice that says that the Document is released under this License. If a section does not fit the above definition of Secondary then it is not allowed to be designated as Invariant. The Document may contain zero Invariant Sections. If the Document does not identify any Invariant Sections then there are none.

The "Cover Texts" are certain short passages of text that are listed, as Front-Cover Texts or Back-Cover Texts, in the notice that says that the Document is released under this License. A Front-Cover Text may be at most 5 words, and a Back-Cover Text may be at most 25 words.

A "Transparent" copy of the Document means a machine-readable copy, represented in a format whose specification is available to the general public, that is suitable for revising the document straightforwardly with generic text editors or (for images composed of pixels) generic paint programs or (for drawings) some widely available drawing editor, and that is suitable for input to text formatters or for automatic translation to a variety of formats suitable for input to text formatters. A copy made in an otherwise Transparent file format whose markup, or absence of markup, has been arranged to thwart or discourage subsequent modification by readers is not Transparent. An image format is not Transparent if used for any substantial amount of text. A copy that is not "Transparent" is called "Opaque".

Examples of suitable formats for Transparent copies include plain ASCII without markup, Texinfo input format, LaTeX input format, SGML or XML using a publicly available DTD, and standard-conforming simple HTML, PostScript or PDF designed for human modification. Examples of transparent image formats include PNG, XCF and JPG. Opaque formats include proprietary formats that can be read and edited only by proprietary word processors, SGML or XML for which the DTD and/or processing tools are not generally available, and the machine-generated HTML, PostScript or PDF produced by some word processors for output purposes only.

The "Title Page" means, for a printed book, the title page itself, plus such following pages as are needed to hold, legibly, the material this License requires to appear in the title page. For works in formats which do not have any title page as such, "Title Page" means the text near the most prominent appearance of the work's title, preceding the beginning of the body of the text.

The "publisher" means any person or entity that distributes copies of the Document to the public.

A section "Entitled XYZ" means a named subunit of the Document whose title either is precisely XYZ or contains XYZ in parentheses following text that translates XYZ in another language. (Here XYZ stands for a specific section name mentioned below, such as "Acknowledgements", "Dedications", "Endorsements", or "History".) To "Preserve the Title" of such a section when you modify the Document means that it remains a section "Entitled XYZ" according to this definition.

The Document may include Warranty Disclaimers next to the notice which states that this License applies to the Document. These Warranty Disclaimers are considered to be included by reference in this License, but only as regards disclaiming warranties: any other implication that these Warranty Disclaimers may have is void and has no effect on the meaning of this License.

2. VERBATIM COPYING

You may copy and distribute the Document in any medium, either commercially or noncommercially, provided that this License, the copyright notices, and the license notice saying this License applies to the Document are reproduced in all copies, and that you add no other conditions whatsoever to those of this License. You may not use technical measures to obstruct or control the reading or further copying of the copies you make or distribute. However, you may accept compensation in exchange for copies. If you distribute a large enough number of copies you must also follow the conditions in section 3.

You may also lend copies, under the same conditions stated above, and you may publicly display copies.

3. COPYING IN QUANTITY

If you publish printed copies (or copies in media that commonly have printed covers) of the Document, numbering more than 100, and the Document's license notice requires Cover Texts, you must enclose the copies in covers that carry, clearly and legibly, all these Cover Texts: Front-Cover Texts on the front cover, and Back-Cover Texts on the back cover. Both covers must also clearly and legibly identify you as the publisher of these copies. The front cover must present the full title with all words of the title equally prominent and visible. You may add other material on the covers in addition. Copying with changes limited to the covers, as long as they preserve the title of the Document and satisfy these conditions, can be treated as verbatim copying in other respects.

If the required texts for either cover are too voluminous to fit legibly, you should put the first ones listed (as many as fit reasonably) on the actual cover, and continue the rest onto adjacent pages.

If you publish or distribute Opaque copies of the Document numbering more than 100, you must either include a machine-readable Transparent copy along with each Opaque copy, or state in or with each Opaque copy a computer-network location from which the general network-using public has access to download using public-standard network protocols a complete Transparent copy of the Document, free of added material. If you use the latter option, you must take reasonably prudent steps, when you begin distribution of Opaque copies in quantity, to ensure that this Transparent copy will remain thus accessible at the stated location until at least one year after the last time you distribute an Opaque copy (directly or through your agents or retailers) of that edition to the public.

It is requested, but not required, that you contact the authors of the Document well before redistributing any large number of copies, to give them a chance to provide you with an updated version of the Document.

4. MODIFICATIONS

You may copy and distribute a Modified Version of the Document under the conditions of sections 2 and 3 above, provided that you release the Modified Version under precisely this License, with the Modified Version filling the role of the Document, thus licensing distribution and modification of the Modified Version to whoever possesses a copy of it. In addition, you must do these things in the Modified Version:

A. Use in the Title Page (and on the covers, if any) a title distinct from that of the Document, and from those of previous versions (which should, if there were any, be listed in the History section of the Document). You may use the same title as a previous version if the original publisher of that version gives permission.
B. List on the Title Page, as authors, one or more persons or entities responsible for authorship of the modifications in the Modified Version, together with at least five of the principal authors of the Document (all of its principal authors, if it has fewer than five), unless they release you from this requirement.
C. State on the Title page the name of the publisher of the Modified Version, as the publisher.
D. Preserve all the copyright notices of the Document.
E. Add an appropriate copyright notice for your modifications adjacent to the other copyright notices.
F. Include, immediately after the copyright notices, a license notice giving the public permission to use the Modified Version under the terms of this License, in the form shown in the Addendum below.
G. Preserve in that license notice the full lists of Invariant Sections and required Cover Texts given in the Document's license notice.
H. Include an unaltered copy of this License.
I. Preserve the section Entitled "History", Preserve its Title, and add to it an item stating at least the title, year, new authors, and publisher of the Modified Version as given on the Title Page. If there is no section Entitled "History" in the Document, create one stating the title, year, authors, and publisher of the Document as given on its Title Page, then add an item describing the Modified Version as stated in the previous sentence.
J. Preserve the network location, if any, given in the Document for public access to a Transparent copy of the Document, and likewise the network locations given in the Document for previous versions it was based on. These may be placed in the "History" section. You may omit a network location for a work that was published at least four years before the Document itself, or if the original publisher of the version it refers to gives permission.
K. For any section Entitled "Acknowledgements" or "Dedications", Preserve the Title of the section, and preserve in the section all the substance and tone of each of the contributor acknowledgements and/or dedications given therein.
L. Preserve all the Invariant Sections of the Document, unaltered in their text and in their titles. Section numbers or the equivalent are not considered part of the section titles.
M. Delete any section Entitled "Endorsements". Such a section may not be included in the Modified version.
N. Do not retitle any existing section to be Entitled "Endorsements" or to conflict in title with any Invariant Section.
O. Preserve any Warranty Disclaimers.

If the Modified Version includes new front-matter sections or appendices that qualify as Secondary Sections and contain no material copied from the Document, you may at your option designate some or all of these sections as invariant. To do this, add their titles to the list of Invariant Sections in the Modified Version's license notice. These titles must be distinct from any other section titles.

You may add a section Entitled "Endorsements", provided it contains nothing but endorsements of your Modified Version by various parties—for example, statements of peer review or that the text has been approved by an organization as the authoritative definition of a standard.

You may add a passage of up to five words as a Front-Cover Text, and a passage of up to 25 words as a Back-Cover Text, to the end of the list of Cover Texts in the Modified Version. Only one passage of Front-Cover Text and one of Back-Cover Text may be added by (or through arrangements made by) any one entity. If the Document already includes a cover text for the same cover, previously added by you or by arrangement made by the same entity you are acting on behalf of, you may not add another; but you may replace the old one, on explicit permission from the previous publisher that added the old one.

The author(s) and publisher(s) of the Document do not by this License give permission to use their names for publicity for or to assert or imply endorsement of any Modified Version.

5. COMBINING DOCUMENTS

You may combine the Document with other documents released under this License, under the terms defined in section 4 above for modified versions, provided that you include in the combination all of the Invariant Sections of all of the original documents, unmodified, and list them all as Invariant Sections of your combined work in its license notice, and that you preserve all their Warranty Disclaimers.

The combined work need only contain one copy of this License, and multiple identical Invariant Sections may be replaced with a single copy. If there are multiple Invariant Sections with the same name but different contents, make the title of each such section unique by adding at the end of it, in parentheses, the name of the original author or publisher of that section if known, or else a unique number. Make the same adjustment to the section titles in the list of Invariant Sections in the license notice of the combined work.

In the combination, you must combine any sections Entitled "History" in the various original documents, forming one section Entitled "History"; likewise combine any sections Entitled "Acknowledgements", and any sections Entitled "Dedications". You must delete all sections Entitled "Endorsements".

6. COLLECTIONS OF DOCUMENTS

You may make a collection consisting of the Document and other documents released under this License, and replace the individual copies of this License in the various documents with a single copy that is included in the collection, provided that you follow the rules of this License for verbatim copying of each of the documents in all other respects.

You may extract a single document from such a collection, and distribute it individually under this License, provided you insert a copy of this License into the extracted document, and follow this License in all other respects regarding verbatim copying of that document.

7. AGGREGATION WITH INDEPENDENT WORKS

A compilation of the Document or its derivatives with other separate and independent documents or works, in or on a volume of a storage or distribution medium, is called an "aggregate" if the copyright resulting from the compilation is not used to limit the legal rights of the compilation's users beyond what the individual works permit. When the Document is included in an aggregate, this License does not apply to the other works in the aggregate which are not themselves derivative works of the Document.

If the Cover Text requirement of section 3 is applicable to these copies of the Document, then if the Document is less than one half of the entire aggregate, the Document's Cover Texts may be placed on covers that bracket the Document within the aggregate, or the electronic equivalent of covers if the Document is in electronic form. Otherwise they must appear on printed covers that bracket the whole aggregate.

8. TRANSLATION

Translation is considered a kind of modification, so you may distribute translations of the Document under the terms of section 4. Replacing Invariant Sections with translations requires special permission from their copyright holders, but you may include translations of some or all Invariant Sections in addition to the original versions of these Invariant Sections. You may include a translation of this License, and all the license notices in the Document, and any Warranty Disclaimers, provided that you also include the original English version of this License and the original versions of those notices and disclaimers. In case of a disagreement between the translation and the original version of this License or a notice or disclaimer, the original version will prevail.

If a section in the Document is Entitled "Acknowledgements", "Dedications", or "History", the requirement (section 4) to Preserve its Title (section 1) will typically require changing the actual title.

9. TERMINATION

You may not copy, modify, sublicense, or distribute the Document except as expressly provided under this License. Any attempt otherwise to copy, modify, sublicense, or distribute it is void, and will automatically terminate your rights under this License.

However, if you cease all violation of this License, then your license from a particular copyright holder is reinstated (a) provisionally, unless and until the copyright holder explicitly and finally terminates your license, and (b) permanently, if the copyright holder fails to notify you of the violation by some reasonable means prior to 60 days after the cessation.

Moreover, your license from a particular copyright holder is reinstated permanently if the copyright holder notifies you of the violation by some reasonable means, this is the first time you have received notice of violation of this License (for any work) from that copyright holder, and you cure the violation prior to 30 days after your receipt of the notice.

Termination of your rights under this section does not terminate the licenses of parties who have received copies or rights from you under this License. If your rights have been terminated and not permanently reinstated, receipt of a copy of some or all of the same material does not give you any rights to use it.

10. FUTURE REVISIONS OF THIS LICENSE

The Free Software Foundation may publish new, revised versions of the GNU Free Documentation License from time to time. Such new versions will be similar in spirit to the present version, but may differ in detail to address new problems or concerns. See http://www.gnu.org/copyleft/.

Each version of the License is given a distinguishing version number. If the Document specifies that a particular numbered version of this License "or any later version" applies to it, you have the option of following the terms and conditions either of that specified version or of any later version that has been published (not as a draft) by the Free Software Foundation. If the Document does not specify a version number of this License, you may choose any version ever published (not as a draft) by the Free Software Foundation. If the Document specifies that a proxy can decide which future versions of this License can be used, that proxy's public statement of acceptance of a version permanently authorizes you to choose that version for the Document.

11. RELICENSING

"Massive Multiauthor Collaboration Site" (or "MMC Site") means any World Wide Web server that publishes copyrightable works and also provides prominent facilities for anybody to edit those works. A public wiki that anybody can edit is an example of such a server. A "Massive Multiauthor Collaboration" (or "MMC") contained in the site means any set of copyrightable works thus published on the MMC site.

"CC-BY-SA" means the Creative Commons Attribution-Share Alike 3.0 license published by Creative Commons Corporation, a not-for-profit corporation with a principal place of business in San Francisco, California, as well as future copyleft versions of that license published by that same organization.

"Incorporate" means to publish or republish a Document, in whole or in part, as part of another Document.

An MMC is "eligible for relicensing" if it is licensed under this License, and if all works that were first published under this License somewhere other than this MMC, and subsequently incorporated in whole or in part into the MMC, (1) had no cover texts or invariant sections, and (2) were thus incorporated prior to November 1, 2008.

The operator of an MMC Site may republish an MMC contained in the site under CC-BY-SA on the same site at any time before August 1, 2009, provided the MMC is eligible for relicensing.

How to use this License for your documents

To use this License in a document you have written, include a copy of the License in the document and put the following copyright and license notices just after the title page:

> Copyright (c) YEAR YOUR NAME.
>
> Permission is granted to copy, distribute and/or modify this document
>
> under the terms of the GNU Free Documentation License, Version 1.3
>
> or any later version published by the Free Software Foundation;
>
> with no Invariant Sections, no Front-Cover Texts, and no Back-Cover Texts.
>
> A copy of the license is included in the section entitled "GNU
>
> Free Documentation License".

If you have Invariant Sections, Front-Cover Texts and Back-Cover Texts, replace the "with...Texts." line with this:

> with the Invariant Sections being LIST THEIR TITLES, with the
>
> Front-Cover Texts being LIST, and with the Back-Cover Texts being LIST.

If you have Invariant Sections without Cover Texts, or some other combination of the three, merge those two alternatives to suit the situation.

If your document contains nontrivial examples of program code, we recommend releasing these examples in parallel under your choice of free software license, such as the GNU General Public License, to permit their use in free software.

Free Documentation License Version 1.2, ember 2002 Copyright (C) 2000,2001,2002 Software Foundation, Inc. 59 Temple e, Suite 330, Boston, MA 02111-1307 USA yone is permitted to copy and distribute atim copies of this license document, but ging it is not allowed.

EAMBLE

urpose of this License is to make a manual, textbook, or functional and useful document "free" in the sense of m: to assure everyone the effective freedom to copy and bute it, with or without modifying it, either commercially or nmercially. Secondarily, this License preserves for the and publisher a way to get credit for their work, while not considered responsible for modifications made by others. icense is a kind of "copyleft", which means that derivative of the document must themselves be free in the same It complements the GNU General Public License, which is left license designed for free software. We have designed cense in order to use it for manuals for free software, se free software needs free documentation: a free program come with manuals providing the same freedoms that the re does. But this License is not limited to software manuals; be used for any textual work, regardless of subject matter ther it is published as a printed book. We recommend this e principally for works whose purpose is instruction or ice.

LICABILITY AND DEFINITIONS

License applies to any manual or other work, in any n, that contains a notice placed by the copyright holder it can be distributed under the terms of this License. Such ce grants a world-wide, royalty-free license, unlimited in n, to use that work under the conditions stated herein. The nent", below, refers to any such manual or work. Any er of the public is a licensee, and is addressed as "you". ccept the license if you copy, modify or distribute the work ay requiring permission under copyright law. A "Modified n" of the Document means any work containing the nent or a portion of it, either copied verbatim, or with cations and/or translated into another language. A ndary Section" is a named appendix or a front-matter of the Document that deals exclusively with the nship of the publishers or authors of the Document to the nent's overall subject (or to related matters) and contains g that could fall directly within that overall subject. (Thus, if cument is in part a textbook of mathematics, a Secondary n may not explain any mathematics.) The relationship could matter of historical connection with the subject or with matters, or of legal, commercial, philosophical, ethical or al position regarding them. The "Invariant Sections" are Secondary Sections whose titles are designated, as being of Invariant Sections, in the notice that says that the nent is released under this License. If a section does not fit ove definition of Secondary then it is not allowed to be ated as Invariant. The Document may contain zero nt Sections. If the Document does not identify any Invariant ns then there are none. The "Cover Texts" are certain short ges of text that are listed, as Front-Cover Texts or Back- Texts, in the notice that says that the Document is ed under this License. A Front-Cover Text may be at most ds, and a Back-Cover Text may be at most 25 words. A parent" copy of the Document means a machine-readable represented in a format whose specification is available to eneral public, that is suitable for revising the document htforwardly with generic text editors or (for images sed of pixels) generic paint programs or (for drawings) widely available drawing editor, and that is suitable for input formatters or for automatic translation to a variety of s suitable for input to text formatters. A copy made in an ise Transparent file format whose markup, or absence of p, has been arranged to thwart or discourage subsequent cation by readers is not Transparent. An image format is ansparent if used for any substantial amount of text. A copy not "Transparent" is called "Opaque". Examples of suitable s for Transparent copies include plain ASCII without p, Texinfo input format, LaTeX input format, SGML or XML a publicly available DTD, and standard-conforming simple PostScript or PDF designed for human modification. les of transparent image formats include PNG, XCF and Opaque formats include proprietary formats that can be nd edited only by proprietary word processors, SGML or or which the DTD and/or processing tools are not generally ble, and the machine-generated HTML, PostScript or PDF ced by some word processors for output purposes only. The Page" means, for a printed book, the title page itself, plus ollowing pages as are needed to hold, legibly, the material cense requires to appear in the title page. For works in s which do not have any title page as such, "Title Page" the text near the most prominent appearance of the work's receding the beginning of the body of the text. A section ed XYZ" means a named subunit of the Document whose ther is precisely XYZ or contains XYZ in parentheses ng text that translates XYZ in another language. (Here XYZ for a specific section name mentioned below, such as wledgements", "Dedications", "Endorsements", or y".) To "Preserve the Title" of such a section when you the Document means that it remains a section "Entitled according to this definition. The Document may include nty Disclaimers next to the notice which states that this e applies to the Document. These Warranty Disclaimers nsidered to be included by reference in this License, but s regards disclaiming warranties: any other implication that Warranty Disclaimers may have is void and has no effect meaning of this License.

RBATIM COPYING

nay copy and distribute the Document in any medium, commercially or noncommercially, provided that this e, the copyright notices, and the license notice saying this License applies to the Document are reproduced in all copies, and that you add no other conditions whatsoever to those of this License. You may not use technical measures to obstruct or control the reading or further copying of the copies you make or distribute. However, you may accept compensation in exchange for copies. If you distribute a large enough number of copies you must also follow the conditions in section 3. You may also lend copies, under the same conditions stated above, and you may publicly display copies.

3. COPYING IN QUANTITY

If you publish printed copies (or copies in media that commonly have printed covers) of the Document, numbering more than 100, and the Document's license notice requires Cover Texts, you must enclose the copies in covers that carry, clearly and legibly, all these Cover Texts: Front-Cover Texts on the front cover, and Back-Cover Texts on the back cover. Both covers must also clearly and legibly identify you as the publisher of these copies. The front cover must present the full title with all words of the title equally prominent and visible. You may add other material on the covers in addition. Copying with changes limited to the covers, as long as they preserve the title of the Document and satisfy these conditions, can be treated as verbatim copying in other respects. If the required texts for either cover are too voluminous to fit legibly, you should put the first ones listed (as many as fit reasonably) on the actual cover, and continue the rest onto adjacent pages. If you publish or distribute Opaque copies of the Document numbering more than 100, you must either include a machine-readable Transparent copy along with each Opaque copy, or state in or with each Opaque copy a computer-network location from which the general network-using public has access to download using public-standard network protocols a complete Transparent copy of the Document, free of added material. If you use the latter option, you must take reasonably prudent steps, when you begin distribution of Opaque copies in quantity, to ensure that this Transparent copy will remain thus accessible at the stated location until at least one year after the last time you distribute an Opaque copy (directly or through your agents or retailers) of that edition to the public. It is requested, but not required, that you contact the authors of the Document well before redistributing any large number of copies, to give them a chance to provide you with an updated version of the Document.

4. MODIFICATIONS

You may copy and distribute a Modified Version of the Document under the conditions of sections 2 and 3 above, provided that you release the Modified Version under precisely this License, with the Modified Version filling the role of the Document, thus licensing distribution and modification of the Modified Version to whoever possesses a copy of it. In addition, you must do these things in the Modified Version: A. Use in the Title Page (and on the covers, if any) a title distinct from that of the Document, and from those of previous versions (which should, if there were any, be listed in the History section of the Document). You may use the same title as a previous version if the original publisher of that version gives permission. B. List on the Title Page, as authors, one or more persons or entities responsible for authorship of the modifications in the Modified Version, together with at least five of the principal authors of the Document (all of its principal authors, if it has fewer than five), unless they release you from this requirement. C. State on the Title page the name of the publisher of the Modified Version, as the publisher. D. Preserve all the copyright notices of the Document. E. Add an appropriate copyright notice for your modifications adjacent to the other copyright notices. F. Include, immediately after the copyright notices, a license notice giving the public permission to use the Modified Version under the terms of this License, in the form shown in the Addendum below. G. Preserve in that license notice the full lists of Invariant Sections and required Cover Texts given in the Document's license notice. H. Include an unaltered copy of this License. I. Preserve the section Entitled "History", Preserve its Title, and add to it an item stating at least the title, year, new authors, and publisher of the Modified Version as given on the Title Page. If there is no section Entitled "History" in the Document, create one stating the title, year, authors, and publisher of the Document as given on its Title Page, then add an item describing the Modified Version as stated in the previous sentence. J. Preserve the network location, if any, given in the Document for public access to a Transparent copy of the Document, and likewise the network locations given in the Document for previous versions it was based on. These may be placed in the "History" section. You may omit a network location for a work that was published at least four years before the Document itself, or if the original publisher of the version it refers to gives permission. K. For any section Entitled "Acknowledgements" or "Dedications", Preserve the Title of the section, and preserve in the section all the substance and tone of each of the contributor acknowledgements and/or dedications given therein. L. Preserve all the Invariant Sections of the Document, unaltered in their text and in their titles. Section numbers or the equivalent are not considered part of the section titles. M. Delete any section Entitled "Endorsements". Such a section may not be included in the Modified Version. N. Do not retitle any existing section to be Entitled "Endorsements" or to conflict in title with any Invariant Section. O. Preserve any Warranty Disclaimers. If the Modified Version includes new front-matter sections or appendices that qualify as Secondary Sections and contain no material copied from the Document, you may at your option designate some or all of these sections as invariant. To do this, add their titles to the list of Invariant Sections in the Modified Version's license notice. These titles must be distinct from any other section titles. You may add a section Entitled "Endorsements", provided it contains nothing but endorsements of your Modified Version by various parties--for example, statements of peer review or that the text has been approved by an organization as the authoritative definition of a standard. You may add a passage of up to five words as a Front-Cover Text, and a passage of up to 25 words as a Back-Cover Text, to the end of the list of Cover Texts in the Modified Version. Only one passage of Front-Cover Text and one of Back-Cover Text may be added by (or through arrangements made by) any one entity. If the Document already includes a cover text for the same cover, previously added by you or by arrangement made by the same entity you are acting on behalf of, you may not add another; but you may replace the old one, on explicit permission from the previous publisher that added the old one. The author(s) and publisher(s) of the Document do not by this License give permission to use their names for publicity for or to assert or imply endorsement of any Modified Version.

5. COMBINING DOCUMENTS

You may combine the Document with other documents released under this License, under the terms defined in section 4 above for modified versions, provided that you include in the combination all of the Invariant Sections of all of the original documents, unmodified, and list them all as Invariant Sections of your combined work in its license notice, and that you preserve all their Warranty Disclaimers. The combined work need only contain one copy of this License, and multiple identical Invariant Sections may be replaced with a single copy. If there are multiple Invariant Sections with the same name but different contents, make the title of each such section unique by adding at the end of it, in parentheses, the name of the original author or publisher of that section if known, or else a unique number. Make the same adjustment to the section titles in the list of Invariant Sections in the license notice of the combined work. In the combination, you must combine any sections Entitled "History" in the various original documents, forming one section Entitled "History"; likewise combine any sections Entitled "Acknowledgements", and any sections Entitled "Dedications". You must delete all sections Entitled "Endorsements".

6. COLLECTIONS OF DOCUMENTS

You may make a collection consisting of the Document and other documents released under this License, and replace the individual copies of this License in the various documents with a single copy that is included in the collection, provided that you follow the rules of this License for verbatim copying of each of the documents in all other respects. You may extract a single document from such a collection, and distribute it individually under this License, provided you insert a copy of this License into the extracted document, and follow this License in all other respects regarding verbatim copying of that document.

7. AGGREGATION WITH INDEPENDENT WORKS

A compilation of the Document or its derivatives with other separate and independent documents or works, in or on a volume of a storage or distribution medium, is called an "aggregate" if the copyright resulting from the compilation is not used to limit the legal rights of the compilation's users beyond what the individual works permit. When the Document is included in an aggregate, this License does not apply to the other works in the aggregate which are not themselves derivative works of the Document. If the Cover Text requirement of section 3 is applicable to these copies of the Document, then if the Document is less than one half of the entire aggregate, the Document's Cover Texts may be placed on covers that bracket the Document within the aggregate, or the electronic equivalent of covers if the Document is in electronic form. Otherwise they must appear on printed covers that bracket the whole aggregate.

8. TRANSLATION

Translation is considered a kind of modification, so you may distribute translations of the Document under the terms of section 4. Replacing Invariant Sections with translations requires special permission from their copyright holders, but you may include translations of some or all Invariant Sections in addition to the original versions of these Invariant Sections. You may include a translation of this License, and all the license notices in the Document, and any Warranty Disclaimers, provided that you also include the original English version of this License and the original versions of those notices and disclaimers. In case of a disagreement between the translation and the original version of this License or a notice or disclaimer, the original version will prevail. If a section in the Document is Entitled "Acknowledgements", "Dedications", or "History", the requirement (section 4) to Preserve its Title (section 1) will typically require changing the actual title.

9. TERMINATION

You may not copy, modify, sublicense, or distribute the Document except as expressly provided for under this License. Any other attempt to copy, modify, sublicense or distribute the Document is void, and will automatically terminate your rights under this License. However, parties who have received copies, or rights, from you under this License will not have their licenses terminated so long as such parties remain in full compliance.

10. FUTURE REVISIONS OF THIS LICENSE

The Free Software Foundation may publish new, revised versions of the GNU Free Documentation License from time to time. Such new versions will be similar in spirit to the present version, but may differ in detail to address new problems or concerns. See http://www.gnu.org/copyleft/. Each version of the License is given a distinguishing version number. If the Document specifies that a particular numbered version of this License "or any later version" applies to it, you have the option of following the terms and conditions either of that specified version or of any later version that has been published (not as a draft) by the Free Software Foundation. If the Document does not specify a version number of this License, you may choose any version ever published (not as a draft) by the Free Software Foundation. ADDENDUM: How to use this License for your documents To use this License in a document you have written, include a copy of the License in the document and put the following copyright and license notices just after the title page: Copyright (c) YEAR YOUR NAME. Permission is granted to copy, distribute and/or modify this document under the terms of the GNU Free Documentation License, Version 1.2 or any later version published by the Free Software Foundation; with no Invariant Sections, no Front-Cover Texts, and no Back-Cover Texts. A copy of the license is included in the section entitled "GNU Free Documentation License". If you have Invariant Sections, Front-Cover Texts and Back-Cover Texts, replace the "with...Texts." line with this: with the Invariant Sections being LIST THEIR TITLES, with the Front-Cover Texts being LIST, and with the Back-Cover Texts being LIST. If you have Invariant Sections without Cover Texts, or some other combination of the three, merge those two alternatives to suit the situation. If your document contains nontrivial examples of program code, we recommend releasing these examples in parallel under your choice of free software license, such as the GNU General Public License, to permit their use in free software.

CPSIA information can be obtained at www.ICGtesting.com
Printed in the USA
LVOW041745090112

263055LV00007B/94/P